The Warping of
Government Work

The Warping of Government Work

◆ ◆ ◆

JOHN D. DONAHUE

HARVARD UNIVERSITY PRESS

Cambridge, Massachusetts

London, England

2008

Library of Congress Cataloging-in-Publication Data

Donahue, John D.
The warping of government work / John D. Donahue.
p. cm.
Includes bibliographical references and index.
ISBN-13: 978-0-674-02788-6 (alk. paper)
1. Civil service—United States.   2. Public administration—United States.   I. Title.
JK692.D66 2008
352.6'7—dc22
2007042329

For Ben

Contents

Acknowledgments

AS THE THEMES of this book took shape I benefited from discussions with Alan Altshuler, George Borjas, Suzanne Cooper, David Ellwood, John Haigh, Elaine Kamarck, Steve Kelman, Dutch Leonard, Joe Nye, Mark Ramseyer, Bob Reich, and a long list of former students. Richard Zeckhauser has been a particularly valuable sounding board. A series of research and administrative assistants, including Bernie Cahill, Michael Coullahan, Minoo Ghoreishi, Patience Terry and—most recently and indispensably—Erica Jaffe helped to assemble data and track down sources. Michael Aronson, Mary Jo Bane, David Beard, Bob Behn, Joe Bower, Steve Goldsmith, Jerry Grossman, Derek Kirkland, Mark Moore, Joe Nye, Clyde Pax, Maggie Pax, Jeremy Rosner, Rafe Sagalyn, Max Steir, Bill Straus, Frank Weil, Richard Zeckhauser, and three anonymous referees read the manuscript in draft—sometimes multiple drafts—and were generous with comments and suggestions that have made this a better book than it otherwise would have been.

Beyond the thanks owed to specific friends and colleagues I am more diffusely indebted to two institutions. Harvard's Kennedy School is a monument to good government in all its aspects. Much of what I know, and much of what I care about, is anchored in this extraordinary institution. My sojourn at the U.S. Department of Labor was briefer, but my years there both equipped me to build the empirical foundation for this book and offered memorable cases in point that spanned the range of government work.

Finally, I acknowledge the special contribution of my son, Benedict Pax Donahue. When Ben first learned to read he found on the living room shelves earlier books dedicated to my parents, wife, and daughter and asked rather pointedly where *his* book was. In the years since, amid many competing claims on my time, Ben has nudged me, very helpfully, to get this one done. Neither Ben nor any of the other people acknowledged here are responsible for error of fact or judgment in this book, which are exclusively mine.

ONE

◆ ◆ ◆

Two Worlds of Work

FOUR EPISODES, SEEMINGLY unlinked, combine to hint at the peculiar standing of government work in America's economy. Three of the stories were thoroughly obscure, even as they played out in the early 2000s, while one was splashed across just about every front page and television screen. A long parade of comparable cases-in-point could be marched out, but four should suffice to set the stage.

PRIVATE LYNCH'S AMBITIONS: In the tense early days of the war in Iraq Americans were riveted, cheered, and charmed by the story of Private First Class Jessica Lynch. She was a winsome blond volunteer who had grown up—though at nineteen, she was just barely grown up—in a hardscrabble West Virginia village. Private Lynch fell prisoner when her truck convoy was ambushed in Nasiriyah. For days her photo was the public face of America's armed forces in this strange new war. Pentagon press releases spread the word that she had gone down fighting, blazing away with her M-16 until the rifle jammed and she was overwhelmed. Eight days later Special Forces mounted a dramatic midnight raid to liberate Private Lynch from the hospital where she was held. A film crew accompanying the rescue team recorded her wan smile as heavily armed comrades carried her on a stretcher to a whirring helicopter, an American flag layered over the blanket covering her battered body.

Some amendments to the original reports, issued quietly while Private Lynch healed, drained away a bit of the drama. She had been

1

knocked unconscious at the start of the ambush and never fired a shot, for example, and when Special Forces blasted into the hospital the only Iraqis on the scene had been doctors and nurses. Yet her ordeal was still a heart-stirring episode, retold in a movie and a best-selling biography. Many have been moved by her story, but few focus on (or even know) what brought her to Nasiriyah in the first place. She was a patriotic young woman, of course, but one with a special motive for taking up arms, a motive that might well seem bizarre in other places and times: she wanted to be a kindergarten teacher. A job nurturing five-year-olds at a public school was a tantalizing prospect compared to her other options, a worthy and agreeable career with a steady paycheck. But to become a kindergarten teacher, Jessica needed to go to college. And her route to college required a detour through Iraq, so she could earn the military education benefits that came along with the M-16.[1]

THE ROBERTSONS' COMPLAINT: America had been very good to the Robertson family—they made a fortune from their A&P supermarket chain—and they wanted to give something back. In 1961 Charles and Marie Robertson donated $35 million in A&P stock to Princeton University to establish "a graduate school where men and women dedicated to public service may prepare themselves for careers in government."[2] The gift, the biggest ever to any U.S. college, let Princeton launch the Woodrow Wilson School of Public and International Affairs, staff it with distinguished academics, house it in a handsome building, and handpick the most promising few from a flood of applicants to prepare for public service.

Thirty years later the value of the Robertson endowment had soared to $525 million, even after paying out more than $200 million to operate the Woodrow Wilson School. Princeton's school of government had cemented its reputation as a world leader, boasting a stellar faculty and a student body drawn from the upper tiers of the best undergraduate institutions, with the Robertson Foundation covering their tuition. There was only one discordant note: few of these supremely talented young men and women, when they finished their splendid education, ended up working for the government. William Robertson (Charles and Marie's son) charged that "these folks are turning up their noses at government service," and complained that Princeton was not delivering on the mission that had motivated his parents' gift.[3] The

Robertson family mustered a team of lawyers and informed Princeton that they wanted their money back.

MS. PEYTON'S LAWSUIT: Monica Peyton was not much older than Jessica Lynch, and not much more prosperous, when she first went to work for the Government Printing Office (GPO). Peyton spent ten years in menial jobs at the lower rungs of the civil service scale, helping to keep the vast river of federal paper flowing along. Then came her big break: she was picked for an apprenticeship program that would lead to a career as a government proofreader, with a steady middle-class paycheck. But as she set to work learning the finer points of the trade, fate sent her a boorish and vengeful boss. Peyton's supervisor annoyed her with lewd comments about her anatomy and later, when she filed a complaint, undertook a concerted and wholly successful effort to make her life miserable.

Continued harassment, and malevolent bureaucratic maneuvers by the supervisor, led to Peyton flunking out of the apprenticeship program. Shortly thereafter she sued the GPO. Everyone connected with the lawsuit, which eventually reached a federal appeals court, agreed that Monica Peyton had been treated abominably, and the GPO didn't try to deny that she had been harassed out of a job. When the suit was tried in a Washington, D.C., district court, the jury awarded her $482,000 as compensation for the hostile work environment she had endured. But the jury, and the court, looked to the future as well as the past in weighing the harm done to Ms. Peyton. They concurred that she had lost an "optimum and unparalleled occasion to earn a handsome living." Judging that it would be "ill-advised" to order her reinstalled at an employer that had dealt with her so shabbily, the court instead told the GPO to compensate her for the gap between her lost prospects as a government proofreader and her actual job at the printing business where she ended up after leaving the GPO. The court ordered a lump sum payment of $378,000 to make up the difference between a career at the GPO and Peyton's private-sector fallback.[4]

THE NATIONAL INSTITUTES OF HEALTH'S DILEMMA: The National Institutes of Health (NIH) is a cluster of twenty-seven federal research centers dedicated to understanding, and eventually ameliorating, afflictions such as AIDS, cancer, heart disease, and mental illness. With congressional appropriations exceeding $25 billion, the NIH is the conduit for nearly half of all federal spending on research and development and is, by general consensus, the world's reigning champion in the struggle against disease.[5] Its labs in Washington's suburbs hum with cutting-edge research, and the NIH catalyzes top science nationwide through its grants to medical schools and other research institutions.

A minor scandal erupted in 2004 concerning the salaries the NIH was paying its directors. The NIH had grown adroit at exploiting loopholes in federal compensation rules—offering "retention incentives" and other supplements—to boost directors' pay packages well beyond the civil-service norm. Critics in Congress and elsewhere pointed to reports showing that NIH directors were collecting annual salaries ranging from $142,500 to $293,750. This was more (sometimes much more) than was paid to members of Congress, Supreme Court justices, Cabinet secretaries, and other people ranking higher in the federal hierarchy than research institute directors and glaringly in excess of the average American's salary.[6] Clearly, the NIH directors were being paid far too much. Other observers, however, stressed the imperative for the NIH—as the crucial point of leverage for America's health agenda—to hire medical experts able to lead research campaigns into the most promising directions. The NIH had been finding it hard to recruit and retain top talent, and the salaries that were drawing Congress's ire were only a little more than half what these top government scientists could expect if they left NIH for equivalent work in the private sector.[7] Clearly, the NIH directors were being paid far too little.

These disparate stories share a subtext. Government has become something separate from the rest of America's economy in ways that are complex, consequential, and not in the least healthy.

An Island Apart

What we now call the island of Bali was, rather recently, just a chunk of the Asian mainland. During the late Pleistocene epoch, about 12,000 years ago, today's Malay Archipelago (with Bali near its tip) formed a hilly peninsula curving off the continent's southern edge. South Asian animals—sun bears and leopards, rhinos and tigers, elephants and wild pigs—flourished in an unbroken domain from the northern reaches of their ecological ranges down to the bottom of the peninsula.

Then the world changed. The earth warmed by a few crucial degrees, in one of the periodic climatic wobbles that make ice ages come and go, and glaciers and polar ice caps started to melt. Water trickled into the seas—enough, over time, to deepen the planet's oceans by a few hundred feet. The peninsula's valleys were transformed into seabed, and the peaks turned into islands. Among the smallest of these islands was Bali. When the waters rose, the animals on Bali became separated from their fellows on the mainland, and cut off from the bulk of their habitat. Most species died out. Others evolved, molding themselves to fit the peculiar circumstances of their isolated existence. By 1856, when naturalist Alfred Russel Wallace stepped ashore to study life on the island, the species on Bali had grown sparse and strange.[8]

Something along these lines has happened over the past generation or so to America's public sector. A gap opened between the worlds of work in government and in the rest of the U.S. economy. This gap was not carved by any coherent or even conscious set of policy decisions. Much of it is due to economic forces that policy affects weakly, indirectly, or not at all, and to the accumulated side effects from choices made (or not made) to address entirely separate issues. The segregation of the public and private working worlds has been incremental, largely accidental, and like other gradual transformations less noticed and hence less understood than its consequences warrant.

Mapping the dynamics of this isolation and exploring its implications constitute the work of this book, but the basics are simply stated. In about the mid-1970s the long postwar trend of shared prosperity began to unwind. Slowly at first, and then with gathering speed, the prospects for American workers diverged. People endowed with native wit, education, ambition, and luck discovered ever-wider opportunities and ever-richer rewards. As the economy became more global, more diverse, more sophisticated, technologically complex, and flooded with information, some workers surged ahead. Others fell behind. Laws, institutions, and norms that had constrained the highs and the lows of working life were swept away. Inequality increased, through boom and bust, until by the early years of the twenty-first century the economic distances separating Americans were wider than they had been in living memory. Employment became a game with higher and higher stakes, and Americans learned to play the game hard. More hours in the week and steeper shares of energy and passion were drained from the rest of life and invested in the workplace. Winners win big. Losers fall hard. Those are the rules today.

This didn't happen in government. Today's public sector mostly missed the transformation that swept over the rest of the working world. Government jobs, for good and for ill, tend to operate under the rules that defined the middle-class economy in the decades following World War II. Risk is dampened. So is opportunity. Rewards at the top are not all that different from those below. Nearly all workers, from janitors to governors, earn middle-class salaries. Unions thrive. Change is gradual. Layoffs are rare. Promotions come slow. The role of money—as a motive and as a symbol—is circumscribed.

Some workers—those for whom this work world is more hospitable than today's private alternative—seek out and cling to government jobs. Other kinds of workers find the public sector world dull and stingy and opt for the private sector. Certain commentators believe that it is the business world that has turned its back on a healthy balance, breaching a vague but vital social contract. Others charge that the public sector has foolishly lagged behind as business blazes new trails of efficiency and opportunity. We will engage some of these debates later but the essential point, for now, is not to decide which working world is better and which is worse but to recognize that they are *different*.

This would not matter, or not matter so much, if the isolated enclave were small and self-contained. Asia can get along without Bali. America can handle the propensity of churches or communes or family farms to treat workers in ways that depart from the national norm. But the public sector is a large part of the economy and is intimately intertwined with the rest of it. Government's work involves all of us, even if we never draw a public salary. Since Americans want government to be competent, people who work in government should be good at what they do. Since Americans want government to be thrifty, people who work in government should be no greater in number, and no more generously compensated, than is required to accomplish the work. Since Americans want government to be efficient, government workers should be motivated to find the best ways to get each task done, even if the best way involves fewer government workers. Since Americans want government to be fair, the burdens and the rewards of government jobs should conform to widely shared views about what's right. The isolation of the public sector makes all of this much harder.

Sharply different futures can be imagined for government work. In one of them America's two separate economies become reconnected—by the public sector yielding to contemporary business standards for how people should be treated and paid, or by the private sector undoing the transformation of working life, or by some compromise between the two. The difficulties of forging this convergence, in any of its variants, are considerable. In the other scenario, government work remains an island apart. If this is the future we turn out to inherit we must either improvise ways to cope with a segregated economy, or accept that the gap between government's performance and citizens' legitimate expectations will continue to widen. This book aims to clarify where we are and how we got there, to stimulate and to inform a wider conversation about where we want to go from here, and to suggest some better options than the binary choice between the two worlds of work.

We will start with a quick tour of the curiously obscure terrain of public-sector employment.

A Profile of Government Work

A lot of people collect government paychecks. A recent official tally reported nearly 23 million public workers in the United States, and government employees constitute about 8 percent of the U.S. population. This proportion has been remarkably stable since 1975, through war and peace, boom and bust, exuberant governmental initiative and diffident retrenchment. It was about 8 percent during President Gerald Ford's improbably activist administration. It was about 8 percent when President Bill Clinton declared "the era of big government is over." And it was about 8 percent in 2005.

But this seeming stability hides a complicated story about the scale and structure of the public sector. To understand the present, the recent past, and almost certainly the future of public work, it is important to recognize that the District of Columbia's prominence as a symbol of government is rather sharply at odds with reality. Ask an American about government and the chances are good that the first image summoned to mind will be a "Washington bureaucrat," a white-shirted denizen of some vast office building constructed in a style that manages to be at once grandiloquent and drab. Some people—those particularly inclined toward a kindly view of government—may imagine this bureaucrat focused on an arcane but vital mission of national security or environmental protection or airplane safety. Others are more likely to picture a sluggish time-server shuffling papers.

The interesting thing here is less the discrepant details people invest in this American archetype than the fact that it is so wildly unrepresentative. Fewer than 150,000 people in 2002—a good deal less than 1 percent of the public workforce—were white-collar civil servants based in Washington.[9] Most federal employees work outside the capital (patrolling borders, managing parks, tracking spacecraft, inspecting food) and even the nationwide total of federal workers constitutes a decided minority of public employment. The number of Americans working as federal civil servants (about 1.9 million) is actually smaller than the number serving time in prison (about 2.2 million).[10] Thus Bill Clinton could honestly brag of sharp reductions in federal jobs, but without moving the needle on government's share of the population. George W. Bush could preside over an equally sharp expansion and see it practically disappear within the rounding error of the government-wide workforce.

Public employment as a share of the population is the standard benchmark in political rhetoric, and a meaningful answer to some kinds of questions. But it is not a particularly good gauge of the government's weight in the working world. Among the 300 million or so people living in the United States are a great many who are so young or so old or so sick or so busy with unpaid tasks that they are not going to work for the government or for anyone else. There are many noncitizens ineligible for most government jobs (and uncounted numbers of illegal aliens facing the same constraints).

A more relevant basis for calibrating the public payroll is relative to total employment. By this measure there has been some change since 1975, though still nothing to match the sound and fury of speeches about the urgency of new programs, or of holding the line on public spending. The trend is clear, even if punctuated by a few twitches here and there: government has lost ground as an employer. In 1975 the public sector accounted for more than 22 percent of all jobs. At the beginning of the twenty-first century it was around 17 percent. While this may seem like a minor decline, for public work to figure as prominently in the labor market as it once did there would need to be 6.2 million more government jobs than there actually are. This is equivalent to about four times the strength of all the armed forces, or twice the federal civilian sector (including the post office), or all state workers plus a slice of local government. Government jobs are not quite as common as they used to be.

This is not, however, because government has shed workers during the past generation. Except for slight dips in 1981 and 1982 the public payroll has grown every year since 1975. The average increase has been about enough to add a new U.S. Postal Service every four years. Government employment has grown. But other employment has grown even faster. The swelling of the private workforce has been driven by changes on both the supply and the demand sides of the labor market. As the twenty-first century began about 45 percent of America's population held a paid nonfarm job (the rest were children, retirees, disabled, students, farmers, homemakers, prisoners, and so on). A generation earlier this had been about 35 percent. During the intervening years an extra 10 percent of the population had joined the payroll. This was largely a matter of women surging into paid employment amid the cultural changes of the late twentieth century. Immigration increased, too, and people who forsake their homelands for life in America tend to have a special ardor for work. The growth in overall jobs also reflects what was on balance a benign economic climate during the 1980s and 1990s, which were generally good decades to be in the workforce. Most of the ups amid the general downward trend in the public share of employment reflected unusual *shrinkage* in total jobs (in the slumps of 1983 and 2002, for example) rather than unusual growth in government jobs. So even though government employment increased by more than 6 million between 1975 and 2005, and public payrolls held their own relative to the nation's population, the public sector surrendered more than a fifth of its share of total employment.

This completes the thumbnail sketch of the size of the governmental economy. Next, we turn to the broad contours of its structure.

American government is remarkably bottom-heavy. Cities, towns, municipalities, and other local jurisdictions account for 60 percent of public employment. The fifty states (plus, to a small extent, the District of Columbia and other jurisdictional odds and ends) claim about 22 percent. And the federal sector, which looms so large in the popular image of government, comes in last with just over 18 percent of the total. (If only civil service jobs are counted—excluding the military and the post office—the federal share falls well below 10 percent.)

The predominance of local government is unsurprising, and goes way back. Most public tasks that require a lot of labor—teaching, policing, tending to parks and streets—are done, as they must be done, close to the ground. Local jobs were already more than half of the total in 1955 (the earliest year for which the Bureau of Labor Statistics can provide comparable data on the three levels) and dominated the public sector prior to the mid-twentieth century. But the relative rise of the *states* is a more recent thing. In 1955 there were nearly twice as many federal civilian workers as there were state workers. Then state payrolls began to surge, while the federal payroll stagnated. Part of this was Washington's aggressive use of "intergovernmental grants," starting with the Great Society era, as federal money paid for state and local personnel. Part of it was the increasing scale and importance of state education efforts. And part of it reflected one cycle in America's endless argument about the right balance between nation and state in its flexible federal system.[11] By 1972 state employment had surpassed federal civilian employment. And by 2002 the two sectors had traded places compared to 1955: state workers outnumbered federal workers by roughly two to one.

What do all these people *do?* This question, perhaps surprisingly, is readily answered, at least in rough terms. Every five years the Census Bureau assembles a detailed accounting of the number of people engaged in each kind of civilian work at each level of government; complete data are available for 2001. Combining this with Defense Department statistics on military force strength produces a tally of government jobs by function. Fully exploiting this mine of information would risk a drastic loss in readership before the first chapter of this book is well under way—not everyone longs to know that 8,807 people work in state liquor stores—so those with a thirst for detail are encouraged to peruse the sources identified in the endnotes.[12] For everyone else, it is better to group the thirty-six separate functions into seven broad categories, plus a catch-all:[13]

- **Education** covers teachers at local elementary and secondary schools, faculty at state colleges and universities, all support staff (from janitors and bus drivers to principals and chancellors) at state colleges and local schools, federal education officials and

administrators, and people working in libraries at all three levels
of government.

- **Law and security** includes police, firefighters, and other people
  providing protective services; judges, prosecutors, bailiffs, legal
  stenographers, and everyone else playing roles in the legal system;
  and people working in prisons and jails.
- **Health and welfare** covers people working in public hospitals,
  health departments, welfare agencies, and social insurance organizations.
- **Infrastructure** is a broad category for jobs in public water, gas,
  and electric utilities; roads and highways; air and water travel;
  parks, recreation, and housing; natural resources; and waste
  management facilities.
- **Defense** includes civilians involved in national security or international relations along with people on active duty in the U.S. Army,
  Navy, Marines, and Air Force.
- **Administration** includes a basket of financial and other administrative jobs.
- **Postal service** is blessedly self-explanatory.
- **Everything else** covers the 676,000 or so government workers that
  the Census Bureau couldn't fit into any of its functional categories (including those 8,707 state liquor store workers).

For a summary of the story, see Table 1.1.

Table 1.1 Public Jobs in 2001

	Number	Share (in percent)
Education	10.1 million	45
Law and security	2.7 million	12
Health and welfare	2.5 million	11
Infrastructure	2.4 million	11
Defense	2.1 million	9
Administration	1 million	5
Postal service	860,000	4
Everything else	700,000	3

Source: Census Bureau's Governments Division web site (http://www.census.gov/govs)
and the Department of Defense Active Duty Military Personnel Strength Levels
(http://web1.whs.osd.mil/mmid/military/ms9.pdf), accessed June 2006.

Quite a few Americans, even those knowledgeable about government, would lose a bet about the relative scale of these categories. We all know that there are a lot of public schools to be staffed, but the vastness of the education workforce—five times as big as defense—is particularly startling. Teachers, principals, classroom aides, and other people directly involved in instruction at elementary, middle, and high schools, nearly all of them at the local level, make up close to half of the 10 million education workers. There are also nearly a million faculty members at public colleges and universities, most of them on state payrolls. More than 4 million people have government jobs in education, but play no direct role in the classroom, including 2.3 million noninstructional workers in local education and 1.7 million at the state level. Lost in the rounding error are 11,000 people performing the federal government's role in education, mostly writing rules and writing checks.

The various types of government jobs (as logic would suggest) are distributed unevenly across the three levels of the public sector. More than half of the federal workforce is involved in defense and more than a fifth work at delivering the mail, functions that disappear in the "other" category in state and local governments. It is entirely predictable that 58 percent of local government workers have jobs in education; it is perhaps more surprising that 47 percent of state workers do, too. Other significant categories of local workers are police (6 percent of the total), hospital employees (4 percent), central administration (3 percent), and firefighters (3 percent). At the state level, aside from education, are clusters of jobs in prisons (10 percent), hospitals (9 percent), highways (about 5 percent), public welfare (about 5 percent), public health (about 4 percent), financial administration (about 4 percent), natural resources (about 3 percent), and the legal system (about 3 percent). The federal government deploys about 5 percent of its workers to jobs dealing with natural resources, 4 percent to hospitals (mostly for ailing military veterans), and 3 percent each to health, financial administration, and law enforcement. The rest of the people are spread across job categories; no other function accounts for as much as 3 percent of the workers.

It would be nice to see how the distribution of government jobs, in each of the thirty-six detailed categories, has changed over time. But the Census Bureau gathers this data only every five years, and has been collecting the information in the same way only since 1997. Fortunately the Labor Department has its own annual tally of public-sector employment, and this one goes much farther back, though the categories are coarser. Instead of thirty-six functions, this data source separates government jobs into just a few big groups: local government workers involved in education; other local government workers; *state* government workers involved in education; other state government workers; federal civil servants; postal workers; and (from a different source) active-duty members of the armed forces.[14]

Switching to the Labor Department numbers reveals that the total headcount of government workers grew by more than 6 million between 1975 and 2005. This is not particularly surprising; we've become a bigger country since the mid-1970s. America's population grew by 37 percent from 1975 to 2005. The number of government jobs grew at about the same rate, and government workers' share of the population ended the period pretty much precisely where it began (7.87 percent in 1975 and 7.83 percent in 2005). But the growth has been starkly uneven, as Table 1.2 shows.

Jobs related to education have increased sharply, at both the local and state level. Other state and local jobs have proliferated, too, though at somewhat less impressive rates. The postal service's payroll has grown modestly over this thirty-year period, while other federal jobs have dwindled—civilian jobs down by 11 percent, military jobs down by a third.

Table 1.2 Thousands of Government Workers

	1975	2005	Change	Percentage Change
Local education jobs	4,722	7,864	3,142	67
Other local jobs	4,036	6,194	2,158	54
State education jobs	1,323	2,250	987	70
Other state jobs	1,857	2,771	414	22
Postal service	699	773	74	11
Other federal civilian jobs	2,183	1,951	−232	−11
Armed services	2,164	1,436	−728	−34

Source: Bureau of Labor Statistics' National Employment, Hours, and Earnings Survey Program (May 2006) and the Office of Management and Budget, Budget of the United States Government, Fiscal Year 2007, Historical Table 17.5.

The big increases have been in education-related jobs. At the local level, education workers were already more than 2 percent of the population in 1975. This share slipped a little in the mid-1980s, then commenced a steady climb to 2.7 percent by 2002. One in every thirty-seven Americans, in other words, holds a local-government education job. Demographics—the fact that school-age kids form a shifting share of the population over time—explains part, but by no means all, of this growth in the education workforce. It is true that the children of the baby-boom generation were flooding into local elementary and high schools during this time, and true as well that immigration was surging. But public-school enrollment was only about 5 percent higher in 2002 than it had been in 1975; local education jobs increased by twelve times as much. Some special issues surrounding education will be taken up later. For now, suffice it to note that this disproportionate rise in school payrolls has something to do with falling class sizes (the average number of students per teacher dropped from about twenty to about fifteen during this period); something to do with growing demands for specialists, assistants, and other classroom personnel; something to do with a rising fraction (from 53 to 58 percent) of nonteachers on education payrolls; and something to do with unions' success in fending off threats to education jobs both inside and (no less important) outside the classroom.[15]

A similar story plays out at the state level. State government workers involved in education started out as a much smaller share of the population than did civil servants or soldiers, and ended up considerably above them. Here, too, part of the explanation is demographic. The states specialize in higher education, and as the trailing edge of the baby boom left local schools the demographic bulge moved into the college years. But the sharp increase in the share of high-school graduates going on to college is a bigger factor. The vast ranks of young people, mostly from modest backgrounds, whose counterparts (a generation earlier) would have skipped college, were especially likely to choose state rather than private institutions. Enrollment at public colleges and universities spiked by a quarter in the two decades after 1975.[16] The torrent of incoming students, along with pressures to maintain or boost the quality of state schools' offerings, led to the hiring of more professors, administrators, football coaches, janitors, cafeteria workers, and groundskeepers.

*   *   *

These people work for us. The quality of our lives—how safe we are, how just we are, how well we serve our defining dream of a better America in the years to come—depends on how they do their jobs. The heft of our taxes depends on how many people are employed and how they are paid. We want to do right by them; we want them to do right by us. How well we do at picking the right people for government work, motivating them to act in our interest, and defining their jobs to fit America's needs and values will shape, in no small way, what kind of country we turn out to be as history unfolds. Right now, we are not doing very well.

The next chapter describes a formidable impediment to a fair and sensible approach to government work—the evolution of the *private* economy into a high-rolling sweepstakes very different from the way private work used to be, and from the way public work still remains. It goes on to map the separate island of government work to clarify both the causes and consequences of its growing distance from the rest of the U.S. economy. The last section of Chapter 2 (along with an appendix) focuses on the vexing issues of how to define "fairness" in government jobs, and how to measure the differences in how public and private employers treat their workers. Chapter 3 explores how government has become for millions of U.S. workers a "safe harbor" in an inhospitable economic climate. Chapter 4 examines the flip side of this phenomenon: the diminishing appeal of public work for those most favored by fate. Chapter 5 starts with an overview of the transformative trend that has reshaped much of the private sector but mostly missed government, and then shows how government's isolation warps the public sector's transformation in ways that imperil both the efficiency and the legitimacy of public missions. And the final chapter arrays the hard choices we confront over government's relationship to the wider world of work in America.

TWO

❖ ❖ ❖

Relic of the Middle-Class Economy

CALIBRATING THE GAP between the two worlds of work requires confronting the context—the abrupt unwinding of the middle-class economy. Three decades of surging inequality have transformed public
work into a backwater for the economic elite and a safe harbor for
workers with dimming private-sector prospects. Public employment
echoes a fading era of shared prosperity, and is sharply at odds with today's winner-take-all workplace norms. The separate trajectories of
public and private work have far-reaching and mostly baleful consequences for government's performance.

The debate over growing inequality is a lot like the debate over global
warming: experts argue fiercely over its causes, its consequences, what
can be done about it, and whether anything *should* be done about it.[1]
But the basic facts have become bluntly evident, and few people with
much claim to candor try to deny the divergence in Americans' economic conditions.

What marks today's version of that divergence is not so much squalid
misery at the low end of the scale—the conditions that inspired a war
on poverty a couple of generations ago—as the hollowing-out of the
middle. Until recently "inequality" was a code word for the special
problems of the poor, especially the minority poor, who had been bypassed by the great middle-class boom that followed World War II.
While the poor are still with us, few Americans suffer anything like the

16

absolute poverty that plagues some other parts of the world. Today's inequality has become something less stark but much broader than vestigial poverty amid general prosperity. A wave of economic changes, unleashed roughly a generation ago, gathered force toward the turn of the twenty-first century. This transformation has delivered tremendous economic gains, making the United States a lavishly wealthy nation. But it has bestowed those benefits unevenly. As the transformation continues to unfold the wave of change is presenting Americans with something very different from the way their grandparents encountered work, wealth, and community.

Federal statisticians have tracked how income is divided in essentially the same manner since 1947. For a long time the standard measure of family income inequality—an arcane indicator known as the Gini coefficient—was a decidedly dull statistic, changing little from year to year. The general trend, though, was the consolidation of the broad middle class as the proportion of both rich and poor families dwindled. By the late 1960s, family income distribution was about 8 percent more equal than it had been in 1947. The rising tide of postwar prosperity really did lift all boats, giving a little extra boost to the skiffs and lifting the yachts a bit less. For about a decade, the level of economic equality stayed close to this plateau. Then things changed. After wandering aimlessly a notch up or down from year to year, family income inequality started creeping upward in the late 1970s. By 1982 all the gains made since 1947 were gone, and the growth in inequality started to accelerate. In 2005 the gauge of family income inequality was 17 percent above its 1947 level, and 27 percent above the late-1960s low point.[2]

The "middle class" is a concept of almost mystical resonance in American culture—the vast majority of people consider themselves members of it—but a term with no standard definition. Sometimes the middle class is simply defined by lopping off the high end and the low end of the income distribution. Since the Census data are conventionally arranged by fifths, in practice this means removing the richest fifth and the poorest fifth and declaring the middle class to be what's left over.[3] But the 60 percent in the middle, as a mathematical tautology, comprises the exact same proportion of families over time. Catching any *change* in the prevalence of the middle class requires a different approach. An unscientific but sensible definition of middle-class families might include those earning between *half* and *twice* the average family income. The Census provides a lot of detail at lower levels, but unfortunately compresses the upper reaches into a catch-all category of "$100,000 or more" (measured in inflation-adjusted dollars). So we'll amend the working definition to include families with incomes at least half as large as the average, but below that top category of $100,000 or more. Families getting by on less than half the average may not be poor, but they certainly live with fewer choices and with more pressures than do their more comfortable counterparts. Most families earning $100,000 would not consider themselves wealthy, but they are at the threshold of the most fortunate fifth.

The average family income in 1968 was $48,600, expressed in dollars with 2004 purchasing power. America got considerably richer during the next thirty-six years, and in 2004 the average family income was nearly $70,400. But in contrast to the early decades following World War II, this growth was tilted toward the top. As Figure 2.1 shows, in 1968 three-fourths of American families earned at least half of the average for all families but less than 1968's equivalent of $100,000. By

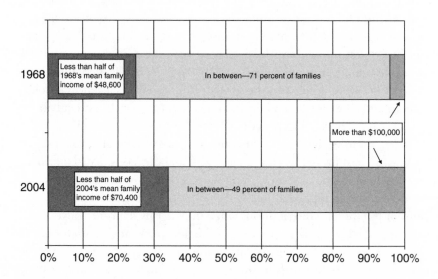

Figure 2.1: Family income ranges, 1968 and 2004 (all figures are in 2004 dollars). *Source:* Current Population Survey Historical Income Tables (Families), Table F-33, "Families by Total Money Income 1967–2004" accessed May 2006 at http://www.census.gov/hhhes/income/histinc/f23.html.

2004 both the bottom and the top had swollen, and less than half of all families remained in the middle.[4]

The gap between the upper and lower reaches of the income distribution in the United States is wide not only relative to our own recent past, but by international standards as well. Two researchers have looked at the earnings of comparable workers (men who work full time) in the seven rich countries that keep sufficiently precise statistics to make comparisons possible. Rather than examining the very top and the very bottom of the earnings distribution (which lets extreme cases dominate the comparison and could make inequality look worse than it is) these countries focus on workers 10 percent up from the bottom, and 10 percent down from the top—the tenth percentile and ninetieth percentile. In the United States, those ninetieth-percentile workers (not CEOs, top doctors and lawyers, movie stars, or home-run kings but simply run-of-the-mill professional workers, middle managers, or technicians) earned 5.7 times as much as tenth-percentile workers. Only in Canada, with a ratio of 4.6, was the multiple anywhere near as large. The dispersal in earning power among American men is so wide that even though *average* earnings in the United States exceeded (sometimes greatly) average earnings elsewhere, tenth percentile American men earned less in absolute terms than tenth percentile men in any of the other countries examined.[5]

Remember that these measures ignore the apex of the pay pyramid. This is in part because the extremes are so stark that including them would obscure what's going on in the middle, and in part because most official income surveys just stop counting at a certain level and miss much of the action in the upper 10 percent. However, it is at the very top that growing disparities in the rewards for work show up most vividly. In the 1970s, big-company CEOs earned about forty times as much as an average worker. Just three decades later the gap had grown nearly tenfold, with top officials collecting 367 times the average paycheck.[6] The United States and, to a lesser extent, other English-speaking countries are also in their own league in the concentration of income at the very top. In the quarter-century ending in 2005 the share of income going to the top tenth of 1 percent grew sharply in the United States, slightly in Canada and the United Kingdom, and not at all in France or Japan.[7]

*   *   *

What happened to America's middle-class economy? The answer is a bit complicated, and more than a bit contested. Let's start out by clearing away a few myths. An article of faith among some on the left is that tax cuts bear the blame for economic inequality. But the timing is wrong. The great divide in incomes began well in advance of cuts in top tax rates made in the 1980s, continued when taxes on the wealthiest were raised in 1986, 1990, and 1993, and didn't accelerate—indeed, if anything moderated a little—with the 2001 or 2003 reductions in top tax rates. Even if the tax-cut explanation were plausible in terms of timing, it would confront the inconvenient fact that the distribution statistics focus on *pre*tax income. Supply-side theory, of course, holds that low tax rates are what motivate people to make money in the first place. A true believer might reason that reducing taxes for top earners elicits more enterprise, and hence more pretax income, among the ablest. Increased inequality is seen as an acceptable side effect, and in any event a mathematical inevitability. But unless tax cuts have an impact on upper-income work incentives that is extravagantly in excess of what most analysts believe—and unless tax *cuts* boost enthusiasm for work among the best-paid but tax *increases* in the 1980s and 1990s conspicuously failed to dampen it—tax policy simply cannot be the core of the story.[8]

Nor, to address another common charge from the left, are we seeing the emergence of an idle upper class whose burgeoning investment gains vault them ahead of the hoi polloi who live by their labor. The income divide is not exclusively, or even primarily, between the coupon-clipping rich and regular working stiffs. Most income is earned through work, not harvested from investments, and economic inequality is chiefly a matter of larger versus smaller paychecks. In 2001 Americans collected a total of about $335 billion from interest, dividends, and other kinds of property income—no small sum, to be sure, and of course heavily tilted toward the wealthy. But investment returns were dwarfed by the $5.3 *trillion* in earned income.[9] Today's well-off Americans, in contrast to their Gilded-Age counterparts, tend to get most of their income from their jobs rather than from their portfolios.[10]

A parallel myth, this one nurtured by the right, is that growing inequality is cancelled out by economic mobility. America's proud tradition of competition and opportunity makes for an ever-changing financial hierarchy, this story goes. The healthy churning of our economy renders all but irrelevant any single year's lineup of rich and poor.

Incomes tend to average out over time, as the man down on his luck one year makes it big the next and the high earning woman is overtaken by eager rivals. If people slip and slide continuously across the income spectrum, from rags to riches and from riches to rages, then the width of that spectrum is a far smaller concern than it might be if the United States shared the rigid class structure that afflicts the Old World's less dynamic economies. Americans can still be overwhelmingly middle class (as a matter of lifetime averages) even if they happen to be rich or poor in any particular year.

There might be something to this story, if it were adequately wrapped in facts. Once upon a time, it was. In the nineteenth century Americans did indeed enjoy more economic mobility than did Europeans. And it is true that the most commonly cited statistics, since they focus on economic standing at a single point in time, could miss any tendency to be middle class, on average, over the years. But other data track a sample of Americans chronologically, and a study based on these numbers followed a large group of men in their prime working years from 1974 to 1991 (long before recent peaks of inequality).[11] The evidence of changing fortunes suffices to complicate the inequality picture presented by any single year's data, to be sure. A few of those who started at the bottom (through whatever combination of education, experience, hard work, good luck, and simple maturation) climbed their way to the top fifth. And a handful of those in the top fifth at the start of the study fell into the bottom fifth at the end.[12] Yet despite these statistical vignettes of trading places, the basic pattern of inequality is altered only a little by factoring in mobility. Even with seventeen years' worth of opportunity, most of those starting out at or near the bottom—and an even higher share of those starting out at or near the top—ended up about where they started. Averaging out earnings over the whole seventeen-year period reduces income inequality by only about one-third, relative to what the snapshot based on a single year's data would suggest.[13]

Taking mobility into account makes the inequality picture look a notch or two less stark, in other words, but comes nowhere close to erasing it. The "opportunity trumps inequality" rejoinder, moreover, loses a good deal of steam when it turns out that economic mobility in the United States is not systematically higher, and is sometimes lower, than in other industrialized countries with far less income disparity. One careful study shows that low-income Americans are less, not more, likely than low-income Germans to earn their way above the bottom rung of the economic ladder.[14] Another finds that the sons of lower-income Americans have worse, not better, prospects for rising beyond their roots than do their counterparts in Denmark, Sweden, Finland, Norway, or the United Kingdom.[15] Nor has mobility accelerated to counterbalance America's post-1980 surge in inequality. In fact, it seems to have slowed in recent decades.[16]

Finally, some argue that inequality is greatly exaggerated, since conventional measures ignore the massive redistribution effected by taxation and transfer programs. It is certainly true that the federal income tax, even after repeated trims in upper-bracket rates, still falls more heavily on high-earning families. So do many (though assuredly not all) other types of taxes. And government benefit programs do, on balance, improve the position of the worse-off. But taxes and transfers turn out to have a rather modest effect on income distribution. Relying on the plain-vanilla definition of income—pretax, pretransfer—doesn't distort matters greatly. An alternative definition of income, employed experimentally by the researchers who run the main income-measurement program, takes into account federal and state income taxes, Medicare, Medicaid, private health insurance benefits, and government transfer programs such as Social Security. Calculations based on this more comprehensive measure of income point to only a little less inequality than the standard definition. And by all measures (not just the conventional one) inequality has increased sharply in recent decades.[17]

If inequality isn't the simple product of tax cuts, or an illusion based on bad statistics, or a matter of the returns to capital outpacing earnings from work, what *is* going on? Efforts to explain the great divide generally point to a set of usual suspects, including trade and immigration, technological progress, and changes in laws, policies, and institutions that govern the workplace. Each of these explanations has something valid to say about why the American economy has become much more hospitable to people with talent, education, ambition, and luck, and much more hostile to people who lack these blessings.

THE GLOBAL MARKET: The erosion of the middle-class economy has coincided with America's ever more intricate integration into the global marketplace. Goods and services produced by low-wage workers in other countries make their way across borders with increasing ease, and frequently so do the low-wage workers themselves. Imports rose from less than 3 percent of the gross domestic product (GDP) in the early 1960s to more than 12 percent in the mid-2000s.[18] As recently as 1970 immigrants accounted for only 4.7 percent of America's population. By early 2002 the immigrant share was 11.5 percent (plus a large but unknown number of illegal immigrants missed by the Census Bureau).[19] Competition from the planet's cheap and plentiful labor pool, by the most elementary economic logic, tends to reduce the earnings of those exposed to the competition. If some Americans face such competition—either because immigrants working in America are willing to do the tasks that would otherwise be performed by natives, or because low-paid workers overseas are willing to make the products or provide the services that otherwise would be produced domestically—while other Americans do not, then globalization will alter relative earning power. And if the workers who are already scraping bottom are especially hard hit by foreign competition, then global integration will exacerbate wage inequality.[20]

We can be pretty sure that some portion of the rise in inequality is due to global integration, though analysts differ over whether this factor accounts for more like 5 percent or 20 percent.[21] International competition has been nipping at the heels of people higher on the skills ladder as software writers, hardware designers, and even medical specialists face pressure from immigrants and foreign outsourcing.[22] Yet the global market remains far kinder, on balance, to Americans near the top of the income distribution than to those farther down the ladder.

THE SOARING DEMAND FOR SKILLS: It is impossible to account for growing inequality without reference to the torrent of technological change that has reshaped America's economic terrain.[23] We have been through this before, but it's different this time. A long, slow slide that commenced in colonial days moved agriculture from mainstay to marginality, in terms of employment. In a similar way, but a great deal more quickly, manufacturing's relative importance has plummeted.[24] Each shift reordered America's income distribution, at least temporarily, since the old economic orders based on growing food or making things had let less-skilled workers collect decent incomes. (This was not intrinsically so—witness plantation farming or the "dark satanic mills" of Manchester or Lowell—but thanks to the structure that American law, culture, and unions imposed on the economy in the middle-class's heyday.) Within the service sector that dominates today's economic scene, technological change has produced a mix of dead-end jobs and sophisticated, high-paying jobs.[25] Physical strength and fidelity to routine count for progressively less; training, flexibility, and initiative count for more.

Stepped-up technological evolution offers glittering new opportunities for those in a position to seize them. But those who had placed their career bets on bypassed industrial structures, and who find themselves ill-equipped to adapt, are left stranded by the shifting economic currents. Workers with the right skills, and with the educational foundations that let them continually improve their skills, discover that new communications and information technologies leverage their ability to create value. Employers bid for the services of these high-skilled workers, and their earning power soars.[26] Meanwhile, the penalty for lacking the right skills is becoming harsher. As workers with limited education discover shriveling demand for the work they are equipped to do, they lose more and more ground to their higher-skilled counterparts.[27]

Consider the differences over time in the "education premium," the extra earning power conferred by higher education. Education has always mattered, but it now matters enormously. In 1976, adult male college graduates collected 44 percent more income, on average, than did adult male high-school graduates. Men with some postgraduate education, in turn, earned 20 percent more than those with just four years of college education. By 2003, college graduates earned more than twice as much as high-school graduates. And men with professional degrees earned close to twice as much as those with a mere college diploma who, not so long ago, had occupied positions near the economic summit.[28] So dramatic and rapid a surge in the payoff to postsecondary education attests to the potency of the forces that are boosting the demand for skills. Yet the widening of the education premium is even more striking when one considers that it occurred while the *supply* of educated workers has been expanding rapidly as well. There were more than four times as many colleges and universities at the end of the twentieth century as at the beginning, and more than *sixty* times more students.[29]

One detail about the payoff to higher education warrants mention, since it turns out to matter for the debate, taken up later in this book, over whether government is less generous than business to its most qualified employees. At the same time as pay gaps were widening *between* more- and less-educated workers, they were also widening *within* the highly educated group. From 1970 to 1995 the variation between college-educated men near the top and those near the bottom of the earnings range grew from about $13,000 to about $50,000 (in constant dollars). What's going on? One part of the explanation is that a bigger slice of each generation is going to college—graduates nearly quintupled as a share of the workforce during the last two-thirds of the twentieth century—so that degree-holders are no longer the uniformly elite group that they used to be.[30] Another is that the changing economy increasingly rewards not just credentials but the innate, unmeasured abilities that lie beneath them—and those differ from one graduate to the next.

But probably the most important reason is ever-sharper segmentation within higher education. A few generations back the children (talented, or less so) of Northern elites went to Harvard or Yale. Princeton and Stanford played the same role for ritzy Southern and Western families, and a few other venerable institutions catered to their respective elite subcultures. Most other ambitious high-school graduates, meanwhile, headed for the nearest college they could afford. But by the end of the twentieth century a clear pecking order had emerged among colleges and universities. A frenzied mating game involving the brightest students and the most prestigious institutions had become a senior-year cultural rite across America. Proximity and tradition count for less in matching students to schools. The ranking of the college, and the promise of the student, count for more. Young Americans sort themselves out into a bright-lined hierarchy of ability through the schools they attend, in a self-reinforcing syndrome of segmentation. If it was once at least roughly true that a sheepskin is a sheepskin is a sheepskin, it is emphatically not the case today.[31] In the 1970s I enrolled at the Midwestern state university from which my father had graduated thirty years earlier, only vaguely aware that more prestigious schools existed. If my children turn out to care a lot about money, they would be reckless not to attend the best school that will take them.

*   *   *

Table 2.1 summarizes some of the story so far.[32] America's best-off families usually include a two-income married couple with plenty of formal schooling. Families that fall behind differ in many ways; the prevalence of single mothers rises as income levels fall, while the number of family members earning a paycheck tends to decline. But the most striking and systematic difference is education. A college education is more than eight times more common among families at the top as among families at the bottom, and graduate education is more than eighteen times more common. Even compared to relatively fortunate families in the second-to-highest fifth, the richest 5 percent of families are more than three times as likely to be headed by someone with a postgraduate degree.

RULES AND INSTITUTIONS: An increase in shoe imports, burgeoning ranks of Internet-savvy workers in South Asia, an influx of illegal immigrants, or the diffusion of automated teller machines will have one set

Table 2.1 Features of Families by Income Category, 2005

	Bottom 20%	Second 20%	Middle 20%	Fourth 20%	Top 20%	Top 5%
Income threshold	$0	$25,616	$45,021	$68,304	$103,101	$184,500
Married couples	48%	69%	80%	87%	92%	94%
Single mothers	43	22	14	8	4	3
No earners	39	19	8	4	2	2
One earner	48	43	31	20	17	20
Two or more earners	13	38	62	76	81	78
Bachelor's or more[a]	9	15	25	37	58	74
Graduate degree[a]	2	4	8	12	26	37

Source: Current Population Survey, Annual Social and Economic Supplement, March 2006, Income Table 6, "Percent Distribution of Families, by Selected Characteristics within Income Quintile and Top 5 Percent in 2005," accessed September 2006 at http://ferret.bls.census.gov/macro/032004/faminc/new06_000.htm.

a. For the designated "head of household."

of consequences if minimum wage laws prop up hourly pay, and another set of consequences if wages are allowed to fall to whatever level the new conditions dictate. Similarly, the ultimate impact on employment and earnings of new telecommunications technologies, or expert systems for bookkeeping, or a merger between a U.S. and a European publisher, will depend on whether affected employees are represented by unions; whether they have legal protection against summary layoffs; and whether (by law, or custom, or contract) they have a voice in corporate decision making. The labor market, like any market, is a simple term for a complex network of organizations, laws, norms, and interests. The details of this network can matter greatly.

Analysts use the term "labor-market institutions" to describe a whole portfolio of factors that shape and constrain the outcomes of deals struck by workers and employers. Studies generally find that such factors—whether institutional peculiarities distinguishing the United States from other advanced countries, or changes over time within America—account for a good deal of the growth in inequality. The narrowing of the earnings distribution in the middle third of the last century was caused partly by the wartime surge in labor demand, but also by the flurry of New Deal policy innovations. The Fair Labor Standards Act of 1938, for instance, put a meaningful federal floor under wages. The National Labor Relations Act was enacted to ease labor organizing, and within a decade the unionization rate had risen from 12 to 35 percent.[33]

But the recent evolution of institutional factors has been in the opposite direction. The minimum wage was nearly half of the average hourly pay in the 1950s and 1960s, but dwindled to less than one-third by the mid-2000s, exerting progressively less influence over labor-market outcomes. The fraction of the workforce belonging to labor unions fell slowly through the early postwar years: 29 percent in 1960, 25 percent in 1979, then plummeted to barely 12 percent overall, and to just 7.4 percent of private-sector workers, by 2006.[34] Labor-market institutions are nested within and shaped by a wider context of laws, organizations, and rules. The long, deep shift toward deregulation (in communication, transportation, finance, and other sectors) has offered enormous benefits to Americans in their roles as consumers, but has also stripped away advantages many used to enjoy in their roles as workers.[35]

Determining the effects of labor-market policies and institutions tends to be both methodologically challenging and ideologically contentious. Minimum-wage laws may raise some workers' pay while pricing others out of the workforce; unions may benefit their members at the expense of unorganized workers. A flurry of good research during recent years, though, has wrung as much truth as possible out of limited data on complex trends, and a surprising degree of consensus exists. The weakening of such institutions in the United States has quite clearly contributed to rising inequality.

One undeniable factor has been the collapse of the labor movement. Collective bargaining generally pushes up pay at the bottom and constrains it at the top within unionized firms by more than enough to counter disparities between workers in union and nonunion workplaces. Something on the order of 10 to 20 percent of the growth in wage inequality among American men seems attributable to the withering away of private-sector unionism.[36] The decline in the value of the minimum wage—relative to the overall price level, and relative to the rewards the market accords higher-paid workers—has probably caused about a tenth of the increase in wage dispersal overall, and may have been a much larger factor for female workers.

The leverage of labor-market institutions can also be calibrated by comparing nations that choose different paths from America's. In Britain, Canada, and the United States labor markets are relatively unconstrained; in Germany, France, and the Nordic countries minimum wages are high, unions thrive, and corporate governance rules grant rights and a voice to workers even if they don't belong to unions. A steep macroeconomic price is paid for such protections, to be sure. While smaller countries sometimes find ways to forge a more favorable tradeoff, social solidarity and slow growth come as a package deal for most of Europe. But the evidence is clear that nations with stronger institutional constraints on labor markets tend to have substantially less wage dispersion and a much tighter pattern of family income.[37]

CULTURE AND VALUES: The trail of hard evidence runs out before the great economic divide can be fully explained, and we must turn to murkier matters of culture and values. One major change in American culture since 1970 actually has had a pretty straightforward impact on inequality. Women's exodus from the kitchen to the workplace explains much of the change in family income patterns. High-earning women tend to be married to high-earning men, which boosts family income at the top. Low-earning women all too often are married to nobody at all, as Table 2.1 shows, dragging down family income at the bottom. But these trends only amplify the central story of widening differences in *individual* earnings power. And much of this dispersion remains a mystery even after accounting for the causes flagged in the previous pages.

Differences in workers' measurable strengths and shortcomings can account for only about a third of the divergence in the rewards to work.[38] In other words, people who seem very similar, in terms of their age, gender, race, educational background, years of experience, and so on, are collecting increasingly *dissimilar* paychecks. The decline of unions and other institutional stories can explain part of this, but only part. Patterns that are well known (though a bit peculiar to those of orthodox economic instincts) can explain a bit more. For example, big companies tend to pay more than small companies, and some industries are systematically more generous than others.[39] But even after these patterns are taken into account much of the great divide is still a puzzle. To some extent this is surely because the pertinent facts about workers, and about the work that they do, are so complex and subtle that much of the data inevitably elude researchers' statistical nets. Even if Bill and Phil have similar résumés and do work that appears identical to an outsider, they may be in entirely different leagues of productivity. Statistical surveys are often blind to differences that are utterly clear in the workplace. What look like random disparities may make eminent sense if we were intimate enough with the details. But dismissing the divide in earnings by reference to our vast ignorance about the realities of the working world begs the question of why this hypothesized realm of perfectly defensible inequality is so much greater now than it used to be, and so much greater in America than elsewhere.[40]

It seems inescapable that culture and values, as they evolve in intimate symbiosis with the American economy, shape how that economy's blessings are shared out. Thirty years ago their manager may well have paid Bill and Phil about the same, overlooking their disparate output, since it eased office tension and seemed, well, somehow fair, whatever the calculus of marginal labor product might dictate. Such practices have become harder to sustain, and for that reason rarer. Even if the manager's own predilection is toward workplace equity, she knows she can't afford to ignore disparities in productivity. If she denies to Bill (the abler of the two) a premium for his extra output he is apt to decamp to a workplace that will recognize and reward his edge. Modern America's competitive, information-drenched labor market makes it easier for Bill to find the highest bidder for his skills. Modern America's hypercharged culture of meritocracy makes it seem only right for him to do so. Meanwhile, if the manager pays Phil more than his output warrants, her unit will be carrying needless costs. Her products will enter the marketplace with a handicap, and she'll have some explaining to do to her own boss. His assessment of *her* worth, after all, will hinge on how well she holds down costs and ramps up output. Happily or not, she will tailor Bill's and Phil's pay packets as precisely as she can to their respective abilities.

A similar dynamic applies, though far more dramatically, to divergent rewards for workers who are demonstrably *dis*similar. A generation or two back even a very talented manager might have felt a little sheepish about a multimillion-dollar salary for himself, and a little ashamed about wringing the last possible nickel out of his company's unskilled workers. But the cultural legitimacy of the market's stern dictates renders such patterns progressively more acceptable.[41] Press accounts of stratospheric paychecks for corporate executives, sports and entertainment figures, and A-list doctors and lawyers have made talented Americans less reluctant to grab for all they can. Cable-fed consciousness about the wider world, including the truly desperate straits of workers in the poorest countries, somehow drained much of the shame away from paying unskilled Americans wages that remain well above starvation levels. Blatant self-dealing on the part of the well-paid and sweatshop exploitation, though both certainly occur, need not be invoked to explain the normalization of wildly unequal workplace rewards.[42] Bit by bit, stark disparities became just the way things are.[43] If you are smart and skilled and ambitious and lucky (and not too squeamish about the fates of your fellows) today's world of work should suit you just fine. If not, you picked the wrong time to be working in America.

There is a crucial coda to this story: the transformation that replaced shared prosperity with a world of winners and losers reshuffled only the private sector. Government is a different deal. Public employment remains a relic of the middle-class economy that is mostly a memory in the private sector.

What's Different about Government Work?

Soon enough we'll dig into the data on public and private employment. But first let's consider why we should expect to find *any* difference between the sectors, and what kind of differences it makes sense to anticipate. Why should the fact that a person works at a local school, a state prison, or a federal bureau—instead of a fast-food outlet, a bank, a foundation, or some other private entity—matter for how he or she is hired, paid, and treated in the workplace? Let's consider some elementary reasons why government employment might differ from private employment in any more-or-less modern, more-or-less market-oriented, more-or-less democratic country.

THE ABSENCE OF MARKET DISCIPLINE:　While it is a myth that there's no accountability in the public sector—if you require convincing on this point talk to a defeated mayor on the first Wednesday of any November, or to a program director pinned in the glare of a press investigation—government does indeed lack the peculiarly precise accountability of the market. In business, wins and losses register on a scoreboard that is well understood and managerially consequential. The obvious fact that this mechanism often fails to work as advertised in the business world complicates, but does not obliterate, this basic distinction between the sectors. A corporate manager can be reasonably confident that more revenue will be regarded as a good thing, and more cost as a bad thing, by those with influence over her fate. For reasons that are to a great extent justified, and to an even greater extent durable, the manager in government has far less cause for obsession with revenues and costs.

The profit motive is a powerful force, and it would be astonishing if its presence in one sector and its absence in the other produced no discernible differences. The diffuse, multidimensional accountability typical of government tends to generate a stance toward personnel that varies from the private-sector norm. Any manager, whether working in business or in government, prefers to employ highly qualified people and to make the most of them. But a private manager will generally feel a more intense imperative to hire with an eye to ability, even if this requires paying top dollar, and to manage for visible results. Likewise, a public manager would rather have low costs than high costs. But she will be less avid than her private counterpart about minimizing headcount and holding down compensation to wring every bit of excess from the payroll. The managers may be very similar people, but they operate within profoundly different matrices of signals, constraints, and incentives. Thus the forces, sketched out in the previous chapter, that have roiled the private economy—globalization, new technologies, shifts in culture, norms, and institutions—apply to government in a greatly attenuated way.

DISPERSED "OWNERS":   It is not merely that private managers are accountable in a focused way that explains the greater precision and intensity of economic motivation in business. It is also that they are accountable to a focused group: shareholders. The owners of a private organization have the right to direct how it is run, coupled with a concentrated stake in having it run efficiently. While nonprofit organizations (churches, foundations, civic associations, museums, and so on) lack the simple scorecard of profit-seeking firms, they share with business a relatively circumscribed and self-selected constituency that is free to provide or to withhold resources. Government is owned by the citizenry at large—a salutary arrangement, on the whole, but one that greatly dilutes any single citizen's proprietary interest in cost control.

Suppose advancing technology renders it possible to replace five hundred receptionists with a sophisticated voice-mail system, generating net savings of $10 million per year. The sole proprietor of a subscription-management company has potent motives to make such a change, and very likely will. If the company, instead of a single owner, had 10,000 equal shareholders the payoff would be less concentrated, and no single shareholder would rationally mount a personal campaign to push automation. Yet the per-owner advantage of $1,000 ($10 million divided by 10,000) would loom large in any reckoning of financial stewardship, and odds are good the system will be installed. Imagine, next, that the same automation opportunity, at the same scale, arises at the Social Security Administration. A $10 million annual savings translates to something approaching three cents per American. Insofar as economic motives are the driving force, it is quite unlikely that any citizen will insist on automation, or indeed even pay enough attention to the agency's inner workings to be aware of the option. Dispersed ownership makes it natural for such opportunities to be seized more slowly in the public sector. And if there are other considerations at stake—for example, the interests of those five hundred receptionists—they may not be seized at all.

Even an occasional glance at any newspaper's business section reveals that owners' interests sometimes get short shrift in the business world. Inattentive or bamboozled shareholders are frequently fleeced by their supposed stewards. Yet one need not pretend that concentrated ownership yields perfect accountability in the private sector to concede that the diluted ownership inherent in government will generate a characteristically different hierarchy of managerial priorities. Running a taut personnel system will trend lower on the list in government than it will in the private sector.

RULES, REGULATIONS, AND SUNSHINE: Precisely because dispersed ownership and the lack of a clear bottom line imperil accountability in such an obvious way, government is permeated with substitute mechanisms for holding stewards to account. To guard against caprice and cronyism, formal regulations lay down procedures for hiring and firing. Such regulations make personnel actions fairer than they might otherwise be, but at the cost of making them slow, cumbersome, and imprecise. Similarly, since managers cannot be expected to have a clear sense of each worker's productivity when goals are complex, long-term, multiple, or imperfectly measurable (and as a further buffer against favoritism), instead of attempting to tailor compensation to each worker's output government relies on rulebooks that specify the pay and benefits associated with each position. This improves the odds that similar workers will be treated similarly. But unless the pay rules are more intricately diverse and flexible than anyone can humanly expect them to be, it also raises the odds that *different* workers will be treated similarly, too. Finally, to compensate for each citizen's diluted motive to scrutinize the inner workings of public organizations, "sunshine" rules mandate disclosure of the details of governmental operations, frequently including the specifics of compensation packages. In the private sector people speculate about the size of the other guy's paycheck, but the number is confidential and it is neither polite nor prudent to pry too aggressively. In government, you can look it up.

MULTIPLE MISSIONS, AMBIGUOUS PRIORITIES: Government often serves more than one goal through some single action it undertakes: teaching basic skills while transmitting culture; acquiring pencils while promoting minority-owned businesses; managing its own workers while sending messages to the private sector about the merits of family leave, or workplace diversity, or continuing education.[44] In the absence of clear metrics of value, the relative importance of each goal embedded in an undertaking becomes a matter of debate, or, to put it less delicately, a matter of politics. Office politics are ubiquitous in every workplace, to be sure, but government stands out as an inherently "employee-owned" enterprise. Public workers have as much right as anyone else, and a good deal more motive than most, to make their voices heard about the terms of employment in the public sector. Unlike employees in a typical private workplace, or even worker-owners constrained by market pressures, government employees' interests are checked by regulations and by broadly parsimonious public opinion rather than by economic counterforces.

You might expect this bundle of factors to produce public jobs that, with far greater frequency than private jobs, are:

- stable and secure, thanks to their insulation from capricious market forces;
- structured and rule-bound, sometimes to an irksome degree;
- less stress-laden than private jobs where the struggle for survival can force tight deadlines and long hours;
- frequently rich with the satisfaction of serving noble goals;
- but (since the scoreboard is murky, rules complex, and games ongoing) short on opportunities for dramatic wins;
- compensated at neither princely nor pauperish levels, since visible pay packets must withstand the scrutiny of coworkers, the press, and fellow citizens without exciting either outrage or pity.

And you would be right. As we'll shortly see in some detail, this is pretty much what we encounter in the data on public jobs, albeit with some important caveats and complications. It is also, to be clear, pretty much what we have always seen. Government work has long been considered tamer than the rough-and-tumble of business, promising slim prospects for getting rich but security and decent pay across the board. Public employment has not changed, in any truly fundamental way, for a long time. What has changed is the context: the world of work in the private sector that serves as an alternative, and as a point of reference, for government work. In a previous version of America, public jobs were already somewhat more secure, somewhat less stressful, somewhat better compensated on average, and somewhat less rewarding at the top, than private jobs. Government work today resembles, in most essential respects, government work of many decades ago. But the private sector has metamorphosed into an ever more extreme version of its basic model. In today's America, with its growingly dramatic economic disparities, the distance between public and private work has widened. It is precisely by not changing much that government employment has become a modern oddity.

How Government Work Actually Does Differ: Sifting the Evidence

Bear in mind the previous section's overview of the fading middle-class economy, and consider some basic facts about the worlds of work in the two sectors, mostly drawn from the data files of the Bureau of Labor Statistics.[45]

Job Security

Public employees have less cause than their private counterparts for anxiety about steady work. Indeed, they have a whole layered list of reasons for confidence that their job will still be there tomorrow. First, government's tasks are relatively enduring. There are always kids to teach, crimes to solve, and borders to patrol, even as many private occupations (producing eight-track cassette players, trading energy futures, selling pet supplies on the Internet) come and go. Second, government's insulation from market pressures means that public workers are less likely to be laid off in response to every twitch in supply or demand, even if a strict economic calculus renders them superfluous. Finally, public-sector employment rules afford workers a degree of protection against job loss (whether arbitrary, economically motivated, or warranted by performance) that is rare, and becoming ever rarer, in the private economy.

Late in 2000 the Bureau of Labor Statistics launched a monthly measure of layoffs and other labor-market turbulence called the Job Opportunities and Labor Turnover Survey (referred to, aptly, as JOLTS). From December 2000 through April 2004—a period that brackets the winding down of an economic boom, a moderately serious slump, and resurgent job growth—about 1.5 percent of the employees in the private sector were fired or laid off each month, on average. (The figure ranged from a low of 1.1 percent to a high of 1.7 percent.) The layoff rate in state and local government averaged 0.38 percent over the same period, while in the federal government it was 0.31 percent. Private workers, in other words, faced roughly four times greater risk than public workers of losing their jobs.

A separate data series tracks mass layoffs—plant closings or other misadventures that displace at least fifty workers—and goes back to the mid-1990s. In the private sector the annual total of workers filing for unemployment after such large-scale disruptions averaged about 1.75 million from 1996 through 2005. In the public sector, an average of 75,000 jobs disappeared each year in mass layoffs. Note that a great many private jobs (and very few public jobs) are in small establishments where it is mathematically impossible to lay off fifty workers in one fell swoop since there aren't that many workers in the first place. And consider that even in 2005, when public-sector layoffs were at their recent peak, a private worker was three times as likely as a government worker to fall victim to a mass layoff.

Benefits

Employee benefits—health coverage, pensions, paid vacations—have been dwindling for decades among a broad swath of private-sector workers, particularly those below the middle rungs of corporate ladders. But a government job is still likely to come with a good benefits package. The Bureau of Labor Statistics conducts a periodic survey of employee benefits at both private and governmental workplaces, and some recent comparisons—in each case the latest available data from the 1990s or 2000s—are instructive. (The federal government, which has its own uniform and broadly generous benefits policy, is not covered by the survey, but state and local workplaces account for more than four-fifths of public employment.) Consider first the big, costly items—health-care and pension coverage—that loom largest in any comparison of benefits packages.

HEALTH INSURANCE: An overwhelming majority of state and local government workers—86 percent—have access to employer-provided health coverage, compared with just 45 percent of private-sector workers. Government tends to offer better coverage, moreover, and to pay a larger share of the overall cost. About half of public workers have their own health insurance paid for in full by their employer, and a quarter get their family covered as well at no cost to them. Only about a fifth of private employers pick up the full tab for individual health insurance, and just one in ten pays for family coverage. Governmental employers are more likely than private employers to provide dental benefits (60 percent versus 32 percent) and vision-care benefits (43 percent versus 19 percent). "Wellness" programs are available to more than a third of public workers, compared to 18 percent of private workers. And almost all public workers (96 percent) but just a little more than half of private workers (53 percent) get paid sick leave.

RETIREMENT BENEFITS:　Twice as many public workers (98 percent) as private workers (49 percent) get some kind of retirement benefits on the job. Systematic discrepancies in the *type* of coverage, moreover, matter as well. There are two sharply different kinds of retirement benefits—"defined benefit" plans, in which a worker is promised a fixed level of income upon retirement, and "defined contribution" plans, in which the worker or the employer or both make investments on the worker's behalf, with eventual retirement income contingent on how those investments pan out. Recent decades have seen a massive shift toward "defined contribution" arrangements, including the alphabet soup of 401ks, 403bs, and IRAs that have come to figure so prominently in Americans' financial portfolios. Such plans give people some control over their destinies in retirement, and can pay off handsomely for those who deposit steady, substantial contributions, who make astute investment choices, and who are lucky in the timing of their deposits and their retirement. But defined-benefit plans offer more security, since the worker is guaranteed a set level of retirement income, and coming up with the money is the employer's problem. Just one-fifth of private workers, compared with 90 percent of government workers, have a defined-benefit pension as part of their benefits package. (In fairness to private employers, federal rules require them to fund defined-benefit pensions—that is, sock away the money that will eventually be needed to pay promised pension benefits—while public officials have more latitude to make pension promises that their distant successors will have to deliver on.) Counting only those workers who *do* have defined-benefit pensions, 77 percent of public workers can retire early (before the age of sixty-five) without a reduction in the promised monthly benefit, compared to just half of private workers.

OTHER BENEFITS: The same broad pattern—richer benefits for public than for private jobs—holds up beyond the big-ticket health and retirement items, as summarized in Table 2.2.

Wages and Salaries

A steady job matters, and so do good benefits, but most people care quite a bit about their paychecks. Do government jobs offer scanty pay to counterbalance rich benefit packages? Or are wages and salaries better in government as well? One seemingly straightforward approach to this question is to simply look at average pay in the public and private sectors. The ever-helpful Bureau of Labor Statistics makes this easy to do. In May 2005 (the most recent point at which across-the-board data are available) public-sector pay averaged $21.28 per hour. In the rest of the economy, the average was $18.59.[46] Is the case closed, with a verdict of a 15 percent pay premium for government workers? Not nearly. Indeed, we're just getting started on working through the evidence. Prevailing levels of compensation can differ from one setting to another for all kinds of reasons. Paychecks tend to run higher in urban areas than in farm country, for example, higher in the Northeast than in the Southwest, higher in growing than in shrinking cities, and so on.

Table 2.2 Comparing Benefits other than Health and Retirement

	Public	Private
Average paid vacation (first year on the job)	13 days	9 days[a]
Average paid vacation (ten years on the job)	19 days	15 days[a]
Average paid holidays	11 days	8 days[a]
Share of employees offered:		
Life insurance	89%	47%
Job-related education assistance	63%	38%
Non-job-related education assistance	22%	9%
Paid jury leave	95%	70%
Paid military leave	75%	50%
Paid personal leave	38%	17%[a]

Source: Bureau of Labor Statistics, Public Data Query, accessed June 2004 at http://www.data.bls.gov.

a. Average of separate figures for smaller and larger firms.

Pay also tends, quite systematically, to be higher in big companies than in small ones. Workplaces with more than five hundred employees pay about 50 percent higher wages, on average, than workplaces with fewer than one hundred employees.[47] But this doesn't mean that big operations have sloppy or soft-hearted personnel systems. The roster of small establishments includes a lot of pizza parlors, lawn-mowing services, day-care centers, and the like that for a variety of reasons (some of them clearly legitimate, others open to challenge, but none of them particularly mysterious) tend not to pay very much. Big establishments include law firms, hospitals, major foundations, unionized factories, and banks that tend to compensate handsomely many or most of their employees.

Similarly, government has a distinctive pattern of work and workers—more lawyers and fewer leaf-rakers, more researchers and fewer ranch hands, more teachers and fewer tree-trimmers—that would generate differences in the average paycheck even if both sectors steered by the same hard-eyed economic calculus when setting salaries. To gain any traction on the question of relative compensation we need to push beyond the blunt averages and look first to the principles that underpin notions of fair pay, and then at detailed comparisons of paychecks for particular jobs in both the public and private sectors.

The Puzzle of Fair Pay

What do we mean by "fairness" when it comes to the rewards of work? One simple definition of fairness might be that every worker should be paid exactly the same. But few endorse so extreme a version of egalitarianism; even those who most lament the vertiginous economic disparities of today's America will concede that it can be fair as well as efficient for compensation to vary across individuals. If we depart from lockstep equality as the benchmark, we might first look to differences in the work a person does—variations in complexity, urgency, arduousness, and so on—to justify paying some more than others. Following this approach we could define fairness as equal pay for equal work, and unequal pay for unequal work. If this seemed too simplistic, we could refine the fairness criterion (at the price of making it vastly harder to apply) and call for equal pay for work of equal value, or equal challenge, or some other equilibrating concept. We could also recognize that money is just one element of overall compensation, and accept that pay and benefits could differ, and still be entirely fair, if two otherwise comparable tasks vary in working conditions, or security, or status, or emotional fulfillment, and so on. As the messy history of efforts to codify "comparable worth" policy attests, it can be devilishly difficult to put into practice such richer conceptions of fairness, however valid they may be in the abstract.

Alternatively, we could seek touchstones for fairness by reference to the worker instead of the work. Characteristics of particular individuals— their needs, their credentials, their social standing, their histories (of racial injustice, gender discrimination, military service, and so on)— may be seen as entailing legitimate claims that are separate from the value of the work that they do. Multiple considerations can come into play in a single judgment. For example, we might consider it fair that a college graduate earns more than a high-school dropout because he suffered through all of those lectures in his youth and deserves some recompense, and also because we believe he is likely to be better equipped to do valuable things on the job.[48]

I do not propose to settle the normative debate over fair pay, or even advance the argument to any notable degree, but simply observe that all these issues and perspectives, and more, can come into play. Philosophers, personnel directors, and kitchen-table kibitzers invoke such notions when they talk about what somebody ought to be paid. Whenever there is any room for issues of just-desserts to enter into the conversation about the rewards to work there is no shortage of considerations to fill that space.

Economists, however, have something quite precise in mind when they think about what a worker ought to be paid: compensation should be equal to each worker's "marginal value product." The marginal value product of labor is simply the extra output a worker's efforts make possible, times the price a consumer is willing to pay for that output. Imagine that gadget-savvy home cooks are snapping up automatic carrot-dicers at $20 each (directly from the factory, to sidestep the complicating factors of shipping costs, retail markup, and the like). Production costs other than labor are $5 per dicer. When Betty is at her post on the assembly line a thousand carrot-dicers get made every hour. Only 999 can be produced when Betty takes her lunch break. Betty's marginal value product is revealed to be $15 each hour—one extra carrot-dicer times its price of $20 minus nonlabor costs of $5—and this is exactly what she should collect in wages and benefits.

Multiple chains of logic converge on that $15 point, in the kind of symmetry that economists find so satisfying. First, paying Betty the extra revenue that is attributable to her and her alone puts into effect one plausible conception of fairness: "you get what you give." If we interpret the price someone is willing to pay to acquire the carrot-dicer as a valid measure of the increment in our species' aggregate happiness created by one more such gadget (and who are we to say it isn't?), then Betty is making an even trade with the rest of the human community. Second, a wage equal to her contribution to revenue lets Betty's employer use data both about the demand for carrot-dicers and about alternative production models to inform decisions about how many hours to have Betty on the line, whether to replace her with someone else, or whether to invest in a machine that can replicate her work. Third, a wage anchored in marginal value product helps Betty make good choices as well. If she knows that $15 is the true value of her work on the carrot-dicer line, she is well equipped to decide whether her talents are better applied in this job or in another line of endeavor. A tight link between pay and value creation means that what is good for Betty is good for the world.

Everyone—not least corporate personnel directors and compensation consultants—knows that pay is not always set this way. It is frequently impractical, by the nature of the work itself, to generate a precise estimate of a single individual's contribution. Even when such fine-grained measurement is technically feasible, myriad flaws and complexities in labor and product markets can break the links between value and price, between price and profits, between profits and wages. But the concept is a fundamental touchstone in economic theory, and also has imperfect but real standing in the practical world. The abstraction of marginal value product exerts some gravitational pull over the real paychecks of real people. Compensation that is too far out of line with a worker's contribution to revenue is hard to sustain in business. If a firm pays its workers much above this point of reference it will founder financially. If it pays them much below it, the workers will quit and find employers ready to give them what they're worth. As impediments to market forces have eroded in recent decades, the pull of this abstract ideal has generally strengthened. Vaulting improvements in information technology make it easier to gauge the economic value of each worker's efforts. Intensifying competition at home and abroad toughens the penalties for looking beyond the bottom line when setting wages. Social norms that used to prop up pay on the low end, and hold it down at the high end, have faded.

The link between pay and productivity has always been weaker in the public sector. This is in part because government has more than its share of complicated tasks where it is inherently hard to disentangle any single person's role in producing results. Even if it were possible to parcel out proportionate credit to each person involved in a public mission, though, the fact that government's revenues come from taxes rather than prices makes it hard to fix the value of what's produced. And the market forces that tend to nudge pay into at least approximate alignment with marginal value product, of course, are mostly absent in government. In public workplaces, accordingly, economic considerations compete with other conceptions of fair pay, and always have.

The key question, which I've sidestepped so far, is how much this matters in practice. We'll turn to the Labor Department's Occupational Employment Statistics program for some purchase on this question.[49] The department, working with employment agencies in the separate states, periodically surveys 1.2 million representative workplaces and uses the results to generate fine-grained estimates of employment and compensation levels for seven hundred occupations in 451 separate industries. The industries are organized by the standard North American Industrial Classification System that ranges from the bird's-eye view of broad sectors (such as "construction") to the worm's-eye view of quite specific areas of enterprise ("tile and terrazzo contractors"). The Occupational Employment Statistics marries this industry taxonomy with a comparably detailed roster of jobs called the Standard Occupational Classification system, which similarly drills down from broad groups ("healthcare support occupations") to particular lines of work ("veterinary assistants and laboratory animal caretakers"). Pay levels are tallied on an hourly basis or a full-time equivalent annual basis, with details on the range as well as the average for each occupation in each industry.

The system has some quirks and shortcomings, to be sure. Its definition of wages and salaries includes tips, commissions, and productions bonuses, for example, but excludes overtime pay, which will skew some comparisons. Since it stops counting at a pay level of $70 per hour, or about $150,000 a year, compensation is underestimated in the upper reaches of the labor market. Public education is pulled out of the state and local government sectors and resettled in "education services" alongside private universities, flight training, and cosmetology schools. A whole menagerie of public, for-profit, and nonprofit operations are herded together into the category of "health care and social assistance." And the armed services aren't surveyed at all, nor are farmers, fishermen, the self-employed, or household workers. But even without its big military, health, and education components, the government category—with federal, state, and local breakdowns available—includes pay estimates for nearly 9.5 million workers (as of mid-2005), or about half of the total public workforce. (Most of the missing people work in education, and different data sources exploited shortly will offer some perspective on them.)

Where the Labor Department data get interesting is with their strong suit—apples-to-apples comparisons of particular jobs in the public and private sectors.[50] Consider first the prosaic and ubiquitous occupation "janitors" (or, to be precise, "janitors and cleaners except maids and household cleaners"). About 108,000 of them work in government, and nearly 2 million work in the private economy. The average public-sector janitor earns about $23,700, versus about $19,800 outside government. Or examine another humble job category—"general office clerks." About 330,000 of them work in government, and about 2.7 million work outside government. Average public pay is $26,700; average private pay is $22,800. One of the more prominent job categories in the public sector is "postal service mail carriers." There are about 347,000 of them, and they each earn about $46,300 on average. The private sector doesn't have any people who deliver letters to your mailbox—by law, as it happens. But there are private employees whose mission is to carry documents from where they start out to where they are supposed to go. These 38,000 "couriers and messengers" earn a full-time annual equivalent well under half of a mail carrier's salary.

Plenty of jobs, of course, pay similar wages in the public and private sectors. About 45,000 people get a government paycheck for collecting trash and recyclables, for example, and about 80,000 doing the same tasks draw their salaries from private employers, mostly waste-management contractors. The craft's rewards are only a little higher in government (about $29,700) than in business (about $28,600). In both private industry and government, similarly, the average pay of civil engineers rounds off to $63,000 a year.

And then there are jobs where the pay differential between business and government cuts the other way. The public sector has about 27,000 "appraisers and assessors of real estate" to estimate property values in order to figure out what taxes the owners should be charged. The real-estate industry pays almost exactly the same number of people to do pretty much the same thing, though with an eye to setting prices rather than taxes. Government assessors earn about $43,000; their colleagues in the private sector earn about $57,000. Several thousand economists work in both the public sector and in the "professional, scientific, and technical services industry." In government economists earn an average of $69,000 a year, versus $99,000 in industry. The 34,000 financial managers in government are paid an annual average of $74,000, while their 25,000 counterparts in the securities industry collect about $130,000.

A pattern is starting to emerge, but let's not lean too heavily on these rather random comparisons. Mapping public and private pay patterns calls for a more systematic take on the data. It is a tedious but fairly straightforward matter to determine average pay levels in government as a whole and in the entire private sector for particular jobs. But assuming you don't want to spend the next few hours perusing comparative pay rates for every one of the hundreds of occupations in the public sector, how should a meaningful subset be selected?

It seems sensible to start with jobs that are reasonably prevalent in government. The public payroll does include some upholsterers, animal trainers, and pastry chefs. But the terms of their employment, vis-à-vis their private counterparts, probably do not pose weighty policy issues. So the first decision rule is to include only occupations that account for some reasonable share—let's make it at least half of 1 percent—of total public employment. This should eliminate the fringe cases. It also makes sense to restrict public–private comparisons to occupational categories that exist, to some meaningful degree, both within and outside of government. There are no private mail carriers at all, as noted, and while there are some private-sector court reporters, probation officers, firefighters and air-traffic controllers, the government's preponderance in such professions seems likely to distort any comparisons.[51] The second decision rule, accordingly, is to focus on occupations where government accounts for no more than half of total employment economy-wide.[52] Twenty-five job titles make the cut as prevalent in, but not dominated by, government. Table 2.3 lists these occupations—in ascending order of compensation in the private economy—and gives annual average full-time wages and salaries for both the public and private sectors. It also records, in the final column, the relationship between what government pays and what the private sector pays for each occupation.

Table 2.3 Average Annual Pay (Full-Time Equivalent) in 2005

Job Title	Private Sector Average (in dollars)	Public Sector Average (in dollars)	Private Relative to Public (in percent)
Recreation workers	$19,708	$20,570	95.8%
Janitors	19,825	23,730	83.5
Landscaping workers	20,561	23,860	86.2
Laborers and material movers	20,626	23,910	86.3
Security guards	20,907	25,440	82.2
Nursing aides	21,320	25,260	84.4
Office clerks	22,815	26,730	85.4
Social service assistants	23,819	28,960	82.2
Emergency medical technicians	25,448	27,890	91.2
Secretaries	26,229	31,900	82.2
Typists	28,604	29,700	96.3
Bookkeeping clerks	29,429	31,370	93.8
Maintenance workers	31,180	32,600	95.6
Social workers	34,942	38,130	91.6
Executive secretaries	36,167	35,780	101.1
Construction equipment operators	37,305	32,060	116.4
Managers of office workers	42,056	46,240	91.0
Accountants	52,652	48,500	108.6
Registered nurses	59,853	56,470	106.0
Civil engineers	66,053	66,390	99.5
Computer systems analysts	68,289	68,710	99.4
Management analysts	69,329	62,250	111.4
Managers, not otherwise classified	79,937	77,770	102.8
General managers	83,816	70,820	118.4
Lawyers	108,830	83,650	130.1

Source: Bureau of Labor Statistics, Occupational Employment and Wage Estimates, accessed June 2006 at http://www.bls.gov/oes/oes_dl.htm#2005_m.

Focus for a moment on a job title a little more than midway down the list: "executive secretaries." The Bureau of Labor Statistics defines the duties of this job, with some precision, to be loftier than those of plain old secretaries but within (albeit near the top of) the pink-collar administrative ranks. Executive secretaries "provide high-level administrative support by conducting research, preparing statistical reports, handling information requests, and performing clerical functions such as preparing correspondence, receiving visitors, arranging conference calls, and scheduling meetings. May also train and supervise lower-level clerical staff."[53] The first interesting thing about the executive-secretary category is that there are a lot of them. It is among the more common jobs recorded by the bureau's surveyors, with close to 1.4 million workers. The second interesting thing is that the category is rather neatly divided between the public and private sectors. At 139,000, the ranks of public-sector executive secretaries account for almost exactly 10 percent of the total for the profession, which is not far from the public proportion of all workers (by the survey's definition of government). The third interesting thing is that average pay levels for executive secretaries are very close to the same in the public and private sectors, rounding off to $36,000 a year.

Fourteen job categories come before executive secretaries in Table 2.3—that is, jobs with lower average wages and salaries. For all of these jobs, government pay exceeds private pay. And ten job categories come later in the list, where average private wages and salaries are higher than the $36,000 a typical executive secretary collects. For one of these occupations (front-line office managers), the private sector pays measurably worse than government, and for three others (civil engineers, computer systems analysis, and the grab-bag category of managers falling into any other category) there's basically no difference. But for the other high-level occupations, the private sector is notably more generous than is government.

Figure 2.2 tells the story graphically. If no systematic differences existed at all between public and private pay for specific kinds of work—that is, if the higher overall averages for public work were simply a matter of government having more than its share of high-end occupations—all the dots in Figure 2.2 would march along the 100 percent line. If, alternatively, the higher government average simply meant that the public sector pays more generously across the board, we would expect to see all the dots arrayed in a row above that middle line, like a rank of clouds hovering above the horizon. What we see instead is something more complicated: the less an occupation tends to pay in the private sector, the higher its *relative* rewards in government, and vice versa. Public wages and salaries are quite attractive at the low end of the scale, then droop below the private-sector benchmark at the higher end. Government offers a handsome bonus for janitors, landscapers, and nursing aides, but an inferior deal for accountants, management analysts, and lawyers.

The relationship is not an exact one; we don't see the points in Figure 2.2 arrayed in a straight line slashing up from the southwest to the northeast. In part this is because the picture is incomplete and the data are noisy. But mostly it's because the world is untidy. It would be surprising indeed—when the players include many millions of workers, hundreds of thousands of private employers, and tens of thousands of public employers—for the outcome of the compensation game to be so simple. Bear in mind, too, that this comparison is based on a single fallible data series and that a great many factors can bedevil efforts to

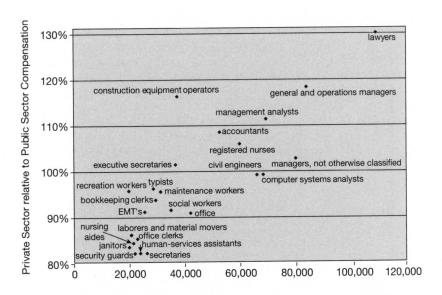

Figure 2.2: Average Annual Pay, 2005. *Source:* Bureau of Labor Statistics, Occupational Employment and Wage Estimates, accessed June 2006 at http://www.bls.gov/oes/oes_dl.htm#2005_m.

strike a fair comparison between public and private pay. We are by no means done yet. But the evidence presented so far should be sturdy enough to motivate at least wary consideration of the main argument here: as the private economy has become less hospitable to workers at the lower end of the labor market, government offers a haven from the economic storm. The most educated, most talented, and luckiest, conversely, must sacrifice more appealing private-sector prospects if they opt for public service.

Government jobs have always been attractive to Americans with few other prospects for reaching or remaining in the middle class. (Consider the economic uplift the Boston Irish enjoyed when they gained political power in the nineteenth century and were able to fill police, fire, and other municipal jobs with their own people.) A public career has never been the fast track to serious wealth, conversely, and throughout America's history the elite who choose government work have had a sense of duty, or modest consumption expectations, or

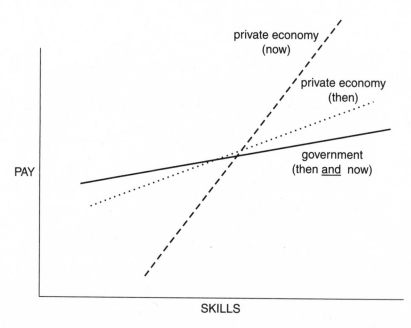

Figure 2.3: Widening Gaps at Both Top and Bottom between Public and Private Pay.

both. But the differences between the public and private worlds of work have widened. Figure 2.3 presents a stripped-down schematic of what's going on. The gradient of public-sector pay with respect to skills (or talent, or ambition, or luck, or other factors that shape relative rewards) has long been shallower than that of the private sector. Gaps between the two sectors have always existed, at both the low end and the high end of the labor spectrum. A generation ago, however, these gaps were narrow. A government job tended to be a little more attractive to the least-skilled, and a little of a sacrifice for the most-skilled. But as government pay patterns have stayed basically the same, the relationship between skills and pay in the private economy has pivoted violently on its axis. And both gaps have widened.

It is conceivable, of course, that the pattern suggested by Figures 2.2 and 2.3—government pay is high at the low end, low at the high end—is a mirage based on faulty and partial data. Gauging the risk that the basic data are deceptive requires going deeper into the research on comparative compensation. The depths are rather murky, alas, and not everyone will want to go there. So a summary of the relevant technical literature, which is inescapably rather denser with academic concepts and language than the rest of this book, is offered up in the appendix. Those who are interested in hearing what the labor economists and other specialists have to say are invited to join me there for a short tour of academic efforts to figure out what's going on with public-sector pay. Others may want to take my word for it that while there are some fascinating details and surprising exceptions, the fancier methods employed by blue-ribbon empiricists essentially support the story told here with unprocessed data and rough-and-ready calculations. The pay-differential literature shows that America's public sector has proven largely impervious to the changes that have roiled labor markets over the past quarter-century.[54] The pattern of government pay, which already tended to be a bit flatter than in the business world, stayed flat, and private-sector disparities intensified.

Academics are trained to maintain an open mind—to forswear declaring that some proposition is proven beyond doubt, and to go for the jugular if anyone else makes such a claim. So even in light of the evidence surveyed in this chapter and the appendix, it could still be the case that there is no systematic difference between the working worlds inside and outside government, or that any differences that happen to exist don't matter much. But I say this in the same cautious spirit that I might concede that the moon could still turn out to be made of green cheese beneath the dust, since we really haven't dug in very many places. It is about as safe an assertion as any can be in this uncertain world that in the private economy—but not in government—the bottom has fallen out and the ceiling has blown off the pay distribution. Gaps have grown between the sectors at both the high and the low ends of the labor market. People notice these gaps as they decide where to spend their energies. Government has become its own working world. And this separation of government work—the gap at the high end, and the gap at the low end—undercuts government's capacity to create value.

THREE

◆ ◆ ◆

Safe Harbor

THE SHIFT IN America's economy over the past few decades has produced a gentle climate for people with education, drive, and luck. But for less fortunate workers it has brought in gale after gale, including global competition, technological transformation, the collapse of the labor movement, crumbling legal protections, all accompanied by subtle cultural mutations that amplify the force of each gust. Many Americans who lack advanced education, the right connections, or good career karma have seen the trappings of middle-class life—job security, health insurance, pensions, a clear path to college for their kids—blown away. But some have managed to find a shelter in the storm. Government work offers a haven from the roiling turbulence of today's economy for many millions of workers. It is eminently understandable that these Americans cherish and cling to a separate working world that still lets them earn a middle-class living. The problem, of course, is that this is not what government is for.

Let's return, for a bit of perspective, to the big Bureau of Labor Statistics survey that tracks the number and nature of American jobs. This data source, recall, has many virtues (fine-grained detail, in terms of both industry and occupation; good estimates of employment levels and earnings for each job title; admirable timeliness, by the glacial standards of many statistical programs), marred by the defect of lumping public and private education together and missing the armed forces entirely. We'll come back for closer looks at the teachers and warriors after surveying the big picture.

51

Table 3.1 lists the top twenty-five job titles in the economy as a whole, along with the 2005 estimates of total employment and median annual pay for each job.[1] Table 3.2 does the same thing for just the public sector.[2] There are hundreds of occupational categories, but the top twenty-five account for more than a third of all jobs.

Table 3.1 Twenty-five Most Common Jobs Economy-Wide, 2005

Job Title	Number	Median Annual Pay (in dollars)
Retail salespeople	4,344,770	$19,140
Cashiers	3,481,420	16,260
Office clerks	2,997,370	23,070
Registered nurses	2,368,070	54,670
Laborers and material movers	2,363,960	20,610
Combined food prep and service (fast food)	2,298,010	14,790
Food servers	2,274,770	14,200
Janitors	2,107,360	19,390
Customer service representatives	2,067,700	27,490
Bookkeeping clerks	1,815,340	29,490
Secretaries	1,744,380	26,670
General managers	1,663,810	81,480
Stock clerks	1,625,430	20,100
Truck drivers	1,624,740	34,280
Elementary-school teachers	1,486,650	44,040
Executive secretaries	1,442,040	35,960
Sales representatives	1,436,800	47,380
Nursing aides	1,391,430	21,440
Office managers	1,352,130	42,400
Maintenance and repair workers	1,307,820	31,210
Teaching assistants	1,260,400	20,090
Assembly team workers	1,242,370	24,120
Receptionists	1,088,400	22,150
Retail sales managers	1,083,890	32,840
Accountants	1,051,220	52,210

Source: Bureau of Labor Statistics, Occupational Employment Statistics program, May 2005 Occupational Employment and Wage Estimates, National Cross-Industry Estimates spreadsheet, accessed June 2006 at http://www.bls.gov/oes/oes_dl.htm#2005_m.
Note: In this version, the economy-wide figures include government as well as the private sector. Teachers and teachers aides are excluded.

Where the same job is common both in government and in the whole economy, the public sector tends to offer a noticeably better deal for relatively unskilled occupations such as janitors and secretaries, in line with the previous chapter. But beyond reinforcing that comparative point, the two lists illustrate how the middle-class economy remains alive and well in government, even as it withers elsewhere. Most of the top government jobs pay enough to offer a family with two wage-earners

Table 3.2 Twenty-five Most Common Jobs in Government, 2005

Job Title	Number	Median Annual Pay (in dollars)
Elementary-school teachers	1,315,650	$47,487
Teaching assistants	1,115,454	20,090
Police and sheriff's patrol officers	609,960	46,470
Correctional officers	394,320	34,390
Mail carriers	347,180	46,330
Office clerks	329,420	26,730
Firefighters	273,540	39,350
Business operations specialists	235,920	59,520
Mail sorters and processors	208,600	43,420
Secretaries	162,500	31,900
Information and record clerks	151,530	41,120
Executive secretaries	139,270	35,780
Registered nurses	136,970	56,470
Highway maintenance workers	134,600	30,310
Maintenance and repair workers	125,270	32,600
Office managers	114,680	46,240
Managers, not otherwise specified	108,740	77,770
Bookkeeping clerks	108,480	31,370
Social workers	108,040	38,130
Janitors	107,880	23,730
Bus drivers	106,930	35,170
Lawyers	105,180	83,650
Recreation workers	102,710	20,570
Accountants	102,110	48,500
Court, municipal, and license clerks	99,060	29,560

Source: Bureau of Labor Statistics, Occupational Employment Statistics program, May 2005 Occupational Employment and Wage Estimates, National NAICS 3-digit Industry Specific Estimates spreadsheet, accessed June 2006 at http://www.bls.gov/oes/oes_dl.htm#2005_m.

middle-class status and many provide one-income families with a toehold on the middle class. Census Bureau data from 2005 identifies $43,400 as the threshold for the middle fifth of families.[3] The entry ticket to the next-lowest fifth, which might be considered lower middle class, was $24,780. Ten of the top twenty-five government jobs pay enough to bring a family into the middle fifth on the strength of just one income—something considered unremarkable in an earlier version of the American economy. Only five of the top twenty-five jobs in the whole economy— registered nurses, general managers, elementary-school teachers, sales representatives, and accountants—paid enough for a family with just one wage-earner to make it to the middle. And one of those five occupational categories (teachers) is predominantly a public-sector job, as to a lesser extent is another (nurses). Indeed, for twelve of the top twenty-five jobs economy-wide, and for six out of the seven most common jobs, a single income is not enough to pull a family out of the very bottom fifth of the income distribution.

The one-paycheck test may be less relevant, to be sure, as dual incomes become the norm. (Just 30 percent of families get by with only one wage-earner.)[4] But government's distinction as a middle-class safe harbor holds up by this standard as well. With only two exceptions— recreation workers and teaching assistants—a pair of paychecks from any job in Table 3.2 would bring a family at least into the middle fifth, and even the two exceptions come within shouting distance of the threshold. For nine of the twenty-five top jobs in the economy overall, however, including six of the ten most common jobs, even two incomes wouldn't do the trick.

This big picture, while affording a general sense of perspective, is both blurred and incomplete. So let's turn to some concrete categories of government work offering shelter to large classes of American workers whose middle-class standing would be vulnerable or worse in the private economy.

The Protectors

"Protective services"—police, firefighters, and other people in uniform who safeguard life, limb, and property—are both a preeminent function of government and a bulwark of the blue-collar middle class. Table 3.2 lists cops—or more properly, "police and sheriff's patrol officers"—as the third biggest job title in government. There are over 600,000 police officers, putting them outside the top twenty-five but easily within the fifty most common jobs in the whole economy. (Police are a little less common than accountants and carpenters, and a little more common than truck drivers and home-health aides.) The law-enforcement workforce also includes about 87,000 detectives and investigators and an additional 100,000 supervisors. Further along the idiosyncratic value chain for this particular industry are the 394,000 correctional officers listed in Table 3.2 (plus *their* 32,000 supervisors and managers) and 83,000 probation officers.

Among the cultural themes entangled with American law enforcement is the notion of police work as a bastion of blue-collar prosperity. Hollywood movies, from *The Big Easy* to *The Bodyguard* to *Cop Land*, pay homage to the tight neighborhoods where cops cluster. Geographic and ethnic variations embellish the same themes: streets where the fathers wear badges and the mothers stay home, where even the kids know the rhythm of day shift and night shift and everyone understands the pride, anxiety, and folkways of the force.[5] A subtext of the story is a decent, though not munificent, paycheck. Cops don't get rich, but they get by. You protect the community, and the community provides a pay packet that lets you reserve your worries for what's down that dark alley instead of meeting the mortgage, paying for braces, or coming up with college tuition.

Patrol officers averaged close to $46,500 in straight-time pay in 2005. Is this a lot, or a little? On the one hand, nobody spotting a patrol car late at night in a dicey neighborhood is likely to be thinking police work is worth less than pile-driver operators, flight attendants, or public-relations specialists (three occupations a little above cops on the earnings scale). On the other hand, $46,500 is quite a bit higher than the $35,725 average for full-time male workers with a high-school education. It exceeds, by a bit, the average for full-time men with some college training, or even an associate degree ($41,900 and $44,400 respectively)[6] without even factoring in the opportunities for overtime available to many cops. A patrol officer's pay is short of the $57,200 average for college graduates, to be sure. But just 15 percent of police departments require any college training at all, according to the Bureau of Justice Statistics, let alone a four-year degree.[7]

Unlike janitors or nurses or secretaries there's no business benchmark for police pay since true-blue cops, more or less by definition, work for the government. There are, however, nearly a million private security guards in America. They work in lots of different industries (about 50,000 each in the retail, health, hospitality, and education sectors, for example) but the bulk of them, about 550,000, are employed by private security firms in the massive administrative and support services industry. Average pay for private security guards overall is about $21,000, while the "rent-a-cops" working for private security firms (rather than directly for the store, restaurant, or hotel they guard) average less than $20,000.

Nobody can claim that a patrol officer and a private security guard do the exact same job. Police work is more dangerous and more demanding, the standards are higher, and the job involves far more than passively standing watch. Even in an alternative universe where cops were paid according to some pristine market calculus, most would collect more than $20,000. But the vast difference in earnings for those who serve and protect on the public payroll hints rather insistently that if police work weren't a government job, it might not be a middle-class job.

The 87,000 detectives working for public police departments earn an average of $52,000, compared to the $30,000 average for America's 31,000 private detectives.[8] You don't need to be a criminal-justice expert to know that this isn't a strict apples-to-apples comparison. Anybody who reads detective novels or watches the occasional crime show on TV has been informed, perhaps to an exaggerated degree, that police detectives and private eyes tend to be different kinds of people doing different kinds of things. But it is improbable that an earnings gap of nearly 75 percent has nothing at all to do with the fact that one draws a government paycheck and the other works in the private economy.

Shifting to a different threat, and a different category of protectors, America has about 270,000 firefighters working in federal, state, and (by far the majority) local governments. They collect an average of $39,000. Even before the heroism and sacrifice displayed by New York City firefighters that grim September 2001 day vaulted the whole profession into iconic status, most people would have agreed that a firefighter earns every penny. Yet the question (for now) is not what they deserve, but what the market would accord them in today's economy, and in this case we do have a business benchmark. The private fire-protection industry, including firms like Arizona's Rural-Metro, employs about 6,000 firefighters and pays them about $25,000.[9] Private fire protection work may not be fully identical to what public fire departments do, but it's close enough for confidence that the distinctive way government treats workers is part of the reason why firefighters—like police officers, and unlike so many other blue-collar jobs—still collect middle-class wages.

One factor (which we'll soon address in general) offers an important explanation for the good wages cops and firefighters earn: collective bargaining. The protective services were in the vanguard of a surge of public-sector unionization during the last third of the twentieth century, and by 2003 protective service workers were the second most heavily unionized group in America, with more than 36 percent belonging to a labor union.[10] State and local laws generally deny protective-service unions the right to strike, but police and fire unions still became forces to be reckoned with in local politics. Police unions have on occasion engineered something very close to a strike through the coordinated resort to sick leave, known as the "blue flu." Such tactics are relatively rare, both because of their borderline legality and because they go against the grain of police culture. Besides, milder measures can be quite effective. The natural sympathy most people have for uniformed protectors means that a police picket line is a daunting barrier. Boston police unions, for example, used the mere threat of picketing at the 2004 Democratic National Convention to engineer a healthy increase in their $53,700 base pay (which already reached an average of $83,700 with overtime and other supplements).[11]

One early study, analyzing compensation and demographic data from four hundred American cities between 1960 and 1970, found that firefighters' wages were about 12 percent higher, and their working hours about 18 percent shorter, than they would have been without union representation.[12] Another examined two hundred cities in 1965, and eight hundred in 1978, and found that states with strong public-sector labor rights feature significantly higher compensation for unionized police forces. But it also found that in the same states, police departments without union representation paid only slightly less than unionized departments.[13] The labor economists who did that study concluded that the potential for police to bargain collectively, even if it remains latent, is a powerful economic lever.

Other research pointed to something more complicated going on with local public unions than the simple economic muscle of collective bargaining. In 1980 (when the imbalance between public and private unionism was less pronounced than it is today) unionized public workers did no better than unionized private workers.[14] Evidence from 614 cities suggests that police and firefighters' organizations exercise political as well as economic leverage. Protective service unions' efforts to muster popular support for their members both amplify the impact of contract negotiations on wage levels and help to cancel any resulting downward pressure on job numbers.[15]

In one of the debates about cause and effect that quite properly preoccupy labor analysts, another scholar suggested the causation goes the other way. A municipal workforce might not be big because it was unionized, but unionized because it was big (thanks to the relative ease of organizing larger departments), exaggerating unions' apparent success in preserving or boosting employment levels.[16] Another careful empirical study in the early 1990s found that unions brought higher wages and more jobs for firefighters; higher wages but no more jobs for police; and more jobs but no higher wages for city finance workers.[17]

There is no consensus among scholars on the details (which is frequently the case) but most studies concur that unionization matters in the public sector, though not as much as in the business world. Research generally finds public-sector unionization to have real, but relatively muted, consequences.[18]

A moment's reflection illuminates the logic of this pattern. In the private sector, where powerful financial forces converge to eradicate every avoidable penny of costs, labor organization is a potent counterweight. The waxing and waning of the American labor movement in the twentieth century, and the parallel rise and fall in blue-collar workers' relative prospects, illustrates the difference a union can make. But in government, as Chapter 2 sketched out, the motive to minimize wages is either greatly attenuated or wholly absent. Government workers, moreover, have tools beyond labor organization to make their voices heard. It makes sense that labor organization for cops or firefighters should matter somewhat less than for truck drivers or auto assemblers. Imagine that a sadly out-of-shape man commits himself to healthy eating and exercise and that his wife, though already fit, joins him in a spirit of solidarity. The new regimen will produce less of a

change in her health than in his. Similarly, unions work to alter labor
market outcomes—to improve them or distort them, depending on
how you feel about such things. The alteration will be greater in settings where market forces would otherwise reign supreme, and smaller
where those forces are already attenuated. (Those disinclined to think
of unions as salutary can simply flip the metaphor: if the plump man
and his thin wife jointly embark on a spree of sloth and gluttony it will
change her more than it changes him.) Their success at labor organization is a real factor, but only part of the reason why cops, firefighters,
and the other protective services have been able to preserve earning
levels that have become increasingly elusive for blue-collar workers in
the private sector.

The Post Office

Now we switch levels, from local to federal, and consider a class of government workers that is a bit less dramatic, perhaps, but nearly as nu-
merous: employees of the U.S. Postal Service. America's postal service
is actually older than the nation itself. It was founded in 1775, antedat-
ing the Declaration of Independence, with Benjamin Franklin as the
first postmaster general. When the Constitution was drafted fourteen
years later, postal matters figured prominently in its text. For much of
American history delivering the mail was by far the most important
peacetime mission of the central government. The postal service is no
longer a federal agency, technically speaking; the Postal Reorganization Act of 1970 turned it into a special government enterprise with
somewhat different finance and personnel systems. But it remains a
salient feature in most people's images of "the government." It delivers
about 100 billion pieces of first-class mail every year, roughly the same
amount of "standard" (otherwise known as "junk") mail, about 10 billion packages, and smaller amounts of certified, priority, and other
mail for an annual total of more than 200 billion items weighing about
25 billion pounds.[19] It is required by law to pick up and deliver whatever anyone wants to mail to or from more than 141 million addresses
in leafy suburbs, mean urban streets, and every isolated village in America's remotest reaches.

The post office is also an enormously important public employer.
The 2002 wage bill for the postal service was $50 billion—ten times as

much as for the legislative and judicial branches put together.[20] Unlike other governmental operations that devote much of their budgets to constructing buildings, buying equipment, or writing checks, the postal service uses most of its money to pay people. Its workforce totaled about 827,000 in 2003, down from more than 900,000 five years earlier but still in the same league as Wal-Mart (and far ahead of General Motors or McDonald's) among America's biggest single employers.

A few of these postal employees are executives, analysts, managers, and other high-end white-collar workers. But most are directly engaged in getting the mail from where it starts out to where it is supposed to go. Recall from Table 3.2 that "mail carrier" is the fifth most common government job, with a total of about 347,000 in 2005, and that the 209,000 mail processors formed the ninth biggest category of workers in the public sector. As big manufacturing firms have faded, fragmented, merged, automated, or turned to foreign sources, the post office stands in a class of its own as a blue-collar citadel.

It is also, and long has been, a bastion of public-sector unionism. Postal unions sprouted almost instantly after John F. Kennedy signed a 1962 executive order lifting barriers to collective bargaining in federal workplaces. The roster of postal unions grew to include the National Association of Letter Carriers (representing 236,000 workers), the American Postal Workers' Union (330,000), the National Postal Mail Handlers' Union (63,000), the National Rural Mail Carriers Association (117,000), and even the National Association of Postmasters. Labor leaders in the postal system tend to be throwbacks to a vanished era of American unionism—blunt advocates for bread-and-butter interests, cagey, aggressive, and remarkably effective. The 1970 legislation that shifted the post office from a federal department to a separate enterprise gave postal workers nearly the same rights to organize as industrial workers then enjoyed, with the exception of the right to strike.[21] (An ugly postal strike that same year had precipitated the reorganization.) Instead, the law required the postal service to "maintain compensation for its officers and employees comparable to the rates and types of compensation paid in the private sector" while sidestepping the vexing details of just what this means in practice.[22] The same legislation equipped postal workers with potent grievance and arbitration procedures they could invoke whenever they disagreed with managers' interpretation of comparability.

If you are ever bored and itching for an argument, look up any leader of a postal union and hint (even in a friendly, congratulatory way) that postal employees might be doing a little bit better than the strict parity with comparable private workers that the law requires. When a 2003 Presidential Commission on Postal Reform questioned both the process and the results of reckoning comparability—citing estimates that the average new hire got a 28 percent pay increase on joining the post office—it triggered a storm of protest.[23] (My tentative reference in Chapter 2 to private couriers as a vaguely similar, and vastly less lucrative, point of reference would be dismissed as an insult and an outrage.) So without wading into the technical and political thicket of how to truly reckon comparability, I will simply observe that a worker without a college education could do much, much worse than a job with the post office.[24]

The intricate personnel system of the USPS features a hierarchy of fifty-five levels of work, not counting the upper reaches of management. The first ten levels, which include by far the majority of the workforce, are overwhelmingly blue-collar occupations. Levels 1 to 4 are "unskilled laborers" doing jobs that require no special training. This range covers big groups like mail handlers, as well as smaller categories like the groundskeepers and garage laborers any far-flung operation requires.[25] Level 5 covers "semiskilled operatives" who operate sorting machinery and perform other tasks that may be beyond the immediate competence of the average temp but can be mastered in short order. Levels 6 through 9 are "skilled operatives," manual workers who need little book learning but have a "thorough and comprehensive knowledge of the processes involved in their work." Most of the workers in these nine levels are eligible for overtime and some can earn modest performance bonuses, but the core of their compensation is their annual salary, a fixed scale that rises steadily in line with time on the job. Table 3.3 summarizes the story, giving base salaries for both the first year on the job and at full seniority for the various blue-collar ranks. (Since postal workers generally stay in their jobs for a long time, the average tends to run toward the high—that is, more senior—end of each range.)

Once again we confront the question: Are the salaries summarized in Table 3.3 a lot or a little? Not everyone reading this book would consider a postal paycheck to be a king's ransom. But it compares quite favorably with median earnings for full-time workers who lack any college education. There were nearly 37 million such workers in 2002, collecting an average of $22,350 for dropouts and $29,187 for high-school graduates.[26] Fewer than one in six high-school educated workers had total earnings in excess of the USPS range for straight time annual pay.

But hasn't it always been the case that the post office offered good jobs? For the story told in Chapter 2 to hold up, we need to see a difference over time—a *rise* in the relative appeal of government work for less-educated workers as their alternatives worsen in the private sector. Long-term statistics on postal pay are elusive, but the Commerce Department's Bureau of Economic Analysis keeps extensive historical and current data on average wages and salaries for "federal government enterprises." This category includes a few odds and ends, such as the Tennessee Valley Authority, but the post office accounts for nearly all of it, about 97 percent of the workers, as of 2000. If we take this as a good-enough approximation of postal pay, and compare it to average income for full-time working men twenty-five or older with a high-school education, we can get some sense of the trend over time, shown in Figure 3.1.[27] In 1970, before the collapse in private sector opportunities for workers without advanced training, postal pay was about 10 percent above the average for high-school educated men. The postal premium doubled by 1980, approached 60 percent by 1990, and was higher still in 2000, even as a strong economy boosted private-sector pay.

The story is not, let us be clear, that postal workers have recently managed to elbow their way past their private-sector counterparts. Instead, political and bargaining-table victories in the 1970s brought them

Table 3.3 Postal Service Full Time Annual Rates as of November 2002

Blue Collar Jobs in the U.S. Postal Service	Annual Pay Scales, 2002 (covering range from entry level to full seniority)	Number of Workers, 2002
Unskilled laborers	$25,700 to $40,700	305,877
Semiskilled operatives	$31,100 to $42,500	237,037
Skilled operatives	$32,800 to $49,400	65,330

Source: Dennis V. Damp, *Post Office Jobs* (McKees Rock, Penn.: Brookhaven Press, 2003), and U.S. General Accounting Office, "U.S. Postal Service: Data on Career Employee Diversity," September 15, 2003, GAO-03-745R, calculated from 2002 tables of employees by grade, race, and gender on pages 34–38.

into rough parity with private production workers. As shifting economic currents swept blue-collar private workers out of the middle class, the governmental safe harbor let postal workers keep their middle-class status. It is possible, of course, that labor leaders are correct in their claims that postal employees are utterly unlike other blue-collar workers and postal jobs wholly different from other tasks that can be done without college training. But it seems more likely that these very leaders have earned their pay (with an assist from the peculiar dynamics of government labor practices) and preserved for their members the modest prosperity that has slipped away from so many otherwise simi-

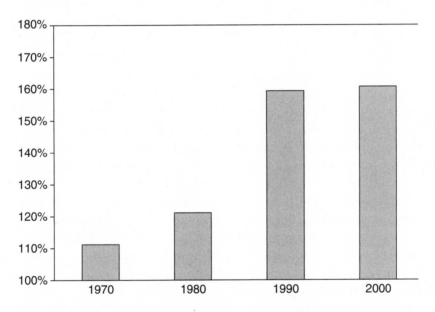

Figure 3.1: Average Postal Earnings Relative to Median Income for Full-Time Male Workers with a High-School Education. *Source:* Current Population Survey, March 2002 supplement, PINC-03: Educational Attainment— People 25 Years Old and Over, by Total Money Earnings in 2001, Work Experience in 2001, Age, Race, Hispanic Origin, and Sex. The data were collected in 2002 but refer to 2001, and so are not strictly comparable to the 2002 postal service salary number, though the gap is slight. Also, National Income and Product Accounts, Commerce Department, Bureau of Economic Analysis, Tables 6.6B and 6.6C, various years, and on Current Population Survey Historical Tables, Tables P-17 (for 1990 and earlier) and P-24 (for years after 1990).

lar workers. A pertinent observation, in this regard, is the backlog of more than 400,000 applicants clamoring to join the postal service (and the extreme reluctance of current postal workers to make room for them by quitting).[28]

One final feature of the postal workforce warrants mention. Among the groups most battered by the economic transformations of the past generation are African-American males, particularly the lamentably large fraction of black men without higher education. Thirty years ago, despite still-lingering discrimination, abundant factory jobs let many of these men earn enough to be able to support a family. As the factories closed, automated, or moved abroad, and as black men (unlike black women) proved slow to embrace the service economy and the higher education it demanded for decent jobs, the impacts—economic, social, cultural, and in every case personal—have been devastating.

Nearly 2.4 million African-American men with a high-school education or less worked full-time in 2001. Their earning power was limited, with an average pay of about $23,000 for drop-outs, and about $28,000 for graduates.[29] Not until their education reached to the master's degree level did average earnings for black men exceed a letter carrier's straight-time salary. It is salient, in this light, that a greatly disproportionate number of postal workers are black men. This is partly due to conscious efforts by USPS leadership, partly a matter of the location of major processing centers, and partly a side effect of veterans' preference in postal hiring. Black males constitute 5 percent of the American workforce but 14 percent of blue-collar postal workers. Cross-walking between postal-service jobs data and Bureau of Labor Statistics earnings data suggests that those 85,000 blue-collar postal workers account, on their own, for one out of every twelve black men who manages to earn between $25,000 and $45,000 without a college education. For this particular group of Americans, government work offers an especially important refuge from the turbulence of the private economy.

The Military

For more than a generation, the armed forces have been a magnet for working-class Americans. This period is almost certainly coming to an end; once the odds of death or dismemberment reach a certain level a job no longer counts as a "safe harbor." The story starts in 1974 with the abolition of the draft and the advent of the all-volunteer force.[30] Political imperatives drove the abandonment of conscription, but the shift to volunteers proved to be exquisitely well timed in economic terms. As the military, somewhat apprehensively, became dependent on volunteers to fill its ranks, good civilian jobs for unskilled workers began to evaporate. In the last year of the draft adult men with a high-school education earned an average of $11,338—less, but not too much less, than the $14,401 average for men with four years of college. Ten years later college-educated men earned an average of 50 percent more than did high-school educated men, and by 2001 they earned 76 percent more.[31] In the mid-1990s men whose education stopped at high school were earning less, in real dollars, than they had in the mid-1960s.

As other options worsened, a stint in the military became an attractive career move for less-educated Americans. Figure 3.2 shows the trend in pay and basic allowances for enlisted personnel with two or three years of service, compared to average earnings for full-time civilian workers between the ages of eighteen and twenty-four whose education stopped with a high-school diploma.[32] In the early years of the all-volunteer force military pay fell somewhat short of civilian standards. But since the early 1980s it has been comfortably above that benchmark, despite zigs and zags driven by both military compensation policy and trends in the private economy. The military's emergence as the employer of choice for a certain segment of the workforce was partly by default (as other options dried up) and partly the result of efforts by military recruiting officials to sweeten the deal. Military pay, benefits, and allowances rose to levels that would seem austere to more fortunate Americans, but beat the alternatives at the lower reaches of the labor market. A large 2004 survey of army families confirmed standard views that military people tend to be patriotic, conservative, and religious. But it also found that 53 percent reported job opportunities and benefits were the most important reason for joining the military, while less than a third as many cited a sense of duty or patriotism as the primary motive.[33]

The military also offers the kind of excellent medical and dental coverage that has become out of reach for many people too rich for Medicaid, often too young for Medicare, and too unskilled to land jobs providing decent health insurance. In the poll of military families "health care benefits" decidedly beat out "sense of community" and "sense of purpose in life" as areas where the army is superior to the civilian world. Military doctors even deliver, free of charge, the cosmetic surgery that

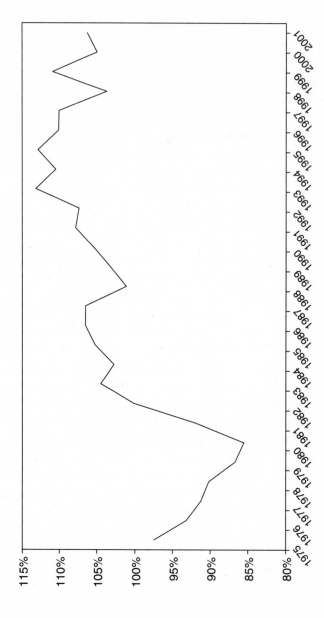

Figure 3.2: Military Pay (Recruits with 2–3 Years of Service) Relative to Average Earnings for Full-Time High-School Educated Civilians Age 18–24. *Source:* Current Population Survey and the Defense Finance & Accounting Service.

only the well-off or the desperate obtain in the private sector. Between 2000 and 2003 the Army provided, among other plastic surgeries, 496 breast enlargements and 1,361 liposuction treatments to soldiers and their dependents.[34]

But for many recruits the most powerful lure was the prospect to remedy the very factor—a lack of education—that made the military a comparatively good job in the first place. (Recall, from Chapter 1, Jessica Lynch's route through one government job in Iraq toward her dream of a different government job, teaching kindergarten.) In the poll of military families, education benefits were cited nine times as often as September 11 as the main motive for enlisting. Television commercials promoting the U.S. Army, Navy, Air Force and Marines stress the opportunities to learn high-tech skills that can boost civilian earning power. Beyond the ample training provided directly by the military, all four services offer tuition assistance that pays for most post-secondary education pursued during off-duty hours, up to an annual ceiling of $3,500.[35] Recruits eagerly seize these offers for in-service education. In 1996 only 3 percent of recruits entered the service with any college training at all, but within a few years of enlisting most had racked up at least a year of college credit.[36]

Even richer education benefits are available to enlistees who have completed their military stint. The GI Bill, administered by the Veterans Administration, provides college scholarships to veterans of all the armed services. Participants in the GI Bill collect enough to fully cover average tuition, room, and board at a public university in about half of the states, according to a RAND Corporation study. The army has a special tuition-assistance program that supplements the GI Bill for selected recruits to bring total education benefits to $50,000.[37] A study by the General Accounting Office in 2002 confirmed that veterans received considerably more federal tuition aid than did non-veterans, and on far more favorable terms. Even for non-veterans with very low incomes most federal college assistance consists of loans that must be paid back; for veterans, assistance packages are larger and are predominantly grants rather than loans.[38]

A report prepared in 2000 for the U.S. Secretary of Defense offered the reassurance that "for an enlistee entering with a high school education, military pay compares well with civilian pay, and an enlisted career holds the promise of significant growth in relative pay."[39] (The same did not hold for officers, who earned more than enlisted personnel but less than their college-educated peers in private work.) A separate, and quite elaborate, academic study found that people joining the military in the 1980s did indeed earn significantly more than comparable people in the private sector, and had better odds of staying employed once they returned to private life. For minority members, though not for whites, military service put veterans on an upward trajectory of long-term earning power.[40] As the distance widened between worsening private-sector options and the package offered by the military, the armed services could be a little pickier about the quality of their personnel. "High-quality recruits"—defined as high-school graduates who scored in the upper half of the Armed Forces Qualifying Test—surged as a share of the total to reach record levels in 1992.[41]

Near the turn of the twenty-first century, military recruiters were worried about what turned out to be an empty threat to the flow of working-class Americans into the military, but failed to anticipate a devastating development. The false alarm was the economic expansion of the late 1990s, which finally produced modest earnings gains even for less-educated workers. Improvements in tuition assistance available to civilians—federal tax preferences for college costs, increases in the Pell Grants less-wealthy students could use to defray tuition expenses, and a wave of comparable moves in many states—simultaneously threatened to narrow the increment of college aid that veterans enjoyed. Would prospects outside the service improve enough to imperil the military's hard-won standing as a working-class employer of choice? That problem turned out to solve itself as an economic swoon erased the gains at the low end of the labor market. Cutbacks in college financial aid and tuition increases at hard-pressed state schools made military education assistance even more valuable. Meanwhile, a precipitous decline in employer health coverage (coupled with rising health-care costs) further burnished the military's appeal.

What shattered the system, of course, was the return of large-scale armed conflict. The decades after the advent of the all-volunteer force had been marked not just by a collapse in private-sector prospects for less-skilled workers, but also by a historically anomalous scarcity of shooting wars. This changed. Massive deployments in Afghanistan and Iraq radically altered the tally of advantages and disadvantages for a military job. Decent pay and excellent health and education benefits had once been ample recompense for a few years' submission to military discipline. For the many young Americans who are adventurous or intensely patriotic or both, the deal was even better. But when high odds of long deployments and family anxiety were added to the equation, along with the real prospect of being killed or maimed, the calculus changed. (In the most searing scene of the film *Fahrenheit 9/11* a mother who had urged her son to join the Army for the college education she could not afford to finance reflects on his death in combat.) By mid-decade recruitment and reenlistment rates were fading, and the armed forces faced a fundamental challenge to the model that had served so unexpectedly well since the mid-1970s.[42]

Teachers

Recall that teachers and other people involved in education comprise by far the largest group of government workers. Recent sections have been mostly silent about teachers, in part because the Bureau of Labor Statistics data series on which we've relied separates education from the rest of government, but mostly because teachers present a very special case. In a book about gaps between the public and private economies at both the high end and the low end, where do teachers fit in? Teaching is clearly no bottom-of-the-barrel occupation. Figure 3.3 traces the relationship between average salaries for public-school teachers and average wages and salaries for all workers.[43] A generation or so ago, teachers were paid nearly one-fifth more than the average full-time worker. They lost some ground in the 1970s, regained it (and more) in the 1980s, then slipped a bit to end the century with about a 10 percent edge.

But this simple comparison is more than a little misleading. For one thing, America's 3 million public-school teachers are among the most highly educated groups of workers in the country. All but a handful have college degrees, and about 45 percent have postgraduate degrees as well.[44] For another, teaching has gone from a profession somewhat tilted toward women to an overwhelmingly female profession. Education is the great exception to a trend of diminishing gender disparities across occupations. In recent decades more and more men have opted for careers as nurses, hair stylists, and other traditionally women's jobs. More women have become chefs, mechanics, and (haltingly) CEOs. In education, conversely, gender segregation has deepened. Women accounted for a little less than two-thirds of all teachers in 1971 but nearly four-fifths (79 percent) in 2001. An even larger share of elementary-

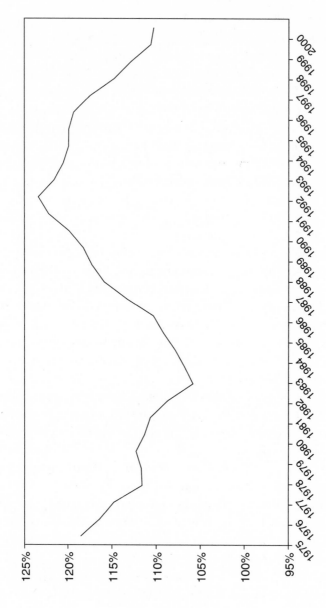

Figure 3.3: Public-School Teachers' Salaries Relative to Average Pay for All Full-Time Workers, 1970–2000. *Source:* U.S. Department of Education.

school teachers (91 percent) and new teachers age thirty or younger (82 percent) are female.[45] Since educated people tend to earn more but women tend to earn less, Figure 3.3 may be a doubly distorted view of teachers' relative economic standing, and a bit more scrutiny is required.

Average base pay for public-school teachers was $43,262 in 2001. Men and secondary-school teachers made a little more; women and elementary-school teachers made a little less. The average teacher earned an additional $3,500 from summer work, outside employment, and other sources. Since most teachers are married, and most of those (especially the women) have working spouses, total household income is higher: $77,739 in 2001, not too far from the $83,500 threshold into the upper fifth of household income.[46] So teachers (unlike police, mail carriers, soldiers, and other groups discussed so far in this chapter) are a fairly advantaged group of workers.

A highly relevant point of reference, and a hint of the niche that teaching jobs occupy in today's economy, can be found by examining educated women in other lines of work. Not so long ago an American woman aspiring to a professional career could be a schoolteacher, a nurse, an executive secretary, or an eccentric. There have always been a few women in traditional male professions, but until the 1970s women were odd exceptions to the Y-chromosome rule in the sciences, law, medicine, finance, and other elite fields.

As recently as 1976, public-school teachers constituted nearly a quarter of all the college-educated working women in America. Gender bias in other professions may have been bad for women, but it was very good for public schools. Barriers to other occupations channeled a steady flow of female talent into the classroom. America's education system grew to depend on this quasi-captive labor force, and has not yet really adjusted to the fact that today's women have other options. In the twenty-five years following 1976 the number of working women with college diplomas, and the number with postgraduate degrees, roughly tripled as opportunities expanded for high-skilled women. Teaching more or less held its own relative to *average* salaries, as Figure 3.3 shows, but it steadily lost its luster, at least in terms of earnings, compared to other choices open to highly trained women. In 1971, female teachers earned nearly 50 percent more than all college-educated working women, and female teachers with a master's or doctorate earned about a third more than the average for women with postgraduate degrees.

But thirty years later this edge had disappeared. Teachers with a BA earned fractionally more, and teachers holding higher degrees, fractionally less than their peers.

During the past generation or so, bucking the general trend, teaching has become more rather than less gender-specific and is now dominated by women. Yet this has happened at the same time as women working as teachers have seen their earnings shrivel relative to equally educated women in other lines of work. What should we make of all this?

Many critics of American public education have one interpretation. They depict public-school teachers as second-raters entrenched behind political barricades, dodging demands for excellence and dooming the future. Teachers may be amply credentialed, this argument goes, but they're not really very good. Only the dimmest college kids choose education majors, and advanced degrees in education are a joke. Given their modest talents, most teachers are grossly overpaid. Blow up the system through school vouchers, these voices demand, and let market forces flush out the parasites.

Teachers and their defenders draw sharply different conclusions. In their view most school districts stubbornly refuse to pay teachers what they're worth. Luckily for the kids, teachers are so committed to education that they stick with it even in the face of better options elsewhere. Women are more inclined than men to put mission ahead of money, which explains the growing tilt in the gender balance. It is only teachers' idealism, defenders say, that protects America from schools that are more expensive, or less ably staffed, than the schools it has today.

Neither account is wholly plausible. Critics' accounts of public schools as sheltered workshops for incompetents is inconsistent with the trend in teachers' intellectual horsepower as gauged by one of the few (admittedly imperfect) metrics of comparative aptitude. Scholastic Aptitude Test scores for education majors ran about 10 percent below the average for all majors a generation ago; they rose to erase half of the deficit in the 1980s, even as the profession's relative rewards eroded, and have been around 95 percent of the overall average for the past fifteen years.[47] A scrupulous economic study has found only a trivial decline in the measured aptitude of the average teacher over the whole period from 1957 to 2000, although the share of those at the very top of the talent distribution has fallen more sharply.[48] At the same time, the defenders' tale of teachers selflessly renouncing greener pastures elsewhere is hard to square with the ferocity of their resistance to any serious alteration of public education.

Let me offer an alternative interpretation, based partly on hard data but partly, I confess, on conjecture, impressions, and partial evidence. Among public-school teachers, as with any group of 3 million people, the best are very good, the worst are very bad, and the middle ground is very large. The typical teacher is a woman who is bright but not brilliant, diligent but not driven, fonder than average of children and less fond than average of money. Teachers' fierce opposition to school vouchers and other threats to public education is inspired in part by pride and in part by honest idealism; most care deeply about education and have sincere doubts about both the judgment and the motives of those prescribing radical surgery for America's schools. But teachers have something personal at stake as well. It is not, as critics suggest, a free pass for mediocrity. While too little top-drawer talent is deployed in the schools, truly bad teachers are uncommon (albeit scandalously concentrated in poor urban schools). What most teachers have to lose, other than a mission they find meaningful, is an interesting and respected job that leaves a little room for other things in life.

Such jobs have become rare. Many professions, including law, medicine, finance, consulting, and most areas of management, offer nothing but the fast-track or the off-ramp. Professionals see other aspects of their lives—family, friends, hobbies, church, community—dry up as job demands escalate. Women probably tend to suffer more than men do when life outside the office shrivels, and also face weaker cultural expectations to suck it up and put work first. Many fast-track women opt for the off-ramp once they have children, particularly if a spouse's earning power makes their paychecks dispensable. This has its own downsides—boredom, tighter family budgets, imperiled self-identity, dim prospects for reentry at the same level—but can seem the better of two bad choices.

Teachers are spared this dilemma. While far from the cushy sinecure some critics depict, teaching is less draining than most other professional jobs. The work day is circumscribed, and a teacher is usually able to care for his or her own school-age kids. Preparation and grading can be done on a flexible schedule. The rhythm of the school year is predictable. Summers offer a chance to recharge, travel, cultivate hobbies, and reconnect with family and friends. Birthdays, book clubs, and charity board meetings are secure against disruption by an insistent client, a looming product launch, or an urgent summons to the London office.

The National Education Association (NEA) has long collected data on how much time teachers spend each week on their official duties, including grading and preparation. The average is closer to fifty than to the canonical forty hours per week, to be sure. (Self-reported working hours tend to run high in general, and this may be the case here.) But the interesting thing is the trend over time—or rather, the absence of any trend over time. For elementary-school teachers the hours claimed by work were the same in 2001 as they had been in 1961, presenting an astonishing picture of stability over the course of a turbulent period. For secondary-school teachers work hours had increased, but by less than 10 percent in forty years.[49]

Teachers' ability to keep a lid on work time, in contrast to most other professionals, may have benefits that go beyond educators' own blood pressure and work–life balance. As my colleague Robert Putnam has documented in his book *Bowling Alone,* Americans in general are in the midst of a headlong retreat from community associations such as the Red Cross, the Boy Scouts, and even (the inspiration for his title) bowling leagues.[50] The NEA periodically surveys teachers about their participation in community and civic activities. In sharp contrast to dwindling rates among other Americans, teachers' involvement in activities outside of work were little different in 2001 than they had been thirty years earlier: 78 percent of teachers were active in religious organizations in 1971, and virtually the same fraction (77 percent) in 2001. Involvement with youth service organizations (such as the Boy Scouts and Girl Scouts) also held fairly steady (16 percent in 1971, 15 percent in 2001). Participation in hobby groups actually increased from 16 percent of teachers to 29 percent. Interestingly, in light of critics' depiction of teachers as raging partisans, the major exception is politics; involvement in political organizations dropped from 13 percent to 9 percent of teachers between 1971 and 2001.[51]

A plausible story that pulls together the various patterns outlined here is that women (particularly married women) have been more willing than most men—and more culturally enabled, perhaps—to stick with teaching as its relative financial rewards faded. The dearth of other professional jobs offering family-friendly hours, predictable schedules, and breaks measured in weeks rather than days has deepened the profession's appeal to many women.[52] Teachers who push back against political threats to public education are fighting in part for their missions, but also in part for work–life balance. It is in this sense, more than as a shelter against plummeting earnings, that government work in the classroom serves as a safe harbor in a stormy economy.

Defending the Harbor

Government workers form and fund labor unions that deploy both the economic muscle of collective bargaining and the political muscle of coordinated voice, votes, and money to preserve employment, improve pay and working conditions, and promote favorable rules and legislation. Public-sector unionism cuts a formidable figure on America's economic and political scene. When Arnold Schwarzenegger decried the influence of "special interests" during his 2003 California gubernatorial campaign he specified that public workers' unions (along with Native American tribes running casinos) were the *only* groups he had in mind.[53] It is a given, in every American election, that public workers' unions will be assiduously courted by Democrats and vociferously denounced by Republicans.

From today's perspective it would be easy to assume that it has always been this way. But in the United States, unlike other countries, public-sector unionism is a quite recent phenomenon. One contemporary observer noted that in the mid-1950s, as private-sector unions were surging from strength to strength, "the subject of labor relations in public employment could not have meant less to more people, both in and out of government."[54] The word "union" did not even appear until halfway through a twenty-page tour d'horizon of public management issues featured by a major journal in 1958.[55] Outside of the Tennessee Valley Authority and the Bonneville hydroelectric complex (where minor appendages of private-sector utilities unions had long existed) there was not a single recognized union in the federal government as of 1960.[56]

This began to change, though at first the changes were glacially slow. In 1962 President Kennedy signed Executive Order 10988 granting some collective-bargaining rights to federal workers. Organizing efforts gradually got under way in a few federal workplaces, with post office workers in the vanguard. Eight years later the Postal Reorganization Act gave postal employees almost the same labor rights as the Taft-Harley Act had long accorded private-sector workers. Executive action by President Nixon further expanded federal labor rights, including strengthening grievance procedures and allowing federal employees to conduct some union activities during working hours.

A parallel flurry of legislative and regulatory shifts in the cities and states loosened constraints on public-sector organizing in the 1960s,[57] their impact intensified by a 1968 Supreme Court ruling that federal labor laws could be invoked by state workers without violating the prerogatives of state governments.[58] The wave gradually gathered force as public union membership more than doubled between 1962 and 1972. In 1970 more than 680 organization ballots were held in federal workplaces, and 92 percent of them resulted in workers opting to join a union. By the early 1970s about 2.3 million government workers were union members, nearly one-fourth of all state and local workforces were organized, and teachers' unions—a startling development at the time—were scoring early successes in campaigns for higher pay and better working conditions.[59]

Public employee unions gradually became consequential institutions at the federal, state, and local levels, and almost certainly contributed to rising relative pay scales in the public sector in the 1970s. Strikes and other labor disruptions—by sanitation workers, postal employees, and especially teachers—dramatized the newfound muscle of government workers and began to spark a political reaction. Resentment of public workers' wage gains helped to inspire tax revolts in several states, and Ronald Reagan's successful showdown with the air traffic controllers' union was one of the defining acts of his first year in office.

Public-sector unions were still decidedly minor players on the national political stage, however. The labor movement as a whole, to be sure, was an enthusiastic and effective source of political contributions and ground troops in the 1980 elections. Union political action committees (PACs) contributed $27 million, most of it to Democratic candidates, during that election cycle. This was nearly 20 percent of all PAC money, though labor was still behind corporations, special-issue PACs, and business groups such as the American Medical Association. But organized labor's political spending was still dominated by private-sector unions. Only a single public employees' group, the American Federation of Teachers, made it into the top-ten list of labor PACs in 1980, and its contributions were dwarfed by those of industrial unions such as the United Auto Workers.[60] A scholarly study of the 1977–1981 political efforts (including get-out-the-vote and lobbying campaigns as well as contributions to candidates) by the major federal unions—the American Federation of Government Employees, the National Federation of Federal Employees, and the National Treasury Employees Union—found them to be both modest in scale and limited in effectiveness. Its author suggested that "federal employee unions may want to consider whether even their current low level of political investment has been worthwhile."[61]

But public workers were poised for a surge to the front ranks of the labor movement as the retreat of their private-sector counterparts turned into a rout. In the American economy overall union membership peaked, in the mid-1950s, at a little more than 26 percent of wage and salary workers. In 1960 the rate of unionization economy-wide was still 24.5 percent, and even by 1970 it had slipped only to 23.4 percent. Then it began an accelerating slide to 18.5 percent in 1980, 16 percent in 1990, and to 12 percent and still falling by 2006.

This story of overall decline, however, masks very different trajectories for unions in the public and private sectors. Outside government the drop was even more vertiginous than the economy-wide figures suggest. Private-sector unions, which had dominated the labor movement in its heyday, claimed as members just 7.4 percent of eligible workers by 2006. Inside government, the unionization rate that year was 36.2 percent, or nearly five times as high. Local government alone had two and a half times as many union members as the entire manufacturing sector that had once been labor's bastion, and the most-unionized industry outside government (utilities) had a lower rate of organization than the least-unionized part of government (the federal sector). The public-sector workforce was less than one-fifth as large as the private-sector workforce, but it had nearly as many union members: about 7.4 million in government versus about 7.9 million outside it. Had the private sector not been able to claim the 1.5 million union members in the (somewhat ambiguous, in terms of sectoral identity) education, health, and social service industries, government would already have the majority of unionized workers. If current trends continue for just a few more years, the public sector will account for most union members by any definition.[62]

As their numbers grew, public employees' unions came into their own as political powerhouses. Labor PACs as a group grew three times faster than other PACs between 1986 and 1996, and within the labor category public employees' unions went from a footnote to the forefront. By the 1996 election the American Federation of State, County, and Municipal Employees (AFSCME) had reached the number-three slot on the list of PAC receipts—ahead of any other labor PAC—while the NEA was ranked number seven.[63]

The nonpartisan Center for Responsive Politics has assembled data on top political spenders from 1989 through 2004, covering money collected through PACs, political contributions from individuals, and the "soft money" that slipped through the cracks of repeated legislative efforts to curb money's role in politics.[64] At the very peak of the list is the AFSCME. It spent just under $37 million during the fifteen-year period, nearly all of it devoted to Democratic candidates. To appreciate the significance of this, ponder the fact that the Center for Responsive Politics data deals almost exclusively with spending on federal races, and that AFSCME represents *state* and *local* workers. The stakes of federal policies affecting state and local employment were sufficiently high that AFSCME had both the motive and the means to spend more heavily, in the effort to shape them, than any other organization in America. Other public workers' unions ranking high on the list of 1989–2004 contributions were the NEA (number five), the American Federation of Teachers (number seventeen), and the National Association of Letter Carriers (number twenty-four)—only the last of them representing people who work directly for the federal government.

Public employees' unions as a class still ranked only thirteenth on the list of political spenders for 1989–2004, with less clout than financial titans such as lawyers, the securities industry, insurance, medical professionals, and banking. But they had grown from political nonentities two decades earlier to far outweigh industrial unions. More than most other interest groups, they were able to amplify the effect of political spending through get-out-the-vote efforts, political education, and the deployment of members as campaign ground troops. It is also worth noting that public-sector unions are exceeded only by industrial unions in the partisan imbalance of their spending. During this whole period, government workers' unions gave 91 percent of their contributions to Democratic candidates. Even the interest group most heavily tilted toward Republicans, the oil and gas industry, directed a quarter of its 1989–2004 money to Democrats.

Much has been said and written about the political influence of public workers' unions. This is not the place, and I am not the writer, to summarize that debate—though I will observe that anyone looking to wax indignant about aspects of American politics could work through a long list of more deserving candidates before directing their outrage toward workers banding together to defend their middle-class jobs. The main reason for discussing public-sector unions' rapid shift from the sidelines to the front lines of politics is that it so vividly illustrates how a government job has become something millions of Americans will fight to defend. This development is both a sorry commentary on the status of the middle class within the private sector, and a chronic impediment to delivering on the public sector's imperatives of efficiency, flexibility, and performance.

FOUR

◆ ◆ ◆

Backwater

GOVERNMENT'S UNHEALTHY IF understandable allure for less fortunate American workers is only half of this story of distortion. As the
middle-class economy unraveled, private-sector opportunities proliferated for people with talent and ambition and the education that un-
leashes these innate assets. Government sat out this transformation.
The public sector retains the fairly tight range of workplace rewards that
characterized both sectors not so long ago. Jobs in government's upper
reaches offer pay and benefits that are only modestly superior to those
collected by midlevel officials, which in turn are not too far beyond the
compensation of lower-level workers. So while public employment has
turned into a safe harbor for many refugees from an unforgiving business world, it is a backwater in the eyes of those whom fate has most
richly blessed.[1]

Nobody is driven solely by material compensation, to be sure, and
people inclined to consider public service tend to be less motivated
than their peers by worldly riches.* This generalization holds only to a
degree, however; most of those who work in politics and government,
like people in general, find compensation to be a reasonably interesting issue. The first day a new web site posted congressional staff salaries

*At the dawn of the American republic Benjamin Franklin argued that senior offi-
cials should not be paid at all, in order to weed out the less public-spirited candidates.
John Adams was less a purist on the point, but he did advise (while conspicuously ig-
noring his own advice) that public service should be an occasional break from a private career rather than anyone's economic mainstay.[2]

the flood of hits—mostly from Capitol Hill computers—crashed the system.[3] A 2006 survey of college juniors and seniors by the Partnership for Public Service found excessive bureaucracy as the biggest perceived downside of civil-service jobs, but low compensation was close behind and ahead of nearly all other factors.[4]

Disparity between high-end public and private compensation is assuredly not the only factor siphoning talent into the private sector. The erosion of trust in government, the decline in its cultural standing, the encrustation of bureaucratic constraints, the transformation of politics into a partisan snake pit, the fun and excitement of today's ever-changing business scene, all play a role. But the pay gap relative to private-sector alternatives is part of the story, both directly and (as we'll see shortly) indirectly.

Why hasn't government followed suit as the business world ramped up the rewards at the top of the labor market? The compensation of members of Congress provides a useful reference point for understanding the dynamics that constrain pay in the public sector. This is so in part because congressional pay scales shape most salaries in the federal government which, in turn, set the tone for state and local governments. Just as no building in Washington, D.C., can be taller than the Capital dome, so too (by law or by custom) a congressperson's salary sets the ceiling for all but a handful of federal jobs. The president and vice president are paid more, as are Supreme Court justices. Deft use of loopholes in federal personnel rules, or waivers from those rules obtained by several agencies or entire departments, allow a few federal workers to exceed the congressional ceiling. (Remember those National Institutes of Health directors mentioned at the start of Chapter 1?) But most high-end federal workers, including cabinet secretaries, sub-Cabinet officials, judges, and virtually all career civil servants, have their pay set in the shadow of Congress. The congressional benchmark has no formal standing for state and local government, but cities and states generally maintain pay scales at or below federal levels. With few exceptions, public employees cannot expect to earn more than a member of Congress.

Congressional pay is also interesting because it illustrates, in all its stark purity, the political forces that keep a lid on governmental salaries. The Constitution (Article I, Section 6) requires Congress to set its own pay scale.[5] This might be an enviable arrangement for a profession operating in obscurity, but for members of America's highly visible and electorally accountable legislative body it has never been very comfortable. For several long stretches of American history—from 1817 to 1855, from 1874 to 1907, and again from 1907 to 1925—Congress lacked the nerve to vote itself a raise. This reluctance is understandable. Representatives face the voters every two years, senators every six, and there is little in a legislator's record that riles the electorate more than voting oneself a raise. Public-opinion polls find resounding opposition, with lopsided margins seldom seen on other issues, to congressional pay increases.[6]

While speaking well of legislators is out of fashion, and while there are certainly some vivid exceptions to my generalization here, representatives and senators tend to be reasonably able people. Most of them would do quite well in the private economy.[7] However ardently they embrace the common folk in campaign rhetoric, furthermore, most legislators set their economic expectations by reference to other successful professionals. As high-end pay has soared outside government, legislators have tried various tactics to keep within shouting distance of private-sector compensation while dodging the electorate's ire. In 1975 Congress enacted legislation to link its own compensation to a neutral cost-of-living index, setting in place a process by which pay would periodically escalate absent a vote to block the increase. But since this system has been established, Congress has affirmatively voted to deny itself a raise twice as often as it has passively accepted the increase.[8]

Figure 4.1 shows the trajectory of congressional pay, from 1975 to 2005, relative to the income of a family in the middle fifth of the distribution.[9] Legislators collected $44,600 in 1975, or a little more than three times the $13,700 income of families in the middle. Amid the ups and downs in this ratio during the next thirty years—as family incomes gradually grew, while congressional pay bumped upward episodically— the only real pattern appears to be a curious gravitational attraction for that three-to-one ratio. Legislators' political antennae seem to sense that this is about the degree of distance between the people and their representatives that voters are willing to stomach. Below that level, Congress can get away with an increase. Much above it, and congressional pay might escalate from a matter of casual grumbling into a ballot-box issue that a challenger could exploit.

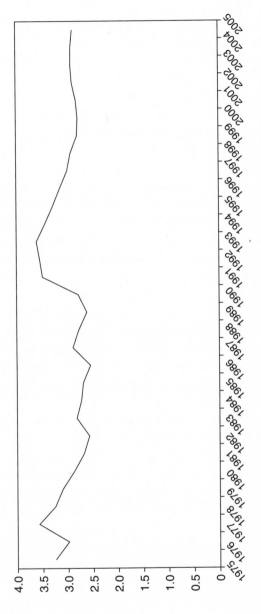

Figure 4.1: Congressional Salary as a Multiple of Average Family Income, 1975–2005. *Source:* Congressional pay data are from Paul E. Dwyer, "Salaries of Members of Congress: A List of Payable Rates and Effective Dates, 1789–2006," Congressional Research Service Report 97-1011 GOV, Library of Congress, updated April 18, 2006. Family income data are from the Current Population Survey, Historical Income Table F-3, "Mean Income Received by Each Fifth and Top 5 Percent of Families (All Races): 1966 to 2005."

But consider a different comparison: to the top instead of the middle. In the mid-1970s, before Americans' economic prospects started to diverge, congressional pay was about equal to average income for the top 5 percent of American families. This was and is a stratum spanning a range from the truly wealthy down to the merely comfortable. To be elected to Congress a generation or two ago meant remaining in—or entering—at least the lower reaches of the economic elite. A member of the House or Senate might not live at the same level as a CEO or a sports star, but he or she kept up with other successful Americans. As the trends discussed in Chapter 2 gathered force, however, average income for the most fortunate twentieth of American families ballooned, exceeding $100,000 by 1985, $200,000 by 1995, $275,000 by 2000, and $300,000 by 2005. Congressional pay, tethered by invisible bonds of political toleration to the slower-growing midrange, fell behind this benchmark. As Figure 4.2 shows, legislators' relative compensation shriveled in just three decades to barely half the average for the top 5 percent. Congressional pay of $162,000 in 2005, situated almost exactly on that gravitational point of three times the average family income, no longer sufficed to make writing the laws of the land a particularly high-end occupation. Indeed, not since the mid-1990s has a congressional salary sufficed for a family to reach even the lower boundary of the top 5 percent.

The goal here is not to inspire any tears for legislators. By any standard *except* that of America's top twentieth they earn a handsome living, in exchange for indoor work with no heavy lifting. Many members of Congress also supplement their official salaries with other income, from working spouses, property, or invested wealth. The Senate, in particular, has notoriously become a millionaire's club. Rather, the point is to illustrate the political barriers against paying public servants too much more than what the typical family gets by on. When top incomes outside government—on which nobody gets to vote—surge ahead, legislators can't keep up. And the rest of the federal government stays behind with them. Cabinet secretaries' pay is pegged to that of congressional majority and minority leaders; the benchmark for deputy secretaries is the salary of run-of-the-mill representatives and senators.[10] Undersecretaries are a little lower; assistant secretaries a bit lower still, and on through the ranks of associate deputy secretaries, principal deputy assistant secretaries and so on. Congressional pay ef-

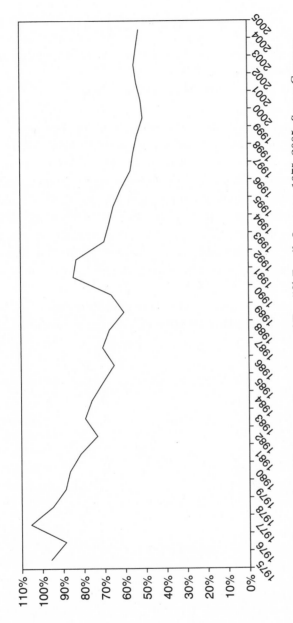

Figure 4.2: Congressional Salary as a Percentage of Top-5% Family Income, 1975–2005. *Source:* Congressional pay data are from Paul E. Dwyer, "Salaries of Members of Congress: A List of Payable Rates and Effective Dates, 1789–2006," Congressional Research Service Report 97-1011 GOV, Library of Congress, updated April 18, 2006. Family income data are from the Current Population Survey, Historical Income Table F-3, "Mean Income Received by Each Fifth and Top 5 Percent of Families (All Races): 1966 to 2005."

fectively sets the ceiling for presidential appointees, and Cabinet pay sets the ceiling for the elite Senior Executive Service, which sets the ceiling for General Schedule workers below.[11] Table 4.1 gives salary data for top federal jobs, and, for a point of comparison, the average first-year salary and bonus of freshly minted Harvard MBA's working at private equity firms.[12]

Few occupational groups have a weaker claim on the American people's sympathy than the best-paid government workers. So what if they earn less than successful players in the private economy? The average voter is far more conscious of the fact that senior public officials are doing a lot better than most of the people who pay their salaries. A majority of those polled by Rasmussen Research in 1999—when public-private compensation gaps were narrower than they are today—endorsed a 10 percent pay cut for all federal employees.[13] The political forces squeezing the high end of public-sector pay are pervasive, durable, and effective.

Most of the figures here refer to the more densely documented federal government, but top salaries in state and local government tend to

Table 4.1 Salaries of Top Federal Officials in 2004

President of the United States	$400,000
Average Harvard MBA starting in private equity (2006)	$289,000
Vice president	$203,000
Speaker of the House	$203,000
Chief justice of the Supreme Court	$203,000
Supreme Court associate justices	$194,300
Cabinet secretaries	$175,700
Appeals Court judges	$167,600
Most federal court judges	$158,100
Deputy secretaries and heads of major agencies	$158,100
Secretaries of military branches	$158,100
Under secretaries and heads of midsized agencies	$145,600
Assistant secretaries and heads of minor agencies	$136,900

Source: Sharon S. Gressle, "Salaries of Federal Officials: A Fact Sheet," CRS Report for Congress 98-53 GOV, Congressional Research Service, Library of Congress, June 25, 2004. Comparison point of first-year salary of Harvard MBA graduates starting in private equity is from Jack and Suzy Welch, "The New Brain Drain," *Business Week*, April 23, 2007, p. 122.

be even lower. Compensation for governors ranges from less than $70,000 in Nebraska on up to New York's $179,000. Many governors also get housing, transportation, and other perquisites, boosting their standard of living beyond what salary figures alone would suggest. But it is still noteworthy that the governor of a large state quite frequently earns less than the marketing director of a small company.

More than a million American men and nearly 200,000 women had incomes exceeding $250,000 in 2005.[14] A medium-sized airplane would comfortably accommodate the government employees earning that much. With few exceptions (such as the commander in chief), most of those highly compensated government workers have jobs at state universities. The number of public universities paying their presidents more than half a million per year nearly tripled (from six to seventeen) between 2002 and 2004. Marquee professors in hot fields at major state universities, and some doctors at state hospitals, can breach the $250,000 barrier. And star football and basketball coaches at state schools, of course, often collect seven-figure salaries.[15]

Like the pay premiums at the lower end described in the last chapter, governmental pay shortfalls at the upper end have consequences—some of them obvious, others subtler and more insidious. As noted earlier, charges of rampant incompetence among American public-school teachers are vastly overblown. But the schools assuredly are not getting the share of top talent that they once attracted and (more to the point) that they very much still need. Between 1963 and 2000 the proportion of women graduating from elite colleges who went on to work as schoolteachers fell by 80 percent.[16] It would be surprising indeed if the tumbling of teachers' salaries, relative to those of comparably qualified workers in other fields, had no effect on the share of each generation's ablest people who opt for education careers. In some countries the enviable social status of teachers allows schools to recruit highly qualified personnel despite richer offers from other employers. But in the United States, status is too intertwined with income to permit such tactics for shoring up quality on the cheap. Hundreds of thousands of managers, consultants, and lawyers out there are desperately needed in the classroom, but are kept away by the chasm between the rewards of public and private work.

Teaching may be one of the most important categories of government work where the private sector bids away vital talent, but it is far from the only one. The Food and Drug Administration (FDA)—long the global benchmark for cautious, scientifically scrupulous pharmaceutical regulation—has been buffeted by historically uncharacteristic failures to spot and block serious risks. Private studies provided clues that some widely used antidepressants worked very differently in children and teenagers than in adults, and could actually increase troubled kids' vulnerability to suicide. But it took the FDA nearly a year to assimilate this evidence and require stiffer warnings for the drugs. At about the same time it emerged that Vioxx, a top-selling pain killer made by Merck, could cause heart damage. Merck pulled Vioxx from the market on its own as the FDA stood passively by amid fierce and unaccustomed criticism of this once respected agency. These failures are well known, but a telling detail is not. For an entire year, as the Vioxx and antidepressant debacles brewed, the crucial post of director of the Office of Drug Safety had been standing vacant. Private drug companies paid much more for experienced safety experts than the $125,000 salary the FDA was able to offer its drug-safety chief.[17]

Following the September 11 attacks and subsequent searing criticism of America's security services, concern grew over salary levels at the Federal Bureau of Investigation. FBI agents are generally older and better educated than other law-enforcement workers. Many have advanced degrees and years of prior experience when they join the bureau. But FBI pay scales run just a little higher than those of medium-sized police departments. Like most governmental compensation systems, the FBI's has not been changed in any fundamental way since before the great divergence in workplace rewards. Thirty years ago it seemed appropriate for a well-educated federal agent to have just a modest edge over city cops with high school diplomas. Today, against the backdrop of sprawling divides in private-sector pay, it is a glaring anomaly.

Low pay for FBI agents—as always, relative to their private-sector peers, not the average worker—means that lateral transfers from the business world usually have to scale back their living standards rather sharply. Agents assigned to the larger, more expensive cities can seldom afford housing close to the office and must spend long hours commuting. The FBI Agents Association has collected scores of reports of agents in grim financial straits: falling behind on student loans, buying groceries on credit, cashing out retirement accounts, depending on subsidies from aging parents. One consequence is an unaccustomed retention challenge. Dale Watson quit his job as the FBI's director of counterterrorism to become an executive at a private security company. "We signed up knowing we weren't gonna get rich," he told a reporter. "But it used to be the FBI was a career that nobody left. It ain't that way any more."[18] More worrisome still is the scenario of vital security workers grown vulnerable to financial temptation. There has always been the occasional traitor, but FBI agents and other trusted personnel used to betray their country out of twisted conviction. According to Bob Graham, former chair of the Senate Intelligence Committee, "our most recent cases, such as Hanssen, have been for money." Robert Hanssen was an FBI intelligence operative in New York City. After years of complaining about tight finances, he was arrested and convicted for selling secrets.

About 2 million government workers can be found in the broad category of "computer and mathematical occupations." A few thousand of these are statisticians, actuaries, mathematicians, and other workers rather distant from workaday information technology (IT). But the biggest groups are computer systems analysts (89,000), computer support specialists (24,000), software engineers, network administrators, and network analysts (each between 11,000 and 12,000). The "professional, technical, and scientific services" industry—the domain of the big government IT contractors such as Electronic Data Systems, Computer Sciences Corporation, Science Applications International Corporation, and the IT branches of Lockheed Martin, Northrop Grumman, and General Dynamics—has about 8.6 million workers in the same category.

IT workers, as a group, are among the better-paid government employees, with average salaries not too far below $60,000. But, in line with the general pattern we have seen, public-sector pay scales for IT workers are far more compressed than in the private sector, and considerably lower at the top. Figure 4.3 shows the annual salary pattern for both government and the professional, technical, and scientific services industry, as of 2003. Government pay is actually a bit better for the bottom of the IT workforce; at the tenth percentile—that is, workers 10 percent up from the bottom, in each sector—government is slightly more generous. The private sector pays somewhat better at the twenty-fifth percentile, with the edge widening more by the median (the worker at the exact midpoint of the distribution), and the gap grows further up the scale. For workers at the ninetieth percentile, the private sector pays about 27 percent more than government, and it is a safe inference that at the very upper reaches that the Bureau of Labor Statistics ignores the gap.

These disparities make it hard for government to get, or to keep, the very best people to run its data systems. (When I took a federal job in 1993 and met the head of my office's computer team for the first time, he told me he was having a hard time staying busy. Given the rapid pace of change in IT systems at the time, this surprised me somewhat.

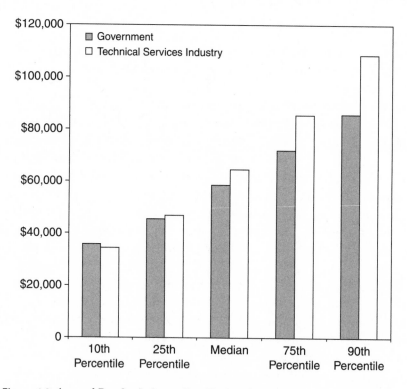

Figure 4.3: Annual Pay for Information Technology Workers, 2003. *Source:* Bureau of Labor Statistics, Occupational Employment Statistics.

He explained that he was waiting for the fad of networked desktops to blow over so he could get back to the good old mainframes in the basement.) As always, there are exceptions: IT wizards who love the special challenges of government work enough to pass up private-sector paychecks, or agencies with enough flexibility in their compensation systems to attract and retain highly qualified IT workers. But in general public employers are shut out of the top of the IT talent pool.

In an evocative, if hopefully extreme, example the deputy chief information officer at the Department of Homeland Security was forced to resign in mid-2004 when it emerged that all three of her degrees, including her doctorate, were from an unaccredited college operating from a former motel in rural Wyoming. "Life experience" substituted for coursework, and a slim essay (submitted by mail in the company of a fat check) counted as a dissertation.[19] In an only slightly happier trend, most of her senior peers at Homeland Security were soon gone as well, though of their own volition. Within three years of its creation, more than two-thirds of the department's top officials had left for private security firms. The deputy administrator of the department's Transportation Security Administration unit, for example, decamped to security contractor Choicepoint and increased her salary from $155,000 to $934,000.[20]

On occasion the public sector's personnel problems manifest themselves dramatically, as empty desks or clear-cut frauds in critical offices. But most jobs do get filled, especially jobs where compensation far exceeds the average, even if it falls short of private pay for similar work. The question is by whom. The fact that upper-level public pay scales are below private benchmarks has both direct and indirect impacts on who works in government. Imagine two smart and idealistic twenty-something acquaintances, Laura and Brian, who have just graduated near the top of their class from an elite professional school. Both are fascinated by big public issues, and neither of them is particularly avid for fancy cars, designer wardrobes, or the other lures implicitly dangled by the corporate consulting firms and venture capitalists with whom they have interviewed. At the same time, they would rather not live *too* differently from their college and grad-school friends—and, besides, each has $70,000 in student loans to pay off.

Now suppose they are both offered positions as legislative analysts at a state budget agency, exactly the kind of job that would make full use of their talents and training. The analyst position, though, starts at $45,000 a year. The recruiter is candid with Laura and Brian that they shouldn't expect rapid salary growth. The state budget is tight these days, and pay raises for bureaucrats (especially bureaucrats already earning more than many taxpayers) aren't a priority for the legislature. If they someday make it to the top of the budget office, they might earn as much as $90,000.

Brian and Laura each eagerly ponder the prospect of helping to shape policies that will make their state a better place. They wonder, though, what kind of living standard they'll be able to maintain and still pay off their loans. Brian calls to mind some high-school buddies from his home town, reminds himself that a lot of them manage to get by on less than $45,000, and decides to accept the budget office job. Laura thinks more about her grad-school friends, imagining (with a distaste that embarrasses her a little) a future of humbler houses in less desirable towns than her peers. At a party after graduation, her study group pledged to climb Kilimanjaro together to mark their five-year reunion. Will she be able to afford the trip? Laura thinks about her other offer, from a consulting firm that does millions every year in contract work for the same state budget office. Sure, if she takes the private job she'll have to do some business consulting as well, and that leaves her cold. But at least she'll spend some of her time on public policy. The pay starts at nearly twice what the budget office can offer. If she's good at the work—and she knows she will be—her salary will rise fast and far. Laura is torn, but she ends up turning down the budget office and taking the consulting job—and using the signing bonus to pay down a healthy chunk of her student loans. The budget office fills the slot it had offered to Laura with a fallback candidate a notch or two below her caliber.

There are a lot of Lauras. But there are a lot of Brians as well, fortunately, willing to pass up the consumption levels their talent could earn them in order to do the work that excites them most. The Brookings Institution studied the Presidential Management Fellows program— the federal government's conduit for channeling the Brians of the world into public service—and found that new presidential fellows were motivated mainly by the chance to do challenging work with leverage over big problems, and by prospects for professional and personal growth. Salary was last on the list of motives, with just 13 percent of these amply qualified fellows considering it to be very important.[21] If we had to worry only about the direct effects of the pay gap at the top, the problem might be manageable.

But there is more to the story. Fast-forward five years. Brian has turned out to be a star at the budget office, rising through the grades at record pace. He loves the work, and he's earning nearly $60,000. He got married a couple of years ago, to a middle-school teacher. With their two incomes they're doing okay. They're not rich, by any means, but they managed to come up with the down payment for their house and they're keeping current on their student loans. True, the schools in their town are only so-so, and they plan to start a family in a year or two. But maybe the local schools will improve, or housing prices will come down in the neighboring town with the excellent schools where Brian's wife teaches, or maybe the legislature will be a little less tight-fisted with civil-service salaries than it has been so far.

The problem is Don, who is Brian's immediate supervisor at the budget office. Don has been assistant director for nearly ten years. That job pays $85,000. More important, it comes with a lot more leverage than the analyst positions below it. Brian wants to be assistant director himself, and knows he'd be good at it—better than Don, actually. With a graduate degree of his own and more than two decades' experience, Don looks pretty impressive on paper. Plug his data into a compensation equation and he would seem underpaid. But lots of things about Don don't show up on paper. He's cranky, disorganized, and hard to get along with, and if he ever had much drive and sparkle he left them behind long ago. As the years have passed, many of his colleagues have decamped for more lucrative private-sector jobs, but the rich offers haven't come Don's way. Brian and Don both know that, whatever his formal qualifications, Don is doing better as assistant director than he ever would outside of government. So he's not leaving.

Having Don as a boss drains much of the joy out of Brian's work. Worse still, Don is sitting in the path of Brian's career advancement. Personnel rules—which the Dons of the world vigilantly safeguard—make it all but impossible for Brian to replace Don or be promoted above him, and Don won't retire for ten or fifteen years. At a conference, Brian runs into his old classmate Laura. They catch up on each other's careers, share news about mutual friends, and Laura shows Brian snapshots from her Kilimanjaro trip. Both of them are aware that Laura's consulting company has recently hired away two of Brian's best colleagues. They'd love to get Brian, too, if he could ever be persuaded to make the switch. Will he join Laura and her boss for a drink after the conference? Sure. Let's talk.

The Brookings study of Presidential Management Fellows—top recruits who are carefully groomed for leadership roles—found that more than half of them were gone within five years. When former fellows were surveyed about their reasons for leaving, a majority said the government fell short on efforts to retain talented workers, but an even larger majority (80 percent) said it did a bad job at dealing with the poor performers who can poison a workplace.[22]

Laura and Brian are invented—or, more precisely, each of them is a composite of a few hundred of my former students—but it's worth touching on a few very real examples. During the first Clinton administration I held senior policy posts at the Department of Labor. (The theme of underpayment at the top isn't personal, by the way. Academia was my point of reference, and I had no complaints about my government salary.) My job was hard but hugely rewarding, not least because of all the smart, patriotic people with whom I got to work, both other political appointees and career civil servants. To list them all, from Secretary Bob Reich on down, would make this a very long chapter. But to make more concrete some of this section's generalizations I will mention a few of the junior stars, people who were then in their twenties or early thirties, poised to be today's public leaders.

Some of those who impressed me most were career employees already at Labor when I arrived. Mark Troppe was an expert in workforce development whom we tapped to help shape a vital initiative for easing the school-to-work transition for America's kids. Mark had a prodigious work ethic and a modest, engaging manner that did not quite hide his piercing intellect. Mark's idealism equaled his abilities. Between college and graduate school he had worked as a volunteer serving low-income kids in a rough section of Portland, Oregon. Kate Kazin, another career civil servant, was the daughter of one of America's preeminent twentieth-century intellectuals, and the bloodline showed. After graduating from law school she had joined the Office of the Solicitor of Labor to help enforce the laws protecting workers' rights. Luckily for me she was detailed to my office, where she proved a powerhouse at policy research and writing.

Three other young stars were people I hired to fill my small quota of political appointees. David Agnew was a gregarious South Carolinian with enough heart and energy for three normal people. He lived and breathed public service, kept a portrait of Martin Luther King Jr. on his desk, and took a leave of absence to run for Congress—unsuccessfully, alas—in his mid-twenties. David could muster a task force and drive it to phenomenal results with no other authority than his own contagious enthusiasm. When I recruited Rob Rodriguez he still had a trace of an accent, and much more than a trace of the diligence and steely discipline that had taken him from working-class immigrant origins to Ivy-League graduate training. Along the way Rob had spent two years in Africa as a Peace Corps volunteer, putting his values into practice and picking up fluency in a third language. Dan Pink was a graduate of Yale Law School who was appalled at the thought of practicing law and determined to apply his incandescent mind to public issues. Dan, a widely read polymath with a lightening wit, was perfect for his job as Reich's speechwriter. He could transform the most convoluted policy announcement into lyrical prose, and had a spooky ability to craft a quotable statement about the monthly unemployment statistic during the few minutes in which he and Reich—locked into a windowless room—knew the market-moving number before it was released to the world.

Each of these five young people had the intellectual horsepower, good judgment, poise, and zest for hard work that would make them treasured assets in any workplace. They would have been on the fast track to the top in law, consulting, or venture capital, but cared more about making a difference than about making money. Most of what I got done was thanks to them and others like them. Over time I got to know these five well enough to understand both the depth of their idealism and some of their misgivings about working in government. Their reservations weren't just about money. Consumption wasn't their priority, and in any case with their advanced degrees they were paid more than other government workers their ages. And they knew they were doing much better than most Americans. But the money wasn't irrelevant. After-hours talk sometimes turned to soaring property values in the Washington area, bid up by lawyers, lobbyists, and technology workers, and somebody would ruefully report that a house he or she had dreamed of buying had just sold for three times what he or she could afford. Another time one of them might mention spending a weekend at a friend's vacation house and being unable to reciprocate, or wisecrack that the Rolex on the wrist of a lobbyist who had come calling outweighed the combined net worth of our office.

The only times any of these five voiced serious complaints about money, though, was when they compared their own paychecks to those of the most senior career people surrounding us who, over the course of three or four decades, had worked their way toward the top of the civil-service ladder. It rankled that these senior careerists were much better paid than the younger stars. It rankled a lot more that some of them just weren't very good. It pained me then to learn, and it pains me now to report, that a significant fraction of the career employees holding key jobs turned out to be pretty unimpressive.

How can this happen, in an organization pursuing an important and exciting mission, where hiring and promotion are guided by rules meant to implement strict merit principles? Suppose you happen to hold a doctorate in economics and have twenty-five years of federal experience. The paymaster's comparability surveys say your job is worth $100,000, and that's what you earn. You grumble that you'd make much more in business, like your former colleagues who have left over the years—but in your heart of hearts, you know otherwise. Maybe your education is out of date, maybe you have a little drinking problem, maybe you're just not quite as smart as your academic credentials advertise. You know this, and you have learned that private employers tend to figure it out. But you also know that government will continue to pay you by your credentials and time in office rather than by your hard-to-measure productive power. So you are anxious to do everything you can—and you have been around long enough to learn the ropes—to preserve the personnel system as it is. Your expectations of a serious raise depend on moving up the hierarchy as those above you are promoted or retire. The last thing you want is for some hot-shot outsider to leap in ahead of you. It does not take a very large fraction of such workers to deepen the sclerosis of public personnel systems, or to ruin the image of public service, and in so doing to repel even those talented people who could content themselves with governmental pay scales.

Here I want to be very careful lest I slander a group that includes some of the finest people I have ever known. Many of those who toil for decades in government are the best of the best, selfless and tireless and vastly able. I could name a long list from my time at Labor alone, and have met countless more in other settings. Some, however, are what might be called "the worst of the best." They have the credentials and experience that qualify them, on paper, for the positions they hold. But behind those formal qualifications, on the dimensions of character and energy and native wit that are opaque to coarse-grained governmental personnel systems, the worst of the best fall short. They know or suspect that the private labor market would be more discerning about their real value-added. So they stay in government, year after year. Meanwhile, a steady flow of the best of the best—their subtler virtues as well as their formal qualifications noticed by other employers—succumb to the lures of private-sector work.

Over time, in many public workplaces, the worst of the best attain a critical mass as their more talented colleagues filter out of government. They are able to shape the organizational structure, the pace of work, and the intricate norms of office culture to suit their preferences. Like an island newly cut off from the mainland, the ecology of the workplace evolves in a separate direction. The population of those best adapted to this environment—one of many rules, formal structures, constrained rewards, and buffered risk—gradually expands. The population of those least suited to such a setting gradually dwindles.

When I returned to academia, Mark, Kate, David, Rob, and Dan were still on the job. The satisfactions of public service still outweighed the frustrations, but the balance was tipping fast. All five were gone well before the end of the Clinton administration. Mark Troppe stunned his colleagues by resigning his civil-service sinecure to join a start-up company. A year or two of freewheeling chaos was enough catharsis for Mark and he settled into a prestigious nonprofit where he does workforce policy consulting for the Labor Department and other clients. The prospect of returning to the Solicitor's Office brought to a head Kate Kazin's long-brewing dissatisfaction with the life of a government lawyer. She ended up leaving not just the Labor Department, but the country. Kate emigrated to Israel, and I've lost touch with her. David Agnew quit Labor to become the mayor's right-hand man in Charlestown, South Carolina. A few years later David cofounded a real estate development company that has become a catalyst for the "livable cities" movement. He's as public-spirited as ever, but when he talks about his time in Washington it's with a tinge of cynicism wholly alien to his nature. Rob Rodriguez left government for a job at a prominent money-management firm where he rapidly rose from trainee to heavy hitter. Today Rob is a well-regarded and very prosperous financial adviser to big pension plans, nurturing his idealism (in his scant free time) by leading volunteer programs at his church. Dan Pink was recruited by the White House to be the chief speechwriter for Vice President Al Gore, did that brilliantly for a couple of years, then quit government altogether and became a celebrated columnist, speaker, and author of path-breaking books.

The loss of these five talented people, and of thousands more like them every year across every level of government, is a quiet calamity for America. As each departs for greener pastures the government becomes a little clumsier, a little dimmer, a little less creative, and a little less attractive to other smart people making choices about their future careers. The world would be a better place today if a clutch of bright kids, doing vital public work, had Rob Rodriguez for a boss. Somewhere in Washington are a lot of workers who lack a certain spark and gumption because they never got the chance to model themselves on David Agnew.

A 2003 survey of more than a thousand college seniors poised to get degrees in the liberal arts and social work found, as one would expect, that young people who chose these majors were not highly motivated by money. Most were eager for work that would change America for the better. But they also tended to be lukewarm about a government career, and most saw the nonprofit sector as a better venue for applying their idealism. By lopsided margins these students thought nonprofits outperformed government at spending money well, helping people, and making fair decisions.[23] Another survey of college students done in 2002 for Harvard's Institute of Politics—this one not restricted to liberal arts and social work majors—also found somewhat more interest in working for nonprofits than for the government. But nearly twice as many of the students were seriously considering working for a large corporation as were considering working for either government or nonprofit employers. In a poll of the general population undertaken for the Council for Excellence in Government in 1997, nearly two respondents thought government workers were generally lower-quality than private-sector workers for every one who thought the reverse.

Even little kids cast jaundiced eyes on government jobs. The venerable children's magazine *My Weekly Reader* surveyed a thousand second- and third-graders, and another thousand fourth-, fifth-, and sixth-graders, about their career aspirations. Interest in public service was low across the board, but dropped by more than a third between the younger and the older group. (This may be in part because the younger kids, but not the older ones, were prompted with "firefighter" as an example of public service.)[24]

It is not news, of course, that government's appeal to top workers has faded, and there have been decades of efforts to restore its luster. The Civil Service Reform Act of 1978 introduced modest performance bonuses into the federal system, updated somewhat the rigid system of job classifications, and provided for waivers to allow agencies to experiment with more fundamental reforms. It also established a new elite layer of career civil servants called the Senior Executive Service (SES) meant to mirror the private sector's mix of risk and reward by loosening both pay constraints and job tenure for the most qualified federal workers. They could earn nearly as much as Cabinet members if they did well, but a healthy chunk of their pay was contingent on excellent performance, and the 1978 law included provisions to make it easy to fire SES members who fell short of the new cadre's exacting standards. (The SES initiative is taken up again in Chapter 6.) Paul Volcker, the savvy former head of the Federal Reserve, led a presidential commission on civil-service reform in 1988. A different president asked him to do it again in 2002, and he once more assembled a commission that met, pondered, and issued similar recommendations for more flexibility, fewer rules, and more emphasis on top performance.[25] But it seems possible that poor Paul Volcker will be called on to chair a commission on civil-service reform every decade or so as long as his health holds up. Comparable efforts to render public service more hospitable to top talent, and less forgiving of mediocrity, have taken place (often recurrently) throughout state and local government.

It would be both churlish and inaccurate to say that these blue-ribbon panels and legislative initiatives—along with the broader reform campaigns discussed in the next chapter—have had no effect. Many have produced improvements; more have stemmed or slowed further declines.[26] A few public-sector organizations do quite well at attracting, retaining, and deploying top talent. In Washington the Office of Management and Budget, much of the Securities and Exchange Commission, and the Government Accountability Office (until recently called the General Accounting Office) are enclaves of excitement and excellence. But the isolated wins have not summed to any systematic breakthrough, and this is no surprise. Efforts to end government's status as a backwater, in the eyes of the most able American workers, are pushing against powerful economic currents. The continuous transformation of the private economy, and the endless escalation in the rewards it offers at the top, too often outmatch reformers' struggles to burnish the government's appeal to talent. So long as the public and private worlds of work differ so profoundly, those straining to upgrade public employment are sailing against the tide.

◆ ◆ ◆

FIVE

A Twisted Transformation

WE ARE LIVING through a transformative economic era. It always seems this way, of course. People who happened to be alive when the steam engine, the railroad, or the telegraph unraveled and then reknit the economy's fabric must have felt, just as surely as we do, that they were watching the birth of modernity. But I suspect historians of the future will record our times as tumultuous beyond the norm. Industries that barely existed a generation ago dominate the landscape. Companies take form, surge to prominence, and mutate or fade away with dizzying speed. Long-established corporations radically remake themselves or blink out of existence. A whole menagerie of new organizational forms has evolved. The spike in economic inequality on which I have dwelt at such length is merely one aspect, and surely among the least welcome aspects, of this technical and institutional ferment. With that admittedly grave exception, the transformation of the private economy has mostly brought good news. Both its bright and dark manifestations, in any case, are dramatic, unpredictable, and exciting to witness.

This is also a transformative era for government, at least on paper, and by intent. Books about the brave new world of government roll off the presses. The public sector has become, or is poised to become, or at the very least *should* become, leaner, more agile, performance-oriented, densely networked, ever more flexible and efficient. At the federal level—as always, overstudied relative to its size—the roll call of major transformation campaigns includes the Grace Commission during the

101

Reagan administration, the National Performance Review pledged to reinvent government under Clinton, and the President's Management Agenda of George W. Bush. Few states have gone without at least one high-level task force dedicated to root-and-branch restructuring. Just touring all of the workshops, seminars, and conferences on governmental transformation could swallow up a career.

I certainly do not want to suggest that all of this is a sham. Some real changes have taken place in how public organizations operate, and many of these changes have been very good indeed. Transforming government is an urgent, noble mission embraced by many people of good will and great talent. It would be quite surprising had the quest proven fruitless. But many aspiring reformers, among whom I count myself, are plagued by a sense that progress has been meager scaled against either the effort applied or the distance to be traveled. The transformation of America's public sector to date is both limited and, perhaps more importantly, distorted. Some eminently sensible changes remain stubbornly stalled. Some second-order, silly, or questionable reforms have outpaced the fundamentals. In part this is just the elemental inertia that torments all would-be reformers and comforts all true conservatives. But the results of the far-flung transformation campaign, both its torpid pace and its peculiar pattern, become easier to understand in light of the segregation between the public and private worlds of work. The trends traced in the past several chapters shape America's political and economic terrain in ways that render the reformers' route a steep uphill climb.

Lumping and Splitting

A bit more attention to the business world's evolution is needed to set the context for parallel patterns in government. There are many conceptual lenses by which to view the transformative thrust of the private economy, and no single one that captures all the subtleties. One of the more revealing of these lenses, though, focuses on the integration or disintegration of economic activity—the degree to which the chain of value creation is lumped together into a unified entity, or split up across separate, specialized units. At the extreme of "lumping," imagine an automobile factory where raw materials pour in at one end (from company-owned mines, on company-owned ships) and finished cars roll out the other, as designers, accountants, and managers direct the whole productive symphony from offices overlooking the shop floor. (Ford's River Rouge plant actually came close to this image of ultimate integration.) At the extreme of "splitting," consider the way many movies reach the screen today. A freelance writer drafts the script and brokers it through an agent to a producer who is aligned (often fleetingly) with a production company. The producer engages a director, cinematographer, and casting director, none of whom may have worked together before. The cast is assembled and the team ramps up for filming. Separate companies provide special effects, wardrobe, film processing, catering, music and sound effects, animal handling, and the like. Once the movie is finished, a different company distributes it to theaters owned by another set of separate organizations, with a network of other firms dealing with shipping, security, insurance, advertising, subtitles for foreign distribution, and on and on.

Scholars have long been fascinated by the forces that account for lumping and splitting in a single industry or the economy as a whole. A seminal episode in the study of economic integration came in 1937 when a young Englishman named Ronald Coase asked himself why companies exist at all. Coase, barely twenty-seven years old, had not yet finished his University of London degree, but he was on the verge of one of the pivotal insights of twentieth-century economics. An economist has been defined as a person who sees something working in practice and wonders if it might work in theory. Coase's elegant little paper, "The Nature of the Firm," is perhaps the happiest application of this professional quirk.[1] It was written during a time of rapid industrial integration, as many of the corporate behemoths of the twentieth century were either forming or undergoing the growth spurts that would take them to their full midcentury sprawl. The executives who were orchestrating this integrative trend seemed to know what they were doing. Despite the speed bump of the Great Depression, most of the big companies were producing things that consumers were happy to pay for and were making money for their investors. What bothered Coase was that economic theory (by the current state of the art) seemed quite clear that nothing of the sort should be going on.

Ever since Adam Smith pinpointed the division of labor as the wellspring of wealth, economists' ideal had been separate, specialized producers guided by the invisible hand of price signals. You don't do what somebody tells you to do; you do what it profits you to do. Buy low. Add the value you are best equipped to add. Sell high. The results are good for you and, thanks to the miraculous clockwork of the market, good for everybody. Prosperity depends on people taking their cues from prices. So long as the crucial links held fast between prices and costs, and between prices and consumers' happiness, it was impossible to improve on this interplay of atomized economic units, getting and spending as their interests inclined them. *Management* was superfluous. When the system was steered automatically by prices, managers had nothing to do except get underfoot. Long before Coase, to be sure, economists knew that the price system could be gummed up by inept public policies or corrupted by monopolists. But the industrial integration that puzzled Coase didn't strike him as a plausible solution to the familiar complications created by taxes, regulation, or monopoly. So what was going on? When theory so clearly prescribed disintegrated production coordinated by prices, why did integrated production coordinated by managers seem to be working out so well in the real world?

The answer, Coase suggested, had a lot to do with gaps and glitches in the flow of information. For the price system to work perfectly, information about what is available on the market, the characteristics of each product, and the alternative ways to obtain them needs to be universally available and consistently accurate. If someone in the value chain doesn't know something significant (or if what he thinks he knows isn't so) then prices are no longer reliable guides. Risks multiply—of being cheated, of surrendering bargaining leverage, of simply making bad choices. When information is imperfect, or imperfectly shared, then mendacity or opportunism or sheer quotidian muddle can undermine the market's efficiency.

In Adam Smith's simpler economy, reality was not so very far from this ideal of everybody knowing everything. A pin is a pin is a pin. Its price is its price is its price. Even in Smith's day prices could lie, of course. A dairymaid might water the milk she sold; her customer might shave some gold from the coin he paid in exchange. Certain industries during Smith's lifetime, such as maritime insurance, were already improvising solutions to information problems that theory would not recognize for a century and a half.[2] But by and large economic life was still straightforward enough that "take your cues from prices" was both a powerful theoretical insight and a fairly reliable practical watchword.

In the modern world of the 1930s, Coase realized, this generalization more frequently failed to hold. A value chain with many links, demanding technologically precise coordination over long periods of time and vast distances, might include so much pertinent information that prices alone couldn't hold it all. Sometimes disintegrated production steered by prices was still the way to go. But in other cases the information stream of the price system became so dammed up, or so polluted, that it was better to retreat to the primitive expedient of enlisting a manager to tell people what to do. A firm, in short, is a fallback—an auxiliary strategy for organizing work when market coordination breaks down. For any productive activity, the choice between lumping and splitting was contingent on how much information was accurately embodied in prices. Coase's emphasis on contingency, rather than some once-and-for-all right answer, was not the least of his contributions.

The more distant you find yourself from the ideal of prices telling everybody everything, the stronger the case for lumping economic activities under the direction of managers. Lumping has its costs—not just the overhead of management and its administrative apparatus but, more seriously, having to forfeit the cost-paring power of market competition for any functions brought into the corporate tent—but under circumstances that are far from rare these costs are less than those of relying on a flawed external market. As "The Nature of the Firm" began to circulate through the profession, the sound of economists slapping their foreheads could be heard on both sides of the Atlantic. Coase's insight helped to spawn whole new subdisciplines dealing with the economics of information, choice, and industrial organization. Legions of disciples and rivals refined and extended the work that Coase continued to do for many decades; he finally got his Nobel Prize in 1991.

The reason for this digression into economic theory is to suggest the role of information technology, and the organizational changes it has enabled, in today's transformation of the private economy. Lumping was the dominant theme when Coase first wrote, because the profusion of economically relevant information outpaced the price system's capacity to capture it. As information becomes more widely shared, easier to access, and simpler to process, one would expect splitting to gain the ascendancy. Even though today's economy is far more complex and data-dense than the economy of the 1930s, our ability to process information has outpaced the growth of the information that needs to be processed. Most questions that matter economically—about the range of providers of some good or service, the prices they charge, their records and reputations—are vastly easier to answer than they used to be.[3] We have cycled back to a situation where, as in Smith's time, the theoretical ideal of fully informed market actors is at least roughly approximated in reality. The more closely we approach this ideal, the more we can harvest the benefits of splitting: flexibility, rich menus of options, rapid innovation, and cost reduction through both specialization and competition.

Lumping is far from unknown in the contemporary economy, of course, but splitting has become a powerful theme.[4] Even the corporate giants of today, such as Wal-Mart and Microsoft, rely far more on subcontractors, partnerships, and alliances than did the big firms of earlier eras. Pressure from hungry rivals or impatient investors motivates firms to outsource or subcontract whenever it can to wring out costs or ramp up production. Ever-improving information technology makes it possible to maintain intricate networks of interlinked organizations that would have become hopelessly entangled in an earlier era. A propensity toward splitting is by no means the only force behind the ongoing evolution of the private sector, but this economic transformation would be greatly dampened had organizational boundaries not become so porous. And, at a sufficiently lofty level of abstraction, there is no reason why this shouldn't apply to the public sector.

Lumping and Splitting Government's Work

In principle, actually, disaggregating the value chain—parceling out each separable function to whomever can perform it best—promises even more of a payoff to government than to business. It is no slur against government to say that productive efficiency is not and should not be its strong suit. The public sector's cardinal virtue—precious when present, crippling when absent—is legitimacy in citizens' eyes. Public organizations, almost by definition, are answerable to a broad range of constituencies whose interests, on a wide spectrum of dimensions, must be taken into account. Let's call this "extensive accountability." Private organizations, conversely, are characterized by what can be termed "intensive accountability." They are answerable to a narrower set of masters, but in a far more focused way. This intensive accountability is inherently more conducive than extensive accountability to pure productive efficiency—rooting out avoidable costs, eking out each tiny improvement that might yield a fleeting competitive edge or add an extra hundredth of a percent to the rate of return, sweating every detail of the production process. Government does the right thing, as the cliché goes, while business does things right. Despite the many vivid counterexamples one could adduce on both sides, this is a generally accurate summary of the different bundles of incentives, constraints, and pressures that shape the behavior of public and private organizations. Expecting government to match business on cost reduction or process refinement is as quixotic, by and large, as expecting business to respond, without the prod of lawsuit or regulation, to the complaints of some unmonied interest its operations happen to injure. There is a built-in tradeoff between intensive and extensive accountability.

Once the ends are established and it's down to a matter of means, therefore, private organizations should have a considerable edge. Shifting some function from one private firm to another may generate gains from specialization, optimal scale, and the spur of competition. Shifting some function from government to a private firm can do this, too, but it also transfers the task from an institutional setting in which productive efficiency is a secondary concern into one in which productive efficiency is the prime directive.

A great deal has been written about the generic make-versus-buy decision in the private sector and the closely related, though not quite identical, choice between direct versus indirect production for government.[5] A bevy of buzzwords and euphemisms refer to indirect governmental production, including outsourcing, competitive supply, contracting out, and privatization. A full account of the criteria that determine whether a task is suitable for privatization would include many layers of rationale, exceptions, nuance, and caveats. But most of it can be summarized as three characteristics whose presence makes a task appropriate for delegation and whose absence renders privatization hazardous.

SPECIFICITY: You can delegate only what you can define. Splitting off a function requires specifying it in sufficient detail to solicit bids, select a provider, and structure a meaningful contract. So tasks that are predictable, stable, and separable from the rest of the value chain are good candidates for contracting out. It is hard to write a sturdy contract for the performance of tasks that are entangled with other functions and subject to continual revision (in timing, scale, or purpose) as circumstances change. For the performance of contingent tasks that are inextricably melded with the rest of the value chain, the appropriate contractual form—you pay me to hang around and follow your instructions as you figure out what needs doing—we call "employment." The choice between employees and outside providers depends crucially on which aspects of an undertaking can and which cannot be well specified. It is logically possible, of course, to rely on outsiders for ill-defined and changeable tasks. But for a range of reasons—most too obvious to mention, and a few too technical to get into here—this is usually not very smart.[6]

EASE OF EVALUATION: To outsource a function you not only need to be able to say what you want (specificity), but you also need to know what you've gotten—clearly enough and early enough to do something about it if what's delivered isn't what was promised. The easier it is to monitor performance and assess the quality of the work, the more safely can a task be delegated. For many functions, fortunately, in both business and government it is not too hard to distinguish between a good job and a bad job, and for such functions a well-crafted contract can enforce accountability. But other tasks resist clear evaluation. Outcomes may be inherently ambiguous or opaque. Consequences may play out over a very long period of time. Results may have multiple causes, making it impossible to infer good or bad efforts from a good or bad outcome. No matter how producers are organized it is inherently tricky to elicit good performance if you can't measure it, but the problems are worse for delegated functions. The special contract called "employment" gives you control over what people do. This isn't so urgent if you know (in real time, and unambiguously) the *results* of what they do. But if evaluation is elusive, murky, or delayed—and if you have some plausible ideas about which actions are likely to produce good results—control over what people do can be a very good thing. As with specificity, there is no logical impediment to outsourcing work you cannot evaluate, but you should keep your expectations modest on matters of accountability.[7]

COMPETITION: Private providers tend to outscore government on productive efficiency not because there is something magic about privateness. They are efficient because they have to be. Market competition weeds out the laggards and keeps the winners in a state of healthy anxiety. The whole point of privatization is to harness for the government the salutary effects of competition. Contracting out can transplant into public undertakings some of the intensive accountability that characterizes the private sector. Without competition much of its rationale collapses. When external providers are comfortably safe from harassment by rivals, privatization offers far fewer benefits and far greater hazards. If government can choose from a list of alternative suppliers for some part of its value chain, both at the start of the relationship, and episodically thereafter, it can hope to meld many of the market's virtues into public missions. Passing a task from a public monopoly to a private monopoly, conversely, is seldom very helpful. Sometimes this criterion can be suspended. A private entity might possess some capacity that is so valuable to government that it is worth obtaining even on unfavorable terms. Or some specialized task may be so distant from government's core competency that its delegation brings gains in managerial focus outweighing the losses from monopoly pricing. Or a private provider may be a nonprofit organization presumed to be merciful in the application of its pricing power. But to opt for privatization when competition is weak or absent is to forfeit, whether knowingly or not, much of its advertised efficiency edge.

Commodity Tasks and Custom Tasks

Determining the degree to which these three criteria—specificity, ease of evaluation, and competition—apply is a matter of careful, case-by-case analysis. The decision to delegate is contingent on the details of the mission, the public sector's specific capabilities and deficits, the number and nature of available private suppliers, and other considerations. Yet in general these conditions will be met more fully for relatively straightforward functions, what might be called "commodity tasks." For more complex and sophisticated functions, or "custom tasks," the odds are generally high that one, two, or all three of these conditions will fail to hold.

The transition of many functions from custom to commodity status has done a great deal to enable the surge of economic splitting in the private sector. Computer components were once exactingly crafted to match the peculiar specifications of a single machine. Most are now so standardized that they can be ordered over the phone by the container-load. In the early 1980s International Business Machines (IBM) ushered in the age of the ubiquitous personal computer. Two decades later thousands of IBM desktops were unpacked every day. But not a single one of them was actually made by IBM. Building a desktop to IBM's design, to a quality standard worthy of the IBM nameplate, had become enough of a commodity function to be handed over to a company called Sanmina-SCI. Sanmina and other low-profile "contract electronic manufacturers" specialized in cranking out electronic goods under contract to name-brand companies.[8] Within their narrow niche, they were able to outperform the IBMs of the world.

In an analogous way, payroll processing used to be an intimate internal chore for nearly all firms. But this function has become so automated, and thus so standardized, that it can be and often is delegated to specialized payroll management firms.[9] Much the same evolution from custom to commodity function has occurred with data entry, claims processing, order tracking, and other relatively routine tasks, and each in turn becomes increasingly likely to be split off from the core company. Some other functions have long been commodity tasks—food service, maintenance and cleaning, plant security—but are now delegated with increasing frequency as the market becomes sufficiently well-populated with supplier firms, as contracting procedures are refined, and as profit pressures reach the point that companies are hungry enough for the cost savings that outsourcing can offer.

The sculptor Jeff Koons is world renowned for his dramatic metal artwork. But many of the museum pieces that bear his signature are produced in a San Fernando factory that Koons rarely visits. The artist sends his designs to a manager at Carlson and Co., one of several firms in the "art fabrication" industry, and the manager oversees hourly workers as they translate Koons's inspiration into polished metal. The arrangement suits Koons, who can concentrate on creativity without the drudgery of all that welding, and also suits the entrepreneur, who takes in $8 million a year managing great artists' grunt work. The disintegration of the artistic value chain also works for the $20-an-hour metalworker laboring away on a Koons original. "It's not the physical act that matters," the worker notes humbly, "it's the idea."[10] Outsourced sculpting is merely one illustration of the degree to which our institutionally sophisticated economy permits the separation of the idea from the act.

It is business orthodoxy that a company should cleave to its core competency, maintaining tight control over those functions on which its fate pivots. This does not preclude the outsourcing of some high-end tasks. Advertising has long been the province of specialized organizations; many companies rely on outside legal counsel; and strategy consulting firms continue to prosper. Often, however, custom tasks that are split off from the rest of the value chain display a reasonable degree of specificity, ease of evaluation, and competition. There are many advertising agencies to choose from, for example, and the trajectory of sales in the wake of an ad campaign is both salient and to some degree measurable. In other cases a company knows a task is ill-defined, resistant to clear evaluation, and available from just one or a few suppliers, but still opts to buy it from the outside. It would be so expensive to replicate the proprietary models and roster of experts that McKinsey and Company possesses, for example, that quite a few corporations seeking strategic direction decide to pay McKinsey's rates and hope for the best. (The fact that the private sector delegates custom tasks, of course, doesn't obviate the downsides of the practice. Businesses can choose badly, too.)

But even though the splitting trend in the private economy applies across the spectrum, it is generally far more pronounced at the commodity end. It has become rare for a company of any size to have its own employees staff the cafeteria, empty the wastebaskets, tend the landscaping, ferry parts and documents between offices and plants, or stand guard at night. One motive for splitting off functions within the private sector, to be sure, is to drive down the unit cost of labor. Supplier firms may have better access to pools of cheap workers, or may be less squeamish than the core company about squeezing compensation down to the bare minimum. But the story does not end with pay cuts, and need not even include them. Separate firms that concentrate on catering, landscaping, security, or some other bundle of commodity tasks can also exploit advantages of scale and specialization that give them a cost edge independent of what they pay for labor. Beyond paring costs, moreover, a major part of the rationale for splitting off routine functions is to tighten manager's focus on those custom tasks that define the company's core. If the purpose of a firm, recalling Coase, is to orchestrate those delicate links in the value chain that cannot be left to the impersonal market, then the more narrowly this core is defined the better. The less distracted managers are by routine chores, the more they can concentrate on those key functions that cannot be delegated. Again, this goes for government, too.

In an alternative universe, where the public and private worlds of work had evolved in the same ways, government would be undergoing a transformation that is not quite identical to that of the private sector but closely parallel. Specialized outside organizations would handle most of the routine commodity work. The transformation would have occasioned some turmoil and sparked some resistance, of the same sort that marks the private sector's reconfiguration. People don't like to have change forced on them, and even amid proliferating alternatives it is usually preferable to retain the status quo as an option. But if sector-switching imposed only modest burdens on government workers—that is, had no gulf developed between the conditions of employment in the two sectors—the turmoil would have been manageable and the resistance short of desperate.

Direct governmental employees would confine their attention to functions that are so intimately entwined with subtle and shifting public missions that they cannot be specified with much precision, or so entangled with other factors that they resist clear evaluation, or that are available on the market, if at all, only from monopoly suppliers. Even in this alternative universe there would still be many such tasks, and government employment would not be limited to a handful of procurement officers. But the public workforce would be appreciably smaller than it had been twenty or thirty years ago—before the technological and organizational enablers of disintegration had matured—and heavily tilted toward the more skill-intensive and sophisticated kinds of work. In our own universe, the picture is very different.

The Pace of Public-Sector Outsourcing

The largest U.S. public employees' union warns that "from city halls, county boards and state houses to our nation's capital, the push for private takeover of public services is picking up steam." As unions point with alarm at the evaporation of public jobs, trade associations representing private contractors celebrate the long boom in profitable opportunities to provide services to the public sector. Yet assertions of a surge in outsourcing—whether gleeful or grim—turn out to lack anything that approaches a convincing empirical base. The record is replete with case studies of both successful and unsuccessful privatization. But the cases may be typical of what is going on in this big and diverse country, or they may be odd exceptions. Without systematic data we simply don't know. There have been a few efforts to survey governments on their outsourcing habits, but these have been spotty, episodic, or marred by low response rates. Some ambitious and generally sensible studies hinge on idiosyncratic definitions and handcrafted data that are hard to test or replicate.[11] So the debate over privatization rests, to a remarkable extent, on simple assemblages of anecdotes.[12] In contrast to other indicators with major policy relevance (the share of industrial capacity that is actually in use; the incidence of serious crime; the rate of health-care cost inflation) as well as matters of perhaps secondary import (opera attendance by Native Americans; per-capita sherbet consumption; the percentage of houses in your immediate neighborhood that lack fully equipped kitchens) there are no official data series focused on direct versus indirect public-service delivery.[13]

The closest approximation is the National Income and Product Account data assembled by the Commerce Department's Bureau of Economic Analysis, which are coarse and imprecise but still of considerable interest. They permit us to track the share of public spending that goes to compensate employees, and the share that goes to engage outside suppliers. The two categories aren't exactly comparable—the costs of external services include equipment and overhead, for example—but close enough to make trends meaningful. For government as a whole, the external share of service spending ran just over 23 percent in the 1950s, growing to a little over 33 percent, on average, between 2000 and 2005. So outsourcing *does* seem to be on the rise in the public sector. But there are several complicating factors to keep in mind.

First, the story differs sharply across segments of the public sector. Figure 5.1 shows the trends for the three big categories: federal defense-related spending, other federal spending, and by far the largest category, state and local government. State and local outsourcing starts low and grows steadily but modestly. Federal non-defense outsourcing

leaps sharply between the 1950s and the 1960s, but changes little thereafter. The most dramatic action is with federal defense spending,
where outsourcing surges from the 1970s onward, and especially after
the turn of the twenty-first century. Such diversity across segments
makes it hard to talk about a single trend.

Second, much of the apparent boost in outsourcing is an artifact of
the soaring share of health-care spending within public-sector budgets.
The Bureau of Economic Analysis implicitly treats Medicare and Medicaid as governmental operations, analogous to maintaining a park or
tracking a missile, which can be either performed by public workers or
split off to private suppliers. But setting up a big public medical system
(instead of having government pay for much of the privately delivered
health services of the poor, the elderly, veterans, and other groups) has
never been a serious option in the United States. The share of external
services including Medicare and Medicaid has grown not because we

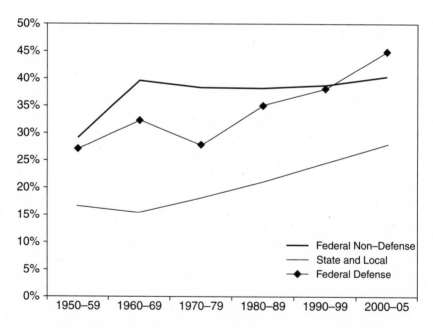

Figure 5.1: External Share of Government's Spending on Services. *Source:*
U.S. Department of Commerce, Bureau of Economic Analysis, National
Income and Product Account, Table 3.10.5, "Government Consumption
Expenditures and General Government Gross Output."

changed our minds about lumping and splitting medical services, but because the big health programs—always heavily private—account for so much more of the government's spending than they used to. An experimental reprocessing of the official data that pulls out Medicare and Medicaid suggests that growth in outsourcing has been only about one-fourth to one-third as great as the raw data suggest.[14]

Much of this modest bump, moreover, reflects the shift in America's demographic center of gravity southward and westward, toward regions that have always been somewhat more inclined to choose private providers, rather than the shift of existing functions from public to private suppliers. It does happen, of course, that a task is wrenched away from public workers and handed to the private sector; the case studies aren't based on hallucinations. It just doesn't happen all that often.

The Bush administration launched a high-profile "competitive sourcing" initiative soon after taking office. This campaign to expose federal workers to commercial competition featured bold presidential statements, task forces and training programs in every agency, noisy exchanges between outraged labor leaders and determined administration officials, and an intricate series of legislative moves and countermoves. The president's Office of Management and Budget issued a report in mid-2004 detailing the agency-by-agency progress of competitive sourcing, hailing the bracing effects of competitive pressure, and projecting the cost savings to be anticipated. The fine print of the report, though, indicates that in the prior fiscal year this unprecedented competitive crusade had moved 2,729 jobs (or about one in a thousand) to the private sector.[15] The Bush team arguably did push the envelope on outsourcing defense functions. But in the rest of the federal sector, and in most of the cities and states, the pace of privatization remains far more modest than the rhetorical *sturm und drang* surrounding the issue would suggest.

Set aside, for now, the debate about whether the outsourcing of public services is on balance a good thing or a bad thing. The point is that it is a much smaller thing than it is generally believed to be. The reasons are not mysterious. It is a constant of life that people resist efforts to alter their jobs. We settle in to what we're used to, and if change is going to happen we want it to be on our own terms. Management is largely a matter of persuading, inducing, or compelling people to accommodate changes they would not embrace on their own initiative.

The bigger and more unappealing the contemplated change, the greater is the motive to resist, and the harder the manager's task of orchestrating any transformation. As the worlds of work in the public and private sector have evolved in different directions many government employees—though not all, as the next section explains—are horrified, with excellent reason, at the prospect of displacement. Their resistance is correspondingly fierce and frequently effective. For aspiring reformers the benefits of restructuring a governmental function are usually marginal and long-term. For public workers the costs are cataclysmic and immediate. It is thus not surprising that even when would-be change agents seem to hold all the cards, imperiled public workers play their hands with grim resolve, and win more often than they lose.

If efforts in recent decades to delegate much of government's work have fallen short of what their champions hope and their critics dread, this may be just par for the course for any reform campaign. Enthusiasts and skeptics alike, however, should still concur that insofar as privatization happens, it should happen where it makes the most sense. Recall the three criteria that permit a function to be split off—specificity, ease of evaluation, and competition—and the distinction, derived from those criteria, between commodity tasks and custom tasks. These suggest a general taxonomy of governmental duties that are stronger or weaker candidates for delegation.

Table 5.1 Sorting Rules for Governmental Tasks

	Custom Tasks	Commodity Tasks
Lump	Direct government performance of functions that are ill-specified, resist clear evaluation, or lack ongoing competition.	
Split		External supply of functions that are well-specified, easy to evaluate, and readily available from competitive suppliers.

Suppose that you happen to be confident that most of the things the government does are clear and straightforward and easily replicated by private firms operating in healthily competitive markets. And suppose I worry a lot about government's complicated goals and the links among functions and all the ways that competition can break down. Whether we believe the northwest quadrant of Table 5.1 should be huge and the southeast quadrant tiny, or the reverse, we should be able to agree that a sensible public-sector transformation should hew to this general pattern.[16] And we will both be disappointed. The dearth of systematic data on who does what makes it impossible to simply list the contents of each box in Table 5.1. But the northeast and the southwest are not the sparsely populated quarters that they ought to be. Pressures set in motion by the separation of public from private work are warping the pattern of government's transformation.

The Retention of Commodity Tasks

Commodity jobs—tasks that are well defined, relatively easy to evaluate, and available from competitive private suppliers—remain plentiful in the public sector. Let's return briefly to the list of the twenty-five jobs most common in government, drawn from the Bureau of Labor Statistics' helpful, if somewhat eccentric, Occupational Employment Survey. While job titles obscure a multitude of detail, it seems only slightly risky to suggest that many of these jobs, in principle, could be split off from the core public sector and delegated to private organizations. There are excellent reasons why this doesn't happen in some cases. It may be imprudent for the president to rely on even a top-of-the-line temp as a personal assistant, and it is probably advantageous to have duly-vetted government employees empty the National Security Council's wastebaskets. But it is doubtful that a persuasive argument against delegation, anchored on the three criteria outlined earlier, could be mounted for every example of every job on the list. Privatization enthusiasts would argue that most or all jobs in the twenty-five biggest categories, from cops to accountants, could easily be turned over to the private sector. Privatization skeptics might caution that very few would pass the tests of specificity, clear evaluation, and truly competitive supply. To advance the conversation, though, let's imagine that fourteen of government's top job categories—see Table 5.2—turn out to contain enough commodity tasks that some large fraction of these jobs are plausible candidates for outsourcing.

The frequency with which commodity tasks are retained in government is due in part to the limited ardor for cost-minimization inherent in public organizations, as described in Chapter 2. But at least as im-

Table 5.2 Twenty-five Most Common Jobs in Government, 2005

Job Title	Number	Median Annual Pay (in dollars)
Elementary-school teachers	1,315,650	$47,487
Teaching assistants	1,115,454	20,090
Police and sheriff's patrol officers	609,960	46,470
Correctional officers	394,320	34,390
Mail carriers[a]	347,180	46,330
Office clerks[a]	329,420	26,730
Firefighters	273,540	39,350
Business operations specialists[a]	235,920	59,520
Mail sorters and processors[a]	208,600	43,420
Secretaries[a]	162,500	31,900
Information and record clerks[a]	151,530	41,120
Executive secretaries[a]	139,270	35,780
Registered nurses	136,970	56,470
Highway maintenance workers[a]	134,600	30,310
Maintenance and repair workers[a]	125,270	32,600
Office managers	114,680	46,240
Managers, not otherwise specified	108,740	77,770
Bookkeeping clerks[a]	108,480	31,370
Social workers	108,040	38,130
Janitors[a]	107,880	23,730
Bus drivers[a]	106,930	35,170
Lawyers	105,180	83,650
Recreation workers[a]	102,710	20,570
Accountants	102,110	48,500
Court, municipal, and license clerks[a]	99,060	29,560

Source: Bureau of Labor Statistics, Occupational Employment Statistics program, May 2005 Occupational Employment and Wage Estimates, National NAICS 3-digit Industry Specific Estimates spreadsheet, accessed June 2006 at http://www.bls.gov/oes/oes_dl.htm#2005_m.

a. Signifies one of fourteen government top job categories.

portant is the vivid awareness that splitting off such functions entails casting workers out into a far harsher world of private work. It is not the least surprising that they resist. There are scores of struggles over service outsourcing every year in the federal, state, and municipal government—some of them dramatic, high-profile confrontations, most of them small-scale and obscure. Public workers doing commodity tasks lose some of these struggles, but not many. To gain a better appreciation of public workers' determination to hold their ground, let's shift the focus from the multitude of commodity tasks marbled throughout government to a few particular functions.

The Postal Service

As defenders of the troubled postal service point out, even in the age of cheap electronic communications the post remains a vital public function. The right of every individual and organization in America to send almost anything from anywhere to anyplace else, for a relative pittance, plays a major role in knitting together the country's economic and social fabric. This is surely true. But it may not be germane. Merely deciding that a task is extremely important does not make it ineligible for delegation. The question, again, is whether it can be specified, evaluated, and competitively obtained.[17] The postal service has traditionally delegated mail delivery in many rural areas to independent contractors, and spends billions of dollars every year on air and land transportation contracts. Many—indeed, most—of its processing and delivery functions are the kinds of commodity tasks that are routinely split off through contracts in the private sector. Retreating again to our alternative universe, where no gulf separates public from private work, it is not hard to imagine a highly disaggregated postal system in which a small number of public workers carry out a core set of custom tasks and orchestrate a network of private organizations charged with the commodity tasks that constitute the bulk of the work. Many other countries have sharply expanded the private sector's role in moving the mail (with Sweden, perhaps surprisingly, near the vanguard).[18] The technical feasibility of splitting up postal functions is manifest in the covert outsourcing achieved by offering "worksharing discounts" to mass mailers who process, sort, or transport their mail before it reaches the post office.[19] It would certainly be possible to bungle the transition to a disintegrated postal system, but there is nothing unsound in concept about a heavily delegated model for moving the mail.

No such shift has happened, and it is unlikely to happen soon. This is not for any want of pressure to change. Unlike most public organizations the postal service is supposed to be self-supporting, and costs have consequences. It is also atypical in facing serious competition. Private courier services such as Federal Express, DHL, and UPS skim away the more lucrative segments of the market, while the inexorable growth of electronic communications chips away at the mundane commercial mail—the torrent of bills sent to households each month and the torrent of checks sent back to businesses—that has kept the postal service solvent. The post office confronts these escalating threats lacking control over its operations (it must offer universal service), its prices (postage rates are set by a separate commission subject to relentless lobbying by mass mailers), or its employment practices.

As of this writing the postmaster-general is leading a determined rescue campaign. But many observers fear for the future of the postal service. A blue-ribbon presidential commission released a report dense with recommendations for shoring up the postal system.[20] Many of its key prescriptions involved labor practices: downsizing by attrition, easing rules against consolidating small post offices, introducing performance pay, adjusting pay comparability rules to consider benefits as well as wages, and limiting (to half a year) the timeline for labor disputes. Its recommendations were rather mild, compared to what private-sector workers have been forced to swallow in recent decades. The commission balked at issuing more radical calls for layoffs, fundamental changes in pay policy, or large-scale outsourcing. The head of the American Postal Workers Union, however, still protested that the commission had "declared war on postal employees" and vowed to "ensure that none of this sees the light of day."[21]

This call to arms (and comparable reactions from other postal unions) provoked charges of perverse pig-headedness. Pay and benefits account for the bulk of postal costs; postal personnel practices, from a business perspective, are relics from a vanished age, and the very survival of the enterprise is in question. How can labor refuse to consider fundamental change? Yet any different stance on the part of postal labor leaders would have been surprising. The goal of the presidential reform commission, in a word, was to make the postal service more "businesslike." The entire rationale of postal unionism is to prevent any such thing. The business world has become a barren realm for the kinds of people postal unions represent. The defining mission of the unions and their congressional allies is to defend a blue-collar redoubt where the old rules still apply. Critics who indict the recalcitrance of postal labor leaders as economically unrealistic and ultimately self-destructive, as the postal service enters what many see as a death spiral, are missing the point. From labor's perspective, a businesslike post office is not worth saving. The prophets of insolvency may be bluffing, after all, or Congress may step in to halt the slide. But if not, postal labor would prefer to go down fighting than to surrender their bastion. Even those who do not share the postal unions' goals should be able to understand them, and to appreciate that they are unlikely to change.

Support Services in Schools

As the tally of government employment in Chapter 1 revealed, fully 45 percent of all public jobs are related to education. This army of education workers includes many teachers, superintendents, principals, and other people dedicated directly to the core mission; Table 5.2 lists teachers as the most common public job, and teaching aides as the second most common. But the educational workforce also includes people performing support functions that are important in enabling, but distinct from, the actual teaching. In 2002 about 3.1 million state and local education employees were doing noninstructional work—a corps of education support workers outnumbering the entire federal civilian workforce, including the postal service.[22]

A fraction of these noninstructional education workers certainly perform what I have termed custom tasks, as senior administrators, counselors, personnel managers and the like. But Bureau of Labor Statistics data point to a great many occupied with relatively straightforward commodity tasks. (This statistical series lumps together public and private education—a minor distortion for K–12 schools, a major one for higher education—so it does not match up directly with other data.) The Bureau of Labor Statistics' occupational statistics include about half a million food-service workers in the education sector, another half-million cleaning and maintenance workers, and more than a million administrative support workers (clerks, secretaries, receptionists, and so on).

There were also more than 300,000 transportation workers—mostly bus drivers, unsurprisingly—and about 200,000 construction and repair workers, such as carpenters, painters, plumbers, and general maintenance workers.

Whether teaching itself should be privatized is the focus of a long and contentious debate. There are respectable arguments on either side. Some special characteristics of primary and secondary education, however—in particular the multiplicity of factors that affect a student's progress and the complexity of measuring performance—suggest that, at best, classroom teaching is a tricky task to delegate well. The core thrust of current national policy, in fact, is to declare teaching to be a commodity task, with simple goals readily gauged with standardized tests—but not to challenge the presumption that most teachers will be public employees. There may be some coherent political logic behind this approach, but it is economically bizarre. If we are confident that standardized test scores are accurate measures of the value we want teachers to deliver, we should open the task to all bidders—and if not, not. If we believe that important dimensions of educational value elude standardized tests, then efficiency and accountability require subtler arrangements.

Educational support functions, in general, present a much simpler case. One can certainly conjure up calamities stemming from careless delegation—a catering company might serve nothing but junk food; a bus contractor might hire child molesters—but to observe that a policy option can be implemented stupidly should not settle the debate. Much of the work of these 3 million noninstructional workers in the education sector consists of the kinds of tasks that are routinely, and for the most part uneventfully, split off by private organizations. Retreating again to our alternative universe, there is no systematic technical reason why many or most of these support functions could not be delegated to private providers. Even in the fantasy world where public and private compensation is the same, this could yield cost savings from specialization, innovation, and economies of scale. The strongest argument for such an approach is not financial, however, but managerial. Principals have better things to worry about than the balky steam table in the cafeteria or the schedule for collating the parent handbooks. The best reason for handing off support functions is to free educators to focus on the schools' core mission. Indeed, an ideal model—while we're still in the realm of make-believe—might be an industry of educational logistics-management companies competing to handle nearly all of a school's functions except for direct instruction.

The pattern we actually see looks nothing like this. Support staff comprised a little more than 30 percent of the workforce in public primary and secondary schools as of 2000, almost precisely the same share as in 1969.[23] A unit of the federal Department of Education maintains statistics on school operations that are wonderfully detailed but, unfortunately, not very current; the most recent available are from the 1999–2000 school year.[24] Spending to buy services from outsiders, for schools as a group, was about 11 percent as great as spending for employees' salaries and benefits. The pattern of lumping and splitting across different functions seems fairly sensible at first glance. Transportation is the most heavily outsourced function, with the purchased-service category about four-fifths as large as employee compensation. Operation and maintenance—another category rich with commodity tasks—comes second, with about half as much spent on external services as on employees. Instruction itself is near the bottom, as it probably should be, with contracts equivalent to just a little more than 3 percent of payroll.

Yet there are some sharp departures from the sorting rule—hold on to custom tasks; split off commodity tasks—established earlier. Outside providers' share of transportation, operations, and maintenance functions actually declined a bit in the second half of the 1990s. Food service (with contracts just 15 percent as large as payroll) was somewhat less likely to be delegated than "instructional staff services," a category that includes curriculum development, teacher training, and other functions closely tied to the core mission. The fastest growth in split-off school support tasks was in this instructional staff services category; the second-fastest growth was for student support functions such as guidance counselors, health services, and speech pathologists, mostly tasks that call for fairly advanced training. And outsourced teaching, while relatively rare, was growing faster than outsourced food services.

These curious patterns become easier to understand by reference to the different ways the public and private sector treats the sorts of workers who carry out commodity tasks in the schools. Food-service workers earn about 13 percent more in the education sector than in the restaurant industry. The "accommodation" industry—covering hotels, motels, and the like—employs about the same number of cleaning and maintenance workers as the education sector, but schools pay these workers about 37 percent more. "Installation, maintenance, and repair" workers earn 24 percent more in education than in the accommodations industry. Clerical and support workers in school offices earn about 12 percent more than their counterparts in the "administrative and support services" industry.[25] Comparably detailed data on benefits are not available, but all the evidence suggests that disparities in job security and in health, retirement, and other benefits are even greater than the pay difference between the two sectors.

Simply put, splitting off support functions would be very bad news for the workers doing commodity tasks in America's public schools. Their resistance is correspondingly ferocious. Attempts to outsource this kind of work tend to be thoroughly miserable political episodes, particularly when the support workers are sympathetic local residents with children in the same school system. Even in Houston during the 1990s—at that time America's undisputed mecca of free-wheeling market approaches, in a state with notoriously weak public-employee unions—Superintendent Rod Paige was forced to backtrack on many of his plans to outsource school support services.[26]

An exhaustive study by the Government Accountability Office found that only 8 percent of public school systems used private food services in the mid-1990s, and that the rate of increase since the mid-1980s had been modest.[27] In a curious departure from the general geographic pattern, the GAO learned that New England states were more likely to outsource food services than were the otherwise more privatization-prone states to the south and west. This may be in part because in New England each separate city or town tends to have its own school system. Even adjacent towns can be sharply segregated by income level. Thus the food-service staff in a wealthier school system is likely to be made up of people who live in humbler communities outside the school district. This political segregation of commodity workers may anaesthetize somewhat the political pain that so frequently precludes splitting off support tasks in the public schools.

Airport Security Screening

In what is no doubt the most instantaneous consensus ever to emerge over any public-service delivery model, Americans found themselves in agreement, on the morning of September 12, 2001, that airport security required reform. It was not obvious, to be sure, that the existing system had fallen short of its specifications; there had been no rules barring the box-cutters that were the hijackers' main weapons on September 11.[28] But those specifications themselves were revealed as grievously flawed. A public mission suddenly perceived to be of paramount import—ensuring that nobody bent on destruction could board an airliner armed—was entrusted to a cheap, rickety delivery system. The airlines, many of them chronically on the verge of insolvency, were required to pay for passenger screening. Preferring to pay as little as possible, they contracted the work to denizens of a highly competitive private security industry. To eke out any profit from their lean contracts with the airlines, these security firms drew their workers from the bottom of the labor pool. Screeners' wages were minuscule and benefits negligible; standards, of necessity, were correspondingly low and turnover correspondingly high. Airport security, pre-September 11, had been a thoroughly low-end business.

Not a single voice was raised for retaining the status quo. But what should replace it? One option was to declare that passenger screening had been erroneously split off from government in the first place, and to move it where it belonged: alongside other crucial security functions carried out directly by the public sector. The other option was to continue to delegate screening to specialized private providers, but with more funding, far higher standards, and direct oversight by government.

The Bush administration and its allies in the House of Representatives proposed an upgraded security system that would still rely on private providers. Rival Senate legislation crafted by Democratic leaders, with the help of Republican maverick John McCain, called for making passenger and baggage screening a governmental function carried out by public employees.[29] The Senate passed its version by a rare unanimous vote, while the House version narrowly squeaked by. Many commentators still predicted that President Bush would get his way, as he had on so much else in the wake of the terror attacks. But as the dust cleared after a House–Senate conference on the airport security bill, it emerged that the proponents of direct governmental delivery had won virtually every point. The final legislation called for nearly all passenger and baggage screening to be performed by federal employees under a new Transportation Security Administration (TSA). Applicants lined up for positions in the TSA, and a year after the law was passed more than 60,000 federal passenger and baggage screeners were on the job in America's airports. Their training was rigorous, their compensation far better than their private-sector predecessors, and their job satisfaction demonstrably higher; once hired at the TSA few workers quit. (Under the old system screener turnover at Chicago's O'Hare International had been more than 200 percent a year; under the new system it was less than 4 percent, and comparably low at other airports.)[30]

This precipitous shift from delegated to direct security screening doubtless owed much to the nation's jittery mood and the consequent political imperative for root-and-branch changes to a system seen as catastrophically flawed. (The editorial board of the *New York Times* had flayed the Republicans for "taking ideological consistency to an absurd extreme" in their opposition to a federal takeover of airport security.)[31] Proponents for the new public agency may have been correct, of course. A recurrence of September 11 was a hideous prospect, and who could prove that an upgraded model for private airport security would really work?[32] But it is quite possible that, whatever their underlying motives, the Republican leadership had the more logical case.

Supreme importance does not, on its own, disqualify a function from being a commodity task suitable for delegation. The gross flaws in the previous contractual model did not preclude structuring a sturdier arrangement. The work, however vital, is readily specified: inspect every passenger and every piece of luggage to ensure that no weapon can be smuggled onto an airplane. Contractual provisions could mandate (at a commensurate price) that screeners be citizens, college graduates, psychiatrists, martial-arts experts, or holders of whatever other qualifications are judged essential. Evaluation is much more straightforward for airport screening than for many other functions that are delegated contractually. The performance of individual screeners can be gauged through devices, now routinely in use, that periodically project the phantom image of a gun, knife, or bomb onto an innocent X-ray screen. The performance of screening contractors could have been evaluated, to almost any desired degree of stringency, by a corps of plainclothes inspectors constantly testing security with dummy weapons or bombs and levying painful financial penalties for any lapse. Several large firms already operate in the industry, and entry is relatively easy, making airport screening far more competitive than many other outsourced functions. Such arrangements are not merely hypothetical; they were and are the norm in many European countries that are sadly familiar with terrorism. Screening contractors earn high fees, pay good wages and benefits, hire qualified workers, and appear to perform about as well as the TSA.

The managerial case for delegating airport screening is subtler but potentially quite significant. America was suddenly confronted with expanded requirements for a vast range of security services. Managing governmental security operations requires a special sort of talent. Skilled managers of security personnel are in limited supply. Structuring airport screening as a commodity task and splitting it off to outside suppliers could spare scarce public managers for myriad security tasks for which delegation is out of the question. Government would still need to manage the contractors adroitly, of course. But the corps of public managerial talent required to structure contracts, monitor performance, and probe for weaknesses would be smaller than that needed to organize, oversee, and manage the day-to-day work of tens of thousands of screeners.

At a minimum, there are respectable arguments for less reliance on direct federal provision than the airport security legislation prescribes. Aside from the predictable reaction against anything resembling the prior model, why were the embrace of public airport screening and renunciation of delegation so close to complete? The gulf between America's public and private working worlds can help to explain the outcome. Creating the TSA brought more than 60,000 workers into the safe harbor of public employment. Most screeners earn between $23,000 and $35,000, depending on their location and specific duties— modest pay by many standards but far superior to private wages under the old arrangement and clearly sufficient, in combination with federal benefits, to draw a flood of qualified applicants. Shifting to governmental airport security gratified a great many voters, while the costs were diffuse and generally small. The vanished jobs at private screening firms were no great loss, as demonstrated by the frequency with which workers had willingly abandoned them. Profit margins for screening contracts were generally too slim to justify a last-ditch political defense. The private firms themselves, in a subtle but significant detail, possessed limited political standing; the three big companies that had dominated the market were all foreign-owned.[33] Had private screening jobs not been so disposable, and public screening jobs not been so desirable, the resolution of the airport security debate might have been different, and possibly more sensible.

The Delegation of Custom Tasks

The sorts of workers most battered by today's private sector find a kinder climate in government, which sets in motion forces that constrain the delegation of government's commodity tasks. Workers with the skills required for high-end custom tasks, conversely, tend to find public employment less appealing. This imposes a second, symmetrical twist in the public sector's transformation. Work that, without these distortions, would be done in-house—whether because it is too entangled with other functions to specify with precision, or hard to evaluate objectively, or sheltered from competitive pressure—is frequently delegated to private firms that are able to access talent pools largely barred to government. Sometimes this works out tolerably well; sometimes delegating custom tasks carries a heavy price.

An obscure agency called the Federal Procurement Data Center keeps detailed statistics on everything Washington buys from the private sector. For fiscal year 2002 the federal government was a party to some 8 million separate transactions summing to almost $250 billion.[34] Many of these acquisitions reflect entirely logical make-versus-buy decisions. It is unremarkable and unobjectionable for the government to buy its aircraft ($15 billion), ships ($7 billion), guided missiles ($4 billion), computer equipment ($6 billion), and live animals (a mere $7 million) rather than setting up its own factories and farms. Even among services (as distinct from goods) many categories are rich with commodity tasks that are quite sensibly split off from direct public service, such as construction ($10 billion), property maintenance and repair ($7 billion), or research and development for defense systems ($14 billion). But there are also many custom tasks for which Washington spends heavily on outside services. The largest single category of federal procurement, at more than $25 billion, is "professional, administrative, and management support services."[35] (One relatively small but telling example within this category is the contract to run most operations at the Federal Procurement Data Center itself.)[36]

The Lockheed-Martin Corporation has long been a preeminent federal supplier, accounting on its own for more than $20 billion in contracts in 2002. It is significant, if little noted, that this famous maker of airplanes, missiles, and cutting-edge defense systems has been furiously diversifying into high-end government services. Its $5 billion in research and development contracts, $1.4 billion in IT services, and nearly $5 billion in "other services," for both defense and civilian agencies, together eclipsed Lockheed's $9 billion in hardware sales. By 2006 Lockheed was responsible for more federal money than either the Department of Justice or the Department of Energy.[37]

The scarcity of internal talent is forcing government to outsource much of its thinking. Markets expand for policy analysis, strategic planning, and other functions that a naive observer might expect agencies to treat as core competencies. Leaving aside scores of smaller operations, three big consulting firms alone (Booz Allen & Hamilton, BearingPoint, and Accenture) billed the federal government for more than $2 billion in 2002. Sometimes such arrangements cross the line from questionable to bizarre. One federal contractor, for example, was engaged to investigate charges of malfeasance against several other federal contractors—a delegation justified in part by the fact that it was able to pay contract specialists roughly double what government could.[38]

A thriving industry provides analysis and strategic advice to state and local government as well. In the wake of the 1996 legislation reshaping the welfare system, the private sector—for-profit as well as nonprofit—has become the mainstay of social services in many cities and states, in part because the staff of social-service agencies proved ill-equipped for the shift from an income-maintenance to a work-based mission.[39] As with the retention of commodity tasks, a bit of detail on a few particular areas may provide more clarity on the delegation of tasks that fall short on specificity, clear evaluation, competition, or all three criteria.

Information Technology Services

"Automatic data processing and telecommunications services" accounted for about $16.7 billion in federal contracts in 2002—an IT service bill nearly three times as large as the cost of IT equipment. There are no comparably complete data for procurement by the cities and states, but IT is a large, growing, and strategically significant category of delegated services at every level of government.[40] It can be wholly rational to outsource some IT services, in both public and private organizations.[41] Certain tasks are so technically exacting and so infrequently performed that delegating them to specialized outsiders makes more sense than developing internal capacity. Other IT functions are so routine and so widely available that they meet every definition of a commodity task. Most well-run organizations maintain a network of IT contractors, but they also take care to retain a strong nucleus of their own highly qualified employees to orchestrate and monitor that network.[42]

The danger lies in crossing the line from commodity to custom tasks, and outsourcing IT functions that are integral to strategic management, resistant to evaluation, or vulnerable to monopoly power. In the private sector this would represent a simple management blunder, which doesn't mean it never occurs. In the public sector, however, the tilt of the economic terrain places government in continual danger of sliding across that line. Many IT services require the sort of high-end labor that is systematically scarce in government. Recall Chapter 4's discussion of pay gaps in IT occupations and their predictable consequences, including the technology chief in my old Labor Department office pining away for his mainframes. If a public organization wants its IT services to be within shouting distance of the state of the art, it often has no choice but to outsource aggressively.

The trend in public-sector IT procurement is away from the healthy pattern of engaging specialized contractors for separate tasks, and toward comprehensive contracts with large "integrated system providers."[43] Such arrangements can be far from ideal, in terms of all three criteria for delegation. It is virtually impossible to specify in advance every requirement for an IT system that weaves throughout an agency's operations. As new requirements emerge and old ones evolve in the course of a contract, the customer agency must either live with the original terms of the deal or renegotiate, at a decided disadvantage, with its contractor. Clear-cut contractor evaluation tends to be elusive, in part because the customer and the contractor are jointly involved in the system's performance, and in part because it is often the case that nobody in the customer agency really understands what the contractor is doing.

Competition for integrated IT service contracts is often vigorous at the start; there are many firms in the government information systems market and the rivalry is fierce. But once a contractor is selected and becomes indispensable to an agency's work, market discipline ebbs. Disentangling an organization from one integrated system provider and bringing in another is so traumatically disruptive a prospect that, short of truly egregious performance or blatant exploitation, it rarely happens.

I do not mean to fault public managers who cross the line from commodity to custom tasks when delegating IT services. Given the constraints within which they operate, this can be the least objectionable option at their command. The point, rather, is to highlight both the causes and the costs of those constraints. IT is an arena where the gap between the public and private working worlds is especially wide. Many agencies cope remarkably well with a degree of IT delegation that, in principle, is strategically unsound. But they would do even better—and produce a public sector that is more efficient, accountable, and managerially coherent—if the great divide in the labor market had not denied them the option of an internal corps of top IT talent.[44]

Human Resource Management

The selection, enculturation, training, deployment, motivation, and assessment of personnel would seem to be the textbook example of a core competency, especially for organizations whose productive capacity is almost exclusively made up of people. This does not preclude delegating certain aspects of human resource management, of course, and earlier sections related how private firms have learned to treat elements of their personnel systems as commodity tasks suitable for outsourcing. The mundane logistics of payroll processing can meet all three criteria (specificity, clear evaluation, and competition) as can preemployment screening, routine training, scheduling, and many other component tasks. Private companies often delegate to executive-search firms the recruitment of their future leaders—a potentially risky practice, perhaps, justified by these firms' special expertise and rendered safer by drawing a bright line between the identification of candidates and the choice among them.

In government, too, human resource outsourcing is a growth industry. The public sector delegates many of the same functions as the private sector, and for many of the same reasons. But as with information technology, government sometimes reaches or breaches the boundary separating commodity from custom tasks as it entrusts personnel work to outsiders. A mid-2004 report by the GAO found examples of outsourcing what it termed "Tier III activities"—aspects of personnel management that "involve the formulation of human capital strategy and policy support."[45] These include assessing the capabilities an agency requires to accomplish its mission; developing strategies for shaping and managing the workforce; and building systems for measuring and managing the agency's performance. Such functions are at the heart of management. They are very far from well-defined, easily monitored, readily available commodity tasks. But the agencies studied by the GAO were quite clear on their motives for delegating this work: they did not possess, and could not obtain, employees with the requisite skills.[46]

Space Shuttle Operations

When it was conceived as a replacement for primitive single-use rockets, the space shuttle was meant to transform space travel into a commodity. The orbiter itself and its solid-rocket boosters, the costly parts of the system, could be reused for mission after mission. Only the massive but relatively inexpensive external fuel tank was jettisoned to burn up in the atmosphere. The National Aeronautics and Space Administration (NASA) expected orbital launches to become cheap and mundane once the shuttle system matured.

The shuttle's evolution from cutting-edge experiment to cut-and-dried routine turned out to be much slower and harder than expected. Blasting people and equipment skyward on a column of flame, and bringing them safely home through the incandescent heat of reentry, involves thousands of technical challenges, and as each was surmounted new ones emerged. The explosion of the *Challenger* in 1986 made clear how very far from routine a shuttle flight remained. Safety upgrades ordered in the wake of the disaster frustrated predictions of steadily declining costs. The three-year grounding of the shuttle fleet required to implement these changes led many launch customers to abandon the shuttle and return to expendable rockets, shattering hopes for the scale economies on which the shuttle strategy hinged.

By the mid-1990s the shuttle program was in deep trouble. Its cost was straining the patience of Congress, and its operational demands were draining resources and management attention from other NASA missions. The Clinton administration's NASA chief seized on a bold strategy of delegation to lower the cost, and the management burden, of running the shuttle. NASA's tangled skein of separate shuttle contracts, along with most NASA personnel involved with the shuttle, were folded into a single Space Flight Operations Contract. A company called United Space Alliance (USA) won what turned out to be an eight-year, nearly $10 billion contract to handle virtually every aspect of a shuttle mission, from astronaut training and system assembly to the management of launch and reentry. A dozen major contracts were consolidated into the deal with USA, which also took on oversight responsibility for those subcontractors that remained independent. NASA technicians and other workers with direct shuttle duties switched their badges to USA, a small remnant staying behind to oversee the contract.

The splitting-off of shuttle flight operations occasioned remarkably little controversy for so radical a change. General acquiescence was partly due to worries that the status quo was unsustainable. It is surely significant, though, that most of the NASA workers affected were at the upper end of the skills spectrum—many of them above the point where public pay exceeds private, and some bumping up against the ceiling on civil-service compensation. No precise reckoning is possible, since USA's compensation data are proprietary. But it is revealing to compare public salaries for these kinds of jobs to salaries prevailing outside government. Private-sector pay for avionics technicians ranges from a little less than government to markedly more, depending on the specific industry, but even at the lower end the difference is outweighed by profit-sharing and other inducements USA can offer. Public and private salaries are comparable for aerospace engineers, and senior managers (eligible for stock options and bonuses) fare considerably better than they had on the public payroll.[47] In contrast to the outsourcing of most commodity tasks, delegating shuttle operations was far from devastating for government workers.

The delegation strategy appeared to pay off. Shuttle operations claimed less of senior managers' attention, while costs declined somewhat as USA deployed its advantages in streamlining procedures and driving hard bargains with subcontractors. Most people are aware, of course, that the subsequent history of the space shuttle has not been a happy one. It is impossible to know, and fruitless to speculate, whether this aggressive delegation contributed to the 2003 loss of *Columbia* and its crew. A shuttle has been lost under both direct and delegated arrangements, after all, and NASA's contract with USA left key decisions, at least formally, in government's hands. The people at USA were no less shocked and saddened by the *Columbia* disaster than those at NASA itself. This is no simple tale of slipshod performance by a cut-rate contractor. It is instructive, nonetheless, to consider how far the shuttle departs from the criteria defining a task's suitability for delegation.

Despite heroic efforts to codify every element of shuttle operations, the contract was not and could not be fully specified. The shuttle system was simply too complex and volatile. Periodic upgrades, altered missions, process improvements, and continuous technological tinkering meant that literally every launch was different. And NASA could not unambiguously evaluate USA's performance, even with a sophisticated set of incentives built into the contract. The operations model continued to evolve following the hand-off, and the remnant of NASA personnel involved was too small—and, to an increasing degree, too unfamiliar with the details of the enterprise—to exercise full oversight.[48] The sharpest shortfall from the criteria for delegation, however, concerned competition. Very few private firms had the scale, experience, and technical know-how to be plausible contenders for the shuttle operations contract. The short list was limited to two companies: Lockheed-Martin and Boeing. United Space Alliance was a joint venture formed by Lockheed and Boeing to bid for the contract, and USA's corporate by-laws specified that neither of its parents would compete against it.[49]

Military Outsourcing

America's military has long struggled to maintain a disciplined boundary between what it does for itself and what it delegates to outsiders. The armed forces have some special features, including the internal split between civilian and uniformed personnel and a tradition of early retirement followed by second careers, which render their make-or-buy practices particularly troublesome. These same features make the services familiar with the troubles, though, and they are thus more conscious than other parts of government of the hazards that lurk along the public–private frontier. But as a post-Cold War wave of military consolidation has been followed by harrowing stresses, some cracks in the coherence of the military's strategies have widened.

When the end of the Cold War made defense downsizing seem both unavoidable and permanent, the armed services moved to concentrate their own personnel on core-war fighting functions. A corollary of this approach involved splitting off to private suppliers anything that could be delegated. Emblematic of this shift was the army's mid-1990s decision to bundle its logistics requirements—including transport, food service, laundry, and a wide range of field support functions—into a single master contract. Outside suppliers had long been responsible for the actual delivery of many of these functions. The rationale for aggregating support functions into a massive master contract was that delegating the management, not just the performance, of military logistics could reserve precious managerial talent for duties closer to the core.

This was quite probably the correct decision at the time it was made, given the constraints the army faced. But things changed in ways the military could not have predicted. A period of peace and military retrenchment gave way to frenzied extensions of the military's mission in the Balkans, Afghanistan, and especially Iraq. Logistical requirements exploded, and the master contract grew into a torrent of goods, services, and invoices that the military struggled to oversee. By 2004 the logistics contract had expanded to encompass more than 30,000 private employees delivering $13 billion in support services. Dozens of contractor employees had been killed on the job in combat zones. Disputes proliferated over the price, quality, and even quantity of services rendered. The contract was held by a unit of Halliburton, which (reflecting either a cynical plot or a nasty twist of fate, depending on your viewpoint) had recently been led by the sitting vice president, Richard Cheney. Logistics contracting became a political, managerial, and public-relations problem of the first magnitude. The army decided to break up the master contract in favor of a set of smaller deals for separate support services.[50] Halliburton moved to sell off the tarnished and marginally profitable unit that had handled the contract.

The saga of Halliburton's logistical contract with the army has aspects far removed from the themes of this book—including the timeless peril, in a changing world, of placing long-term bets on any organizational strategy—but one aspect is certainly germane. Had internal management talent not been so scarce and precious a commodity, the army could have pursued the safer and more conventional course to which it eventually reverted—well-defined contracts for specific commodity tasks, structured in ways more conducive to monitoring, evaluation, and competition. The extra operations managers this option would have required had been pulled beyond the army's reach—to offices at Microsoft and Wal-Mart and Lockheed and even Halliburton—by the widening gulf between public and private pay at the upper reaches of the skills spectrum.

Beyond the sprawling corps of contractor employees providing and managing war-zone logistics, as of 2004 roughly 20,000 armed fighters in Iraq were being paid with public funds but working for contractors instead of the army or the marines. In principle these private warriors were engaged in "security operations"—escorting convoys, guarding key building and industrial assets, protecting civilian leaders against assassination—rather than actual combat. In practice, as an executive for one private firm conceded after a firefight in which his employees exchanged thousands of rounds with insurgents, "the line is getting blurred."[51] Fatal episodes of malfeasance by private contractors, including a notorious 2007 barrage by employees of Blackwater USA, did grievous damage to America's image. The nation's dalliance with mercenary warfare raises political, prudential, and ethical issues far too tangled to engage here.[52] But splitting off military functions sets in motion some labor-market dynamics too pertinent, and too bizarre, to ignore.

The security contractors, oriented to today's sharply divided world of private-sector work, operate in the same arenas and draw on the same labor pools as the armed services that hew to very different rules. Senior members of elite services such as the Green Berets and the Navy SEALS earned about $50,000, as of 2004. Security contractors were offering them two to four times as much to apply their skills privately in Afghanistan or Iraq. This stark disparity in compensation, for closely similar burdens and risks, has proven enough to overcome some fighters' reluctance to abandon their accustomed uniform. Commandos and covert operatives, trained at enormous expense and desperately needed for government work, filter off for more lucrative work with contractors. The Pentagon's chief of special operations has termed private poaching of key personnel, including members of the shadowy Delta Force, "a significant problem." General Wayne Downing, the retired head of Special Operations Command, was philosophical about the problem, but far from content. "They're not leaving out of disloyalty. The money is just so good, if they're going to be away from home that much, they may as well make top dollar."[53]

*   *   *

Multiple causes typically drive decisions to delegate functions that might be better handled internally. One factor, seemingly secondary but often influential, is public managers' urge to transform *something*, as enlisting private competence has been enthroned as managerial orthodoxy. Commodity tasks, where the substantive case for delegation is stronger, tend to be too hard politically, so reformers turn by default to custom tasks. Bids to make custom functions more businesslike, or to turn them over entirely to business, often inspire little or no "defense" from high-end public employees. White House pressure for some kind of action led the Office of Personnel Management to outsource security screening for new federal workers in the second Clinton administration, for example. Pre-employment vetting is at best a borderline candidate for delegation. But worker resistance was limited and, as it happened, many of the former federal employees did a great deal better under private management.

The "offense" from private organizations, meanwhile, can greatly ease efforts to delegate custom tasks. It is not much fun for a company to deliver true commodity services to the government. Tightly specified contracts leave little wiggle room. Close evaluation means constant pressure to perform as promised. Even worse, from the firms' perspective, ongoing competition puts a ceiling on potential profits. Custom tasks that are imperfectly specified, hard to monitor, or secure against competition tend to offer more attractive revenue prospects.

Why the Warping Matters

The divide in the working world imposes distortions at both ends of the labor market. It limits government's access to the human assets required for custom tasks and it hobbles government's flexibility to alter commodity tasks. Public missions that demand highly qualified workers are frequently performed less adroitly than they ought to be (if carried out internally despite skills shortfalls) or performed less accountably than they ought to be (if delegated despite the downsides). Simpler public missions that require unspecialized labor are performed less flexibly and more expensively than they ought to be. This happens both because the outsourcing option is often barred and because rules, institutions, and cultures by which public workers safeguard their status tend, alas, to undermine efficiency. Both aspects of the segregation of government work—its attraction for less-skilled workers, its repulsion of the most fortunate—make government fall short of the performance it could attain had the great divide in the working world never happened.

The same syndrome also contributes to a twisted transformation of American business. As supplying firms shift their strategies to shore up government's deficits of high-end labor, their business models become dependent on the public sector's enduring disabilities. Just 5 percent of Lockheed-Martin's $32 billion in 2003 sales was to private-sector customers.[54] Along with Halliburton, United Space Alliance, and other firms touched on in this chapter are companies such as Corrections Corporation of America (which runs prisons for state and federal customers), Maximus and America Works (welfare services), Electronic Data Systems (integrated IT services), and many more who earn a substantial share of their revenue doing things for government that, by a plausible or even compelling substantive case, government ought to be able to do for itself. One need not credit every charge of cronyism or corruption to perceive the moral hazards inherent in such arrangements.

No less lamentable is the warping of America's labor movement. Labor is hunkering down in its public-sector stronghold as private-sector unionism continues to shrivel. At the tactical level, this focus on government employment is entirely understandable: public workers are easy to organize, intensely motivated to embrace labor's agenda, culturally congenial, and politically reliable.[55] But on the strategic level, it threatens eventual disaster for American unionism. The conscious and conspicuous defense of employment conditions for the delivery of tax-funded services that are superior to what the market offers most taxpayers promises to breed hostility both to government, and to the labor movement.

One might object that my anxious overview of public-sector transformation efforts has focused, too narrowly, on reform ideas that force government to collide with the separate world of private work.[56] The reformers' repertoire includes other options, such as performance measurement, classic reorganization, and electronic government initiatives, which can proceed in substantial isolation from the private economy. It is certainly true that the "lumping versus splitting" framework fails to exhaust all of the options, and many reformers are doing valuable things within the constraints I have sought to describe. But the deepening segregation of government work makes the menu of realistic options a meager one. It is possible to transform government without exposing less-skilled employees to the private world of work they rightly fear, and without expanding the government's share of top talent. It is also possible to write a sonnet without using the letters "E" or "T." But the effort is far more arduous than it would be without the constraints, and the outcome, by long odds, will be less satisfying.

SIX

◆ ◆ ◆

Finding the Future

The Damage Done

ONLY BY DINT of unshakeable ideological fortitude can one claim satisfaction with the performance of American government today. Stead-
fast partisans of one flavor might be convinced that government's
missions are mostly trivial or noxious, and that it is thus no great mis-
fortune for those missions to be carried out badly. Ideologues of a different stripe might cherish government's goals with sufficient ardor to
overlook shabby implementation. But the rest of us are compelled by
evidence to recognize that the performance of America's public sector
falls too short, too frequently, of the caliber that citizens expect and
that a decent commonwealth requires.

The briefest glance at the governmental landscape reveals offenses
against almost any set of priorities, and at every level of government.
One notorious realm of public-sector fecklessness at the local level is
the slow and scandalously uneven improvement of public education,
especially of high schools. Another is the chronic waste of time and
fuel in overburdened, underplanned road networks and the rarity of
either the excellent public-transit systems or the creative market-based
tactics for easing congestion that cities in other rich countries often
manage to operate. A third is the turn-of-the-century recrudescence of
drug trafficking and violent crime in many cities and towns.

Most state governments (with an assist from Washington) run low-
income health-care programs combining ruinous expense with medi-
ocre results. States maintain harrowingly overcrowded prison systems

140

that at best isolate and at worst reinforce criminal inclinations, with scarcely a gesture toward reform. In all but a few states, foster-care and related child welfare systems are so slapdash that children supposedly under state protection are routinely lost to view, frequently neglected, and occasionally slaughtered.

The federal government, meanwhile, suffers from potentially—or perhaps, more accurately, eventually—devastating fiscal imbalances; from a chronic inability to control the borders; and from grievous lapses in drug-safety and pension-security regulation, to note only three instances of federal performance shortfalls, and within just the domestic realm. No great effort would be required to extend this list indefinitely.

It would be fatuous to lay all the blame for government's performance deficits on the labor-market misalignments described in this book. No human organization operates perfectly, and multiple factors typically account for the wedge between the ideal and the real. Government's tasks, we must remember, also tend to be especially difficult tasks; there are more ways to fail at foiling terrorists or fostering education than at developing some new and improved laundry conditioner, or even some new and improved computer architecture. And many governmental shortcomings reflect bad choices on the part of a few top decision-makers, rather than bad follow-through on the part of the many people who put those choices into effect. Some policy decisions (readers are here invited to contemplate whatever examples their political leanings suggest) are so bone-headed that not even the most brilliant implementation can salvage a good outcome. It is also true that dissatisfaction with government is widespread even in countries where the conditions of public and private employment have not diverged to anything like the degree they have in the United States.

Yet the short sample of disappointing governmental performance cited above—and many more such instances—share, amid myriad differences, one unifying factor: they are entrusted to a sector hobbled by inflexibility and starved of talent. All too often American government is not smart enough (because private alternatives drain away the best personnel) and not supple enough (because workers sheltering in government's middle-class bastion quite rationally resist change). The warpage brought about by disparities at either end of the labor market is not the only reason government fails to deliver. But it is an important and underrecognized part of the performance problem.

This factor also does much to explain the distinctive form antigovernment sentiment tends to take in the United States. Prickliness about authority is a widespread and mostly healthy human trait. A jaundiced view of government (among all of the people some of the time, and among some of the people all of the time) can be found in almost every culture blessed with enough freedom to permit the expression of such views. But in countries with narrower gaps between public and private work cultures—including Japan, Singapore, New Zealand, and most of Europe—the targets of criticism tend to be the integrity, the covert scheming, and the financial or sexual shenanigans of top leaders. Such themes arise in the United States as well, but are blended with a heavy dose of disdain for the public sector's competence. In other countries, citizens scorn government mostly for what it does or for what people fear it might do. In the United States, citizens scorn government largely for what it cannot do.

Glaring lapses from adequacy are just the more visible dimension of government's performance deficit. Less obvious than the frequency of clear-cut flaws, though no less significant, is the paucity of conspicuous excellence. Insight, innovation, and breakthroughs are by no means unknown within government, to be sure. But they are rarer than they need to be, given the urgency of government's missions. And they are quite likely rarer than they used to be. Paul Light surveyed scores of experts in American government to identify the fifty greatest public-sector endeavors occurring after World War II for his 2002 book *Government's Greatest Achievements: From Civil Rights to Homeland Defense*. The chapter describing those endeavors mentions specific dates (for the passage of a law, the launching of an organization, the winning of a war, or some other concrete action) 182 times. More than half of these dates were in the 1960s and the 1970s. Year for year there were fewer than half as many exemplary actions prior to 1960 or subsequent to 1979. This is an imprecise gauge, to be sure, but it is no coincidence that these were the decades marking the recent low point for economic inequality and high point for government's appeal to the ablest Americans.[1] Government once was, but for now is not, a full participant in the American enterprise.

A third pertinent point of comparison for government's performance, beyond the benchmarks of other governments today and American government in healthier times, is the U.S. private sector. Periodic

disgraces—Enron, Halliburton, Vioxx, and other such sorry episodes—
cannot conceal a pattern of progress over recent decades (in sophistication, efficiency, variety, and speed) within much of the business
world. Yes, of course a corporation can pick and choose its missions
while government must play the hand it is dealt. Yes, of course the
structure of incentives and constraints endows business with managerial advantages that are independent of personnel disparities. But the
chasm between public-sector and private-sector performance, whether
measured by the achievement of excellence or the avoidance of failure,
is also due to the peculiar tilt of the labor-market terrain that tips
toward business more than its share of the best and the brightest. If government were more amply staffed with top talent, and less hobbled by
the rational conservatism of many public workers, the performance
gap would narrow dramatically. An easing of the forces warping government work would improve the public sector's performance while
no doubt denting, albeit to a lesser degree, that of the private sector.[2]
In light of today's egregious disparities in capability such a rebalancing
would render the American public, on balance, a good deal better off.

How will we respond to this divide between America's stressed and ane-
mic public sector and its well-staffed, more vigorous private economy?
There are at least three different versions of the future, each embodying its own vision of the kind of country we become. The alternatives
vary considerably in their likelihood, though the odds are vanishingly
small that one of them will materialize in its pure form. The best pre-
diction for decades to come is some messy mélange of the three. But
some attention to each scenario in turn will give us a better sense of the
elements from which the alloy of our actual future will be forged.

A Counterrevolution in the Private Economy

One way to mend the breach between the sectors would be to reverse
the workplace revolution that has undermined America's middle-class
economy. Government grew isolated primarily because the private sector changed, after all, and the next generation could undo that change.
In a reprise of the great economic convergence following World War II,
rewards could be shored up at the bottom and held down at the top to

roll back the surge in inequality. Both opulence and penury would become rarer. The winners' circle would be wider and open to most willing workers, though the prizes would be smaller.

Let's add some details to the scenario: Most annual salaries would cluster between today's equivalent of, say, $35,000 and $70,000. In 2005 this range covered less than two-fifths of the workforce; 44 percent of full-time, year-round workers were below it and 17 percent were above it.[3] Health insurance and other benefits would differ little between the top and the bottom. The size of a pension would vary with career earnings, but few Americans would retire bereft of any private pension and few would collect the huge annual payouts now routine among those who retire from upper corporate ranks.

This particular fantasy looks something like an updated version of John F. Kennedy's or Gerald Ford's economy, when earnings dispersion was roughly two-thirds what it is today, rather than the sort of radical egalitarianism that has never played well in America. Drive and discipline would still pay off. Full-time workers would still out-earn part-time workers. Two-income families would still fare better than one-income families. Very able employees would collect several times the average wage. Lucky or brilliant entrepreneurs would earn wealth far beyond the norm, as they always have and always will, in exchange for delivering extraordinary value and accepting extraordinary risk. And some people—illegal aliens, the willfully idle, a few inevitable lost souls— would still fall outside any reasonable definition of the middle class.

But the pattern of workplace rewards would be tighter than it is today. The gradient of earnings, as positions become more demanding, would be shallower than the vertiginous curve that now prevails. Top jobs would be rewarded to a substantial extent by social standing and the timeless pleasure of wielding influence, and elite workers would expect only some modest multiple of average earnings. Except for small numbers of the most and the least fortunate, Americans would inhabit the same economic universe. Their material comfort and security, their children's prospects, and their stakes in a stable economy would be broadly comparable, in contrast to today's glaring discrepancies.

The problems described in previous chapters become easier to solve in this version of the future. Government would have far more luck recruiting and retaining top talent if private alternatives were only a little more lucrative. Opting for public rather than private work might require contentment with a smaller house, but would not force the choice of a cheaper town with worse schools; might imply less lavish vacations, but wouldn't sharply alter college options for the children. Quite a few highly able Americans would view such small-scale sacrifices as well worth accepting in exchange for the satisfaction of public service, including many who find today's price to be prohibitive.

No less important, rank-and-file public workers would have a good deal less motivation to resist reforms that might alter their jobs or dislodge them into the private sector. Workplace change would still spark some opposition, of course—this is a constant in any time and any setting—but if government work were no longer a refuge from a draconian private economy the resistance would be far milder. As the barriers to productivity and innovation became less intimidating, a higher fraction of governmental reform efforts would succeed. Public functions could be sorted more rationally between direct governmental delivery and delegation to the private sector, without the distortions imposed by compensation gaps at both ends of the job market. And the labor movement, liberated from its current preoccupation with defending the safe harbor of government work, could return to its proper role as a buffer against perverse extremes of the market principle within the private economy.

I like this version of the future, and not just because it would improve public-sector performance. Lowering the economic barriers that separate Americans could bring good news on several fronts. Our politics would likely become less fractious. Social interaction would be eased, and empathy amplified, as more of us came to lead materially similar lives. Some of the frenzied anxiety might drain away from our culture if the stakes of the workplace steeplechase weren't quite as high. There would certainly be downsides as well, since at least some of America's characteristic economic vitality stems from the lure of big gains and the fear of big losses. But I suspect the damage would be minor. It is possible that I draw my inferences from an unrepresentative group of rich people, but it seems far-fetched to predict that the ablest Americans' thirst for achievement would disappear if their material rewards were a few multiples of the average, instead of a few orders of magnitude beyond it. Status, satisfaction in accomplishment, and the sheer thrill of the game would still attract talent to key pursuits. Nor is middle-class pay for humbler occupations likely to empty the ranks of managers and professionals and generate a glut of janitors and clerks and nursing-home aides.

Yet it is not worth dreaming in more detail about any imminent restoration of the middle-class economy, since it is quite unlikely to occur. Reversing a third of a century's growth in inequality would require such elaborate economic engineering, maintained for such a long time, straining against such potent counterforces, that it is all but inconceivable that it will happen soon—even if popular revulsion with growing inequality becomes more widespread than it is today. Many European countries are struggling, with limited success, to retain a degree of economic egalitarianism in the face of globalization, technological upheaval, and the other centrifugal forces at work in their labor markets. Even if our commitment to equality were as resolute as theirs, America's size, diversity, and tradition of openness would make an egalitarian agenda a good deal harder to pursue.

The impersonal weight of demographics, moreover, renders this an inauspicious time for an episode of leveling. Deep-rooted trends—strong population growth among groups less prone to advanced education, combined with late marriage, small families, and lavish investments in each child's success among the affluent—all but guarantee that the late-twentieth-century pattern of relatively rapid growth at the highly educated end of the workforce will stall in coming decades. We can anticipate a surplus of less-educated workers and fevered competition to hire the shrinking fraction of the highly skilled.[4] This will make it very hard to forestall the continuation, or even intensification, of diverging workplace rewards. And the recent political climate has not been particularly conducive to the legal, regulatory, institutional, and cultural changes such a reversal would require.

It is possible that the growth in economic disparities will slow over the next generation. The earnings divide may narrow a little, and perhaps more than a little, under some plausible political and economic scenarios. Much as I would like to be proven wrong, however, I do not expect to see America's middle-class economy restored in my lifetime. The odds favor other versions of our future.

Carrying the Workplace Revolution to Government

If it is unrealistic (or, as some certainly believe, unwise) for the private sector to revert to the narrower range of rewards that government never abandoned, America's separate economies could also be reunited by extending into government the full force of the private sector's workplace transformation. Selected aspects of this revolution—the embrace of information technology, experiments with performance management, some steps to reduce bureaucratic rigidities—have already been imported into the public sector. Attempts to transplant other aspects, though, have generally failed, or have not been seriously attempted, because they are inconsistent with the earnings compression and job security that the private sector has renounced but that government retains.

This second possible version of our future hinges on a successful assault against these distinctive features of public employment, in order to align government's workplaces with reigning private-sector norms. Convergence on the business model of working life is already a frequent subtext, and sometimes the headline, of contemporary campaigns for government reform. The turn-of-the-century presidential commission on the postal service, for example, called (obliquely) for cutting the compensation of blue-collar postal workers and (explicitly) for raising the $172,000 salary cap at the top, on the grounds that the post office "simply can't compete in attracting and retaining key managers."[5] The federal government has been whittling away civil-service protections, especially in the Departments of Defense and Homeland Security, and public employees are on the defensive at the state and local levels as well. There is manifestly more momentum behind efforts to align government's labor practices with those of business than there is behind the opposite impulse.

Driving Down the Lower End

Convergence has two aspects: pushing down the low end of the public labor market, and lifting up the high end, each with its own bundle of requirements and ramifications. The first part is fairly straightforward, at least in concept: pay would be lowered, benefits trimmed, and job security weakened until the rewards of public and private employment are equivalent. This could be done by revising the terms of work within government, or by systematically outsourcing lower-end government work, or by a combination of the two. However it is achieved, the shift would clearly entail the enfeeblement of public-sector unions—either breaking them in advance to blunt resistance to the reshaping of public work, or waiting for them to wither once government jobs are no longer worth defending.

While the principle is simple—eliminate anything that gives public workers a better deal than comparable private workers—there is plenty of room for error in implementation. Evidence presented in earlier chapters shows that government's relative generosity rises as you move down the labor-market ladder. But this is a tendency rather than an iron-clad rule, and exceptions abound. When will a leaner deal for labor simply wring out unwarranted rewards, and when will it chase away qualified workers? In many cases we just won't know in advance. Some observers, for example, are convinced that most teachers are overpaid relative to their other options. If we take action guided by these convictions we will learn if our beliefs are sound once we see whether teachers absorb the income loss and stay on the job, or whether the best of them abandon the classrooms. This experiment, and comparable ones in countless bureaus, public-works departments, and post offices, could prove to be rather expensive.

That said, it is eminently plausible that a concerted federal, state, and local campaign to ratchet down the terms of public employment, wherever it exceeds private benchmarks, could reduce the cost of government. It is tempting to fantasize that being tough on labor could solve the public sector's fiscal embarrassments in one fell swoop. There are an awful lot of government workers, after all, and the evidence suggests that some of them are collecting premiums of one-tenth, one-quarter, or even more, in total pay and benefits, relative to what they would command outside government.

The aggregate government payroll was about $810 billion as of 2002—$611 billion for states and localities and $199 billion for the federal government, including the military and the post office.[6] Standard statistics are messier when it comes to benefit costs, but pegging benefits at a little more than one-fifth of payroll suggests $1 trillion as a workable, round-number estimate for the total compensation of government's workforce. To calibrate the potential benefit to taxpayers from shaving public workers' pay and benefits, consider a few points of reference. If the $1 trillion employment bill somehow could be pared by 3 to 4 percent, the savings would be equivalent to state and local gasoline taxes ($33 billion) or federal food assistance ($38 billion). A 5 percent cut could cover veterans' benefits ($50 billion) or state and local spending on school construction ($53 billion).

But even rudimentary arithmetic calls for caution here. Employee compensation accounts for less than one-third of overall public spending, and personnel savings would have to be implausibly dramatic to re-shape government's fiscal landscape. Even if driving a hard bargain with workers became a top priority for politicians at all levels of government, it strains credulity to forecast net savings large enough to alter govern-ment's fiscal picture in any major way. The biggest government com-pensation premiums, in percentage terms, are for low-paid workers who account for correspondingly little of the wage bill. Even a very large fraction of a very small paycheck cannot sum to a big number.

And convergence on the business model, bear in mind, requires gains for some workers along with cuts for others.[7] Suppose we were convinced that a disproportionate share of government workers—say two-thirds, or even three-fourths—are overpaid rather than underpaid by business standards. Raising one financial analyst or midlevel man-ager up to the business benchmark could still wipe out the savings to be gained by pushing two or three clerks down to their going rate. The upper bound on personnel cost reductions is certainly below one-tenth of the wage bill, which translates to around 3 percent of public spend-ing, and is probably much, much lower. Under even the most draco-nian scenario, the budgetary consequences of personnel austerity are not in the same league as looming increases in the costs of Medicare, Medicaid, and debt interest, or the revenues foregone through recent rounds of federal tax cuts.[8] Even if the federal government had fired every single nondefense employee and driven its 2005 compensation costs to zero, after all, most of the deficit would have remained.[9] More-over, compensation spending, especially for workers doing commodity tasks, is largely state and local, while the big fiscal holes are at the fed-eral level.

Driving down the lower end of public compensation thus can deliver only limited direct budgetary payoffs. But citizens would also benefit, and probably more substantially, from the enhanced flexibility likely to result from the extension into government of private workplace norms. A boost in public managers' room to maneuver in search of perfor-mance gains would come about both because of weaker job protections and, more subtly, because much of today's resistance to change stems from the fact that public workers have something to lose. Once they have already lost it, there's less motive to defend the status quo.

Assuming we could toughen the terms of public work to benefit tax-payers at less-educated employees' expense, should we? Some people may find this an easy question to answer, one way or the other. I find it hard. Anyone who laments the erosion of the middle-class economy must dread the prospect of driving millions more Americans out of the safe harbor and into the storms beyond. If the workplace revolution is extended into government it is inevitable that a large number of letter carriers and health aides and clerks and cafeteria workers will tumble from solid citizenship to a more meager, precarious status. Many of these workers, moreover, have paid, in one form or another, for access to the harbor: foregoing maximum earnings during prime working years to get a good public pension; learning the tricks of the hiring game and jumping through procedural hoops to secure a coveted government job slot; putting up with indignities and frustrations in exchange for security, all of which makes a midcareer rule change especially harsh. And it is not hard to think of other options for shoring up public finances at a smaller human cost.

On the other hand, it seems morally random for public workers to be spared from the economic turbulence that their compatriots in the private sector are compelled to endure. And many of the alternative victims of fiscal austerity surely would suffer more grievously than a displaced letter carrier. The extent to which today's arrangements actually shift rewards from richer to poorer is also open to question, moreover, and the answers to the question will vary wildly from case to case. At the federal level, for example, the well-off still pay a disproportionate share of taxes. So if a receptionist at the Department of Agriculture earns $5,000 more than she would at the bank across the street, her boost into the midrange of the income distribution comes largely at the expense of people who remain eminently comfortable despite the extra tax burden. State and local taxation, though, is considerably less progressive, and the middle-class income of a schoolteacher or a state cop is ultimately paid for, in large part, by people lower down the economic scale. It would require both far more detailed data than now exist on the net gains and losses, and a more expert ethicist than I, to tally the moral balance of lowering government's cost and increasing its flexibility at the price of carving another big chunk from America's middle class.[10]

Whether or not we should blow up the harbor, however, it is doubtful that we will—at least not soon, or completely, or easily. It could not be accomplished by one bold stroke, even in theory, however favorable the political context and however resolute the politicians. Even at the federal level an interlinked sequence of legislative and regulatory changes would be required to strip away all the features that make government employment a boon for a broad class of workers. And most public jobs, especially those with a significant compensation edge, are in state and local government. The terms of public employment are largely set statehouse by statehouse, city hall by city hall. Those hoping to carry the workplace revolution into government must brace for a long, hard campaign of separate skirmishes.

The political terrain on which these skirmishes are fought, moreover, may not be as favorable to the offensive as it seems. Jeremiads against overpaid government employees are staples of political discourse, to be sure. But to the extent that citizens really focus on public-sector compensation, other than as an abstract irritation, all the evidence suggests that they direct their ire at the top, toward legislators and agency heads and other senior officials who earn more than the average taxpayer but less than their private-sector counterparts. When the target is not Congress or generic "bureaucrats," views about public workers tend to soften. Even some who thrill to the rallying cry of cheaper government lose some of their ardor when it's a concrete matter of driving down the pay of the postman or the firefighter or the lady behind the steam table at the neighborhood elementary school.

The defenders, conversely, occupy good ground. Their union leaders are dedicated, resourceful, and passionately convinced of the rightness of their cause. The more any group of public workers has to lose, the more focused their motive to resist the extension of the workplace revolution. Few outsiders, meanwhile, take an intense and enduring interest in public employment practices. Public employees tend to win many of their battles as aspiring reformers tire of the trench warfare and turn their attention to targets promising fewer headaches and more visible prizes. Major setbacks for less-skilled public workers may be more probable, during the next decade or two, than major reductions in private-sector inequality. But the most likely scenario is halting, uneven, and partial erosion in the relative terms of employment for government's rank and file.

Lifting Up the High End

The second aspect of integrating the public sector into America's version of the modern economy—raising rewards for the most qualified workers—is likely to prove even more challenging. There are few signs that the citizenry is willing to tolerate, far less that the citizenry is clamoring for, increases in governmental pay ceilings to match ever-escalating business benchmarks. In some countries—notably Singapore, but to a lesser extent New Zealand, Australia, Great Britain, and a few others—pay packages for senior public officials can reach well into six figures without exciting too heated a public reaction. But when the U.S. president's pay was doubled to $400,000 (after decades at half that level) the move had to be carefully engineered so there would be no identifiable target for popular outrage. The raise was not for Bill Clinton, the incumbent who signed the legislation, but for some then-anonymous successor a few years in the future. It may not be rational for us to resist paying the going rate for talented managers, technical specialists, and financial experts, but we seem fairly settled in our stance.

Suppose, however, that government's personnel officials and citizens at large became convinced that, like it or not, the price of talent has risen, and good governance requires paying salaries to the top slice of public servants that soar far beyond the average family's income. There would still be cause for skepticism that the business template of high rewards and tight accountability can be readily applied in government. The multiple goals and complex tangles of cause and effect that characterize many public missions make the appealing principle of pay for performance hard to apply in practice. Without anything comparable to business metrics of profit and loss, assessments of performance in the public sector tend to be plagued by an irreducible element of subjectivity. Public labor leaders routinely charge that pay-for-performance systems will be distorted into partisan tools to reward favorites and enforce ideological orthodoxy. This charge may be politically motivated, but that doesn't make it untrue. And for quite fundamental reasons, personnel officials in government find it as unnatural to be tough on workers at the top as on workers at the bottom.

The history of the federal Senior Executive Service is instructive, and sobering. Legislation enacted in 1978 embodied the ideal of an elite corps separate from both the regular civil service and political appointees. The entirely sensible goal was to build up a layer of highly qualified, well-compensated, stringently accountable leaders to provide the kind of continuity that fleeting political appointees cannot.[11] (Sixteen states also have formal "senior executive" ranks, most of them modeled on the federal service.) The new A-team was to be handsomely paid, roughly on par with comparably senior business managers, and also subject to private-sector performance expectations and job risk. Base salaries were set at the middle of the sub-Cabinet range, which in 1978 was far from shabby even in comparison to prevailing private-sector pay. The SES was also made eligible for a package of bonuses and other incentives that could bring total compensation all the way up to the vice president's level.

But in a bit of historical bad luck, the SES experiment was launched just as top rewards were surging outside government. The reference point for the elevated compensation of the SES was corps of senior political appointees; the reference point for these senior officials' pay was Congress. And, as Chapter 4 related, this congressional benchmark has held steady relative to *average* family income but, as the top pulled away from the middle, has dropped to roughly half the income of the most fortunate 5 percent of families. The SES fell, in relative terms, along with them. Over time most SES members became bunched at or near this politically impermeable pay ceiling.[12]

A 1996 analysis by a leading compensation consulting firm concluded that SES members at the top of the scale would need a 76 percent boost in pay and benefits to attain true parity with the private sector.[13] The business benchmark, of course, has risen sharply since then, while SES compensation has not. Another study found that SES officials at one agency earned less than junior analysts employed by a private contractor at the same organization.[14] It is hard to stir up much popular sympathy for bureaucrats earning $150,000 or more, but contrary to the founding legislation's intent the SES has assuredly not kept pace with senior personnel outside government.

Echoing the bitter joke among workers in the old Soviet Union—"they pretend to pay us, and we pretend to work"—the other side of the SES bargain, tough performance standards backed by the risk of job loss, has also broken down. Many members of the SES perform superbly and serve their country well. If idealism, the hunger for colleagues' respect, and intrinsic commitment to the mission were not such widespread and potent motives among talented Americans, government would be in far worse shape than it is. But these SES stars work hard and well because they want to, not because the terms of their employment really motivate or require them to do so. A study by the National Academy of Public Administration found that SES performance bonuses and other special payments have "become a means of circumventing salary limitations [and] more an expectation than an incentive."[15] In 2002, well into an aggressive campaign against excessive liberality in performance assessments, 75 percent of SES members received the highest possible rating.[16] Both the share of SES members collecting performance bonuses and the average size of each bonus roughly doubled (to 58 percent and $13,700) from the mid-1990s to the mid-2000s.[17] In principle, joining the SES means surrendering civil-service job protections. If an SES worker is rated less than fully satisfactory for three years running, regulations call for him or her to be ejected. Only a fraction of a percent, though, receive ratings this low even for one year, and in 2003 a grand total of two members of the SES (out of about seven thousand) lost their positions due to performance shortfalls.[18]

According to the same National Academy report, which employed language a bit short of full-throated validation, "it appears that poor performance is not pervasive in the SES." But neither is the SES the uniformly top-notch, highly accountable corps its designers had in mind. Studies have found ample evidence of job dissatisfaction, frustration with the tenuous link between performance and rewards, and (in one survey) the sentiment, on the part of 75 percent of senior executives themselves, that the SES experiment had fallen short of its goals. One former deputy director of the Office of Personnel Management, no doubt using less guarded language than had been his habit while in office, has called for the SES to be "flushed."[19]

It is conceivable that parallel state and local efforts to match business standards of pay and performance have turned out better, though there are no serious studies documenting or even hinting at such successes. Or perhaps future attempts to close the gap at the top, including recent and proposed revisions to the SES itself, will succeed where earlier tries have failed. There would be more grounds for optimism here if the SES experiment had fallen short because of obvious errors in design or implementation. But the initiative has probably turned out about as well as could have been expected, given the context. In today's America, harmonizing business and government work for the most demanding jobs would require confronting a maelstrom of political, economic, and managerial forces that can frustrate even well-intentioned and carefully crafted campaigns. At the top as well as the bottom, bringing America's other economy into convergence with the business model remains a tall order.

Dealing with the Divide

It is not hard, as an armchair exercise, to sketch a vision for a fairer, more efficient, more rational public service. Pay and benefits should be closer to private-sector benchmarks. The compensation of unelected officials should be cut loose from the anchor of congressional pay. Cumbersome hiring and promotion rules should be streamlined. Workers at all levels should be held to tough performance standards. Stars should be rewarded. Laggards should be counseled, sanctioned, or eased into another line of work. Government shouldn't hesitate to outsource its commodity tasks, and it should bolster its internal capacity for excellence in core tasks.

The good news is that most Americans across the political spectrum could endorse at least the general thrust of this approach. The bad news is that this outline summarizes the goals of many public-employment reform campaigns undertaken by many officials, of various political stripes, at all levels of government, over the past several decades. Getting public service right, against the backdrop of a starkly divided private economy, is simply hard to do. If noble goals and earnest effort were all it took it would have happened already. There has been progress in the past, and there will be more in the future, and I salute the patriots struggling to engineer a more effective public sector. But this progress has been partial, hard-won, and excruciatingly slow. If the public and private working worlds remain divided for years to come, as it seems prudent to predict, the question becomes how to cope. This third generic scenario—dealing with the divide—itself has several variants, with some decidedly more appealing and realistic than others.

One logical accommodation, if we believe the private sector will continue to claim a disproportionate share of our creativity, flexibility, and productivity, is to lower our expectations for collective action and rely more on what can be delivered through the market. The American version of the good life would differ systematically from that of other cultures with more robust public sectors—better home furnishings and worse homeland security, good private gyms and bad public parks, first-rate cinemas and third-rate schools. Beyond shifting our priorities toward things the private sector already provides, we can also structure market arrangements for education, retirement income security, police and fire protection, and other tasks traditionally handled by government. Some people will embrace this vision with relish; others will find it repellant. But both camps, especially those who lament rampant privatization and dwindling commonwealth, should recognize that the trend is an almost inevitable concomitant of settling for a rigid and talent-starved public sector.

Another way to accommodate the divide, without embracing quite so starkly atomized a version of the future, is to maintain our ambition for shared endeavors but to designate private actors, rather than government, as the stewards of public missions. This notion of "governance without government" summons a great deal of enthusiasm in many quarters, and indeed much can be said in its favor. As observers from Tocqueville onward have noted, Americans possess an uncanny cultural knack for organizing themselves to pursue the public good without waiting around for formal authority.

The most straightforward such scenario is for government to progressively transfer its portfolio to private nonprofit organizations. This would merely intensify a longstanding pattern. Americans' characteristic generosity and our dense network of civic institutions are priceless national assets that offset, to a considerable degree, our disabilities when it comes to government. It is quite plausible that our culture could better survive the crumbling into utter dysfunction of formal government than it could the collapse of the nonprofit sector.

An either-or choice between government and civil society is not the option before us, however. Both sectors will endure. The question is how much farther we can go in our reliance on nonprofits to compensate for an enfeebled state. There are reasons to suspect we have pushed this margin about as far as we prudently can, and perhaps farther. First, it is not at all clear that the nonprofit sector is either more efficient than government or more broadly accountable than business.

Some nonprofits are superlative, others are dreadful, and (absent far more scrutiny than currently prevails) the balance is mostly a mystery. The nonprofit sector suffers to some extent from the same workforce ills that afflict government, including an inability or unwillingness to match corporate pay scales.[20] Where nonprofits *do* pay top dollar for talent, it is by no means evident that accountability is correspondingly intense, or indeed that it can be given the inherent imprecision in evaluation for many of the missions such organizations pursue. Second, the scale and capacity of the nonprofit sector is far from infinitely elastic. Confident predictions that civil society will step forward when government steps back are often disappointed—not least because many nonprofits turn out to be essentially conduits for government funds. Third, there are some profound objections in principle to anointing nonprofits as the dominant stewards of public missions. When goals are set and progress gauged without any nexus to electoral democracy, public value becomes whatever people with resources declare it to be. The boundaries of commonwealth are defined more by the "one dollar, one vote" rubric of the market than by the "one man, one vote" rubric of democracy. For some tasks, this is fine. For others—my list includes primary education, basic research, and many social services; your list may be different—it is deeply problematic.

Another variant of governance without government, more recently in vogue and ultimately more troublesome, envisions a transformative expansion of civic activism among *for*-profits. In this scenario, corporations come to recognize that any apparent conflict between private profitability and the public good is a mirage, since profitability ultimately depends on image and reputation. By forswearing the bad (pollution, labor exploitation, the sale of unsafe or unhealthy products) and embracing the good (nurturing workers, supporting communities, adopting sustainable technologies) corporations may pass up opportunities to maximize short-run profits, but will solidify public support and thus ratchet up their long-term revenues. Social responsibility will also pay off on the human-resources front. People want to be proud of their employer, not embarrassed to admit who signs their paycheck, so solid corporate citizens should have an edge in attracting and retaining talented employees. And many investors, both institutional and individual, will purge irresponsible firms from their portfolios and steer their capital to good actors.

The social contract thus can be negotiated and enforced more and more through markets (for products, capital, and labor) and less and less through the ballot box. As the scenario unfolds, distinctions between the public and private sectors will dissolve and government as we know it will become superfluous. Such a prospect attracts many adherents. Courses on corporate social responsibility and "social enterprise" proliferate at business schools. Business groups, from local chambers of commerce to global organizations such as the World Economic Forum, view it as self-evident that corporations can and should fill in for government's disabilities.

To some degree this is both conceptually healthy and consistent with the facts. America's private sector *is* robust, creative, and equipped to tackle a wide range of tasks. Many public missions can be pursued—efficiently, or at all—only in collaboration with private actors. But today's enthusiasm for replacing government with socially responsible corporations tends to be undiscriminating and ultimately reckless. A regrettable credulity about expanding corporations' social roles is driven, in large part, by the labor-market distortions described here. Many talented Americans care intensely about public issues, but find prevailing conditions of public employment to be unacceptable. They intend to spend their careers in the more exciting, less frustrating, vastly more lucrative private sector. But they are loath to accept that this decision means that their work serves merely to maximize shareholder wealth. Redefining the bottom line to include social goals promises self-fulfillment without self-sacrifice.

It is understandable that idealistic, but not masochistic, young Americans would embrace the notion that corporate employment is just another form of public service. Understandable—but not necessarily sound. Sometimes "corporate social responsibility" is simple hokum, the cynical invocation of conventional pieties meant to camouflage garden-variety avarice. More often it is sincere but incoherent, a sophisticated form of wishful thinking. There is no necessary alignment between the public consequences of a company's actions and the profitability boost from a good image. As flawed as the ballot box can be as a device for defining the public interest, it outshines most comparable corporate approaches. Consciously or not, business leaders—unconstrained by the raucous checks and balances of electoral democracy—are prone to anoint their personal preferences as public priorities. While it is important to respect the sincerity of corporate social responsibility advocates, and to applaud their motives, it remains the case that big brains and good hearts are not all that's required to serve the public interest. At the same time, introducing social objectives that might, in the misty long run, align with shareholder interests threatens to muddy private-sector accountability. A lofty mission can all too easily be invoked to excuse subpar performance. In the terminology introduced in Chapter 5, proliferating social goals can sabotage the intensive accountability that is the private sector's crown jewel in a futile attempt to endow firms with the extensive accountability of healthy public organizations. Corporate social responsibility can thus become both irresponsible and antisocial.

A different strategy for dealing with a persistent divide between government and the rest of the economy—without abandoning electoral accountability for how public missions are designated and pursued—is to reengineer public service to make the most of scarce public-sector talent and to expand options for engaging the private sector to leverage, rather than replace, government's capacity.

A crucial first step is to rehabilitate the prestige of public service. When a career in the classroom, the foreign service, or the transit authority is viewed with special honor, the deterrent effect of relatively low pay loses at least some of its force. Government work's loss of status over recent decades, conversely, amplifies the effect of compensation disparities. This slippage in social standing reflects to some extent the broad trends described in this book and thus resists easy remedy. But it also reflects a widespread and deeply cynical habit of disparaging government workers in order to gain political advantage or assuage status anxieties. A concerted effort to restore the standing of government work, on the part of a president or a coalition of high-profile leaders, could lower an important barrier to talent at the high end of the public labor market and soften the stance of truculent defensiveness prevalent at lower levels. Burnishing the image of public service is a partial strategy, of course, and cannot get very far without improvements in government's actual performance. Forswearing cheap contempt for government workers and fostering proper respect is a necessary but not sufficient measure for dealing with the divide.

We must also concede the folly of expecting the ablest young Americans to devote their entire careers to government work. Some surely will, but the consequent gap in lifetime earnings has grown wide enough to deter most people who aren't exceptionally committed to public service, extraordinarily indifferent to consumption, or born rich. Yet, in an echo of John Adams's prescription more than two centuries ago, a career of episodic public service interspersed with more lucrative private work may be an entirely realistic pattern. A freshly minted analyst or engineer might start with a few years in a corporation or consulting firm in order to whittle down debt and save for a house down-payment, then spend some time with a municipal transit authority; return to the private sector when it's time to worry about college tuition for the kids; and perhaps devote a few years to the Peace Corps before retirement. As serial job-hopping grows more common in the economy as a whole, there is no inherent reason why workers inclined to public service could not sequence their careers in ways that make the lifetime-average financial sacrifice a tolerable matter. Additional tactics on the personal front (a working spouse with the opposite cycle of public and private jobs) or the policy front (such as deferral or reduction of student debt while working a low-paid public job or measures to lessen the hassle and risk of changing jobs) could make such mixed careers even easier to pursue. As a larger fraction of more fortunate Americans spent some of their working lives in the public sector, the elite's alienation from government would ease and efforts to improve the social standing of public service would gain more traction.

Aren't "in-and-outers" already common? Not really, despite decades' worth of predictions that such patterns soon would become the norm, or declarations that they already had. Most vacant public jobs, especially senior ones, are filled by people already working in government.[21] It is true that the few thousand political positions that a president can fill with appointees of his choice tend to come from outside government. This is a tiny sliver of the public sector, however, and even here the share of top appointees with a preponderance of government experience seems to be rising, not falling.[22] One might object that constraining the flow of personnel across sectors is essential to suppress cronyism and corruption. Abuse of the "revolving door" can assuredly undermine the public interest. The greatest mobility today, though, is at the policy-setting levels, where the risk of corruption is

highest, rather than among managers, technicians, and other specialists whose transit across sectoral boundaries poses small risk, and
promises substantial benefit, to the public at large. Conflict-of-interest
rules, cooling-off periods during which ex-officials can't lobby their
former agencies, and other such measures—while of course short of
perfect—can curb corruption at smaller net cost than today's de facto
quarantine between public and private work.

Easing the transition to and from public service requires an ambitious but fairly straightforward set of policy changes. The public sector
needs to rationalize recruitment and hiring to be less cumbersome,
more transparent, more in line with private practices, and more accessible to workers outside government. The federal government has already made progress in this direction, eliminating quirky application
forms in favor of standard resumes and reducing the number of procedural hoops that applicants must leap through. But a great deal remains to be done. With luck, internal reformers and external guides
and advocates, such as the Partnership for Public Service, will perse-
vere with their agendas for change at the federal level and extend the
effort to the far larger workforces in the cities and states.

Changes in professional training are also required. American business schools today put little or no emphasis on preparation for public-
sector work. (In a brave but ill-timed experiment, Yale University
awarded its first graduate degrees in "public and private management"
in 1978, just as public service was losing its appeal to elites. Within fifteen years the hybrid program was abandoned in favor of a plain-vanilla
MBA curriculum.) Most business schools have been offering more cur-
ricular and extracurricular attention to voluntarism, corporate social
responsibility, and other forms of governance without government, but
few grant even a nod to the notion that public employment will, or
should, form any significant part of their graduates' careers. Schools of
public policy and administration, meanwhile, remain for the most part
devoted to a vision of public service that is decades out of date.

Professional schools of government (including the one where I
teach) have watched in frustration as a rising share of their best alumni
migrate to the private sector and never return to government. Absent
a sharp reversal of the trends described in this book, or an abrupt alteration of human nature, there is small hope of dissuading top alumni
from sampling private-sector work. But it is more promising to search

for ways to encourage them to cycle back into public service. Professional schools need to equip their students to pursue cross-sectoral careers as a strategy for coping with the economic divide between the sectors. In part this means emphasizing analytical, technical, and managerial skills that are valuable in both public and private work. And in part it means encouraging students and alumni to think of a mixed career as a normal and honorable thing. Cognitive dissonance leads today's alumni to view a job with McKinsey as either a renunciation of their public-management training or as just another kind of public service. Instead, they should see it as interesting, respectable, and (most important) temporary—a way to gain some perspective and fatten the retirement account for a few years before getting back to the Government Accountability Office.

Easing the flow of personnel across sectoral boundaries can have a positive net impact on government's talent shortage. But it's important to recognize that this impact will be finite. Making mixed careers more common can dilute and compensate for, but cannot fully cure, the features of public work that discourage highly skilled personnel. Even under the most optimistic scenarios the gap at the upper end of the labor market will require government to husband its scarce talent, and the gap at the lower end will continue to sap government's flexibility. Both of these public-sector handicaps argue for engaging private capacity to advance public missions wherever this can be done efficiently and accountably. If we acknowledge that the tilt of today's economic terrain gives private organizations an edge in flexibility and creativity, we are liberated to focus on strategies for harnessing those advantages to the public purpose. This will require a stiff dose of realism about the entirely rational resistance that will greet most efforts to outsource commodity tasks currently assigned to public workers. Likewise, it calls for vigilance against delegating custom tasks that government workers are happy to cede, private organizations are eager to take on, but that cannot be delegated without damage.

Tapping the private sector in order to economize on scarce governmental capacity will frequently involve forms of cross-sectoral collaboration that are related to, but distinguishable from, both outsourcing and voluntarism. In growingly important models of public–private collaboration, in contrast to outsourcing, government does not stipulate every detail of the mission, and private parties may not be driven exclusively, or even primarily, by the prospect of contractual payments. Individuals, businesses, and nonprofits have a mix of motives for collaborating in the production of public value, including intrinsic commitment to the goal itself, a special interest in the process or outcome, reputation, the latent threat of mandates or regulation, and the thirst for good publicity. Unlike voluntarism, conversely, the public sector retains the central role in setting goals, sorting out priorities, and defining success. The government's fundamental challenge is to understand both private motives and private capabilities, and to deploy incentives and influence to focus private energies on public missions.

There is nothing new about turning to private capacity to fill gaps in government's own competencies. Such arrangements go way back, and indeed antedate American nationhood. (Benjamin Franklin organized a private Revolutionary War fighting force, the Pennsylvania Associators, to substitute for the state militia that Quaker Pennsylvania balked at mustering under public authority.)[23] Collaboration is sometimes infeasible, frequently hard to manage accountably, and can decay into plutocracy, noblesse oblige, or simple corruption. But it can be a promising strategy when government itself is sclerotic and starved for talent; when conventional contracts are too coarse and brittle to orchestrate complex public tasks; and when insulation from electoral accountability limits the legitimate reach of pure voluntarism. One complication, to be sure, is the absolute requirement for a nucleus of public personnel with the high-level analytical, strategic, and negotiating skills needed to structure and oversee collaborative arrangements. This circumscribed but steep personnel problem may, or may not, turn out to be easier to solve than a bigger, more diffuse personnel problem. Yet while the challenges and uncertainties are undeniable—and while it would be silly to suggest that it offers any sort of panacea for the challenges posed by government's personnel problems—collaboration can be the best feasible response when the means required to advance public missions reside largely outside government.

There is plenty of room for debate over how best to deal with government's disconnect from the private economy—and, as my guild rules as an academic oblige me to emphasize, much more research is needed. But the divide itself looms as a first-order fact of modern American governance. I continue to scan the horizon for signs that the long, strong tide of rising inequality is beginning to recede. And I continue to cheer on the reformers struggling to structure a fair and effective public sector in spite of the obstacles. But all who dream of easing government's ills will lay their plans more wisely, with better odds of success, if they appreciate the links between the flaws they hope to heal and the workplace upheaval that has reshaped only part of our economy. Government's isolation from the broader working world is an unwelcome, mostly unintended legacy from the past generation, and a formidable challenge to the next. We will surmount the challenge—we have handled far worse—but only if we see it clear.

Appendix

Notes

Index

The Evidence on Comparative Compensation

CHAPTER 2 SKETCHED out a range of reasons why government should tend to be a relatively (albeit unevenly) generous employer. It also adduced some bits of evidence showing that public jobs do indeed tend to offer more security, better benefits, and pay that is high on the low end and low on the high end. But it doesn't definitively nail down the distinction between public and private work. The data arrayed to illustrate those differences might be inaccurate, as numbers (even meticulously collected official statistics) sometimes are. Even if they are correct, in a technical sense, they might be incomplete or misapplied and thus cast a distorting light on features of public employment that, when seen in the proper context, turn out to be entirely warranted.

We know that government pay runs higher, on average, than private-sector pay. But government work differs from private-sector work. Public jobs are disproportionately administrative, professional, technical, or otherwise skill-intensive. Government workers tend to be better-educated, more experienced, and more concentrated in urban areas than are their private-sector counterparts. We have also seen that government workers and private workers in similar occupations often make dissimilar salaries. Bus drivers, janitors, and landscapers earn more in government; accountants, managers, and analysts earn less. But we can't really say that there's anything fundamentally different about government pay practices unless we know that the workers bearing the same job title in the two sectors are doing the same things. It may be a fact (as noted in the chapter) that "inspectors, testers, sorters, samplers, and weighers" in government average nearly twice the pay of food-industry workers in the same occupational category. But what we make of that fact depends on whether they are inspecting, testing, sorting, sampling, and weighing the same things, in the same ways, with the same stakes.

Let's be clear on what it is that we're looking for—sturdy evidence that government compensation practices differ from the private sector's, even after the special characteristics of government work and workers are taken into account. In a perfectly efficient labor market, workers will be sorted across potential jobs so that each is paid just enough to induce him or her to do the work. Each will be adequately, but not excessively, compensated for the productivity contributions of his or her training, experience, talent, and effort. There will be no *systematic* premiums (or "rents," in the economists' jargon) over this walkaway compensation package. Some workers, to be sure, will be earning more than the bare minimum to keep them on the job, because of their affinity or aptitude for a particular kind of occupation. But these rents will be individual and idiosyncratic (Frank is a superlative letter carrier but oddly unsuited for anything else; Lisa loves teaching so much she would do it for free) rather than applying to whole classes of jobs or workers.[1]

Perfectly efficient labor markets, of course, are rare anywhere. But there is a range of reasons, discussed in Chapter 6, to expect them to be particularly rare in government. The public sector broadly lacks the characteristics on the demand side of the labor market (profit-motivated aversion to excess costs; full discretion in hiring, firing, and wage-setting; and the concentrated efficiency incentives of private ownership) that would generate the textbook ideal of just-adequate compensation. So it would not be surprising for government to be more prone than business to pay more, or to pay less, than the precise sum required to attract adequately qualified workers.

To know whether this actually occurs, we need to find out whether public-sector pay differentials still show up once the effect of factors that quite properly shape compensation are taken into account. Relevant factors may pertain to the nature of the work (skill requirements, geographic location, level of responsibility, risk of layoff or dismemberment, whether the job is tedious or gratifying, high status or degrading) or to the nature of the workers (education and training, gender and ethnicity, years of experience, insight, capacity for teamwork, initiative, and so on). Once all such germane features have been controlled for, in a statistically satisfying way, any remaining differential in compensation can be called a public-sector premium or penalty. The hitch, of course, is that some of these complicating factors are measured routinely and well; some episodically and imperfectly; and some are highly resistant to measurement of any sort. Empiricists do what they can with the data they have. The literature is rather sparse—and rather stale, with most of the studies predating recent peaks of economic inequality—but illuminating nonetheless.

The Dialogue of the Deaf over Federal Pay

A spike of academic scrutiny of federal pay practices some years back illustrates the basic approach economists take to the comparability issue, and offers a good point of departure for this tour of scholarly work. The context was the long economic boom that followed World War II, fueling a surge of middle-class prosperity in the private economy and (many feared) leaving federal workers behind. President Kennedy called for reforms that would "assure equity for the [f]ederal employee with his equals throughout the national economy, enable the [g]overnment to compete fairly with private firms for qualified personnel, and provide at last a logical and factual standard for setting [f]ederal salaries."[2] Congress complied, enacting a wave of legislation meant to bring the various federal pay systems into alignment with the business world. The watchword for federal pay was supposed to be strict comparability with the private sector—no more, no less—put into effect through periodic surveys to identify, and then to match, market rates for each kind of work. By 1974, as the reforms took hold, average federal pay was more than double what it had been in 1963, sharply outpacing growth in private wages and salaries.[3]

A young economist (and eventual business-school dean) named Sharon P. Smith, in her doctoral dissertation and publications flowing from it, assessed how well the reforms were doing on the core goal of comparability. If Washington's surveys were successful in matching public jobs with comparable private ones and aligning pay accordingly, then any discrepancies across the sectors should be strictly attributable to the different mix of jobs in each sector—in particular, the need for more educated and experienced workers to undertake high-end federal tasks. Smith assembled Census data on adult civilian workers in Washington, D.C. and three surrounding states, and culled the self-employed and state or local government employees in order to permit as clean as possible a comparison between federal and private-sector workers. This left her with a healthy sample of about 22,000 private workers and 5,000 federal workers. She used multiple regression analysis—a standard statistical strategy for teasing out the impact of each factor when many causes contribute to some result—to disentangle the factors that determine workers' pay levels. Her model took into account the years of schooling each worker had completed, an estimate of work experience, race and gender, marital status, urban versus rural setting, and disability.

If the federal pay reforms were hitting their target, the source of a worker's paycheck (federal or private) should be irrelevant to its size once all of these factors were duly considered. No single number summarizes her conclusions—there seldom are in such studies. But her analysis suggested rather insistently that the comparability surveys were getting it wrong. Only about half of the premium in average federal pay could be traced to differences in education, experience, and other worker characteristics.[4] Even after factoring in characteristics that could plausibly justify premium compensation, federal workers were collecting more, not less, than their counterparts in business.

Smith's study set the pattern for a series of similar academic analyses during the next fifteen years or so that varied in the details of data, method, and conclusions but that generally found federal workers, as a group, to be overpaid.[5] A parallel series of official comparability surveys continued to find federal *jobs*, as a group, to be underpaid. Some observers, in and out of academia, charged that the government's job-comparison system was flawed (either inadvertently or by design). If someone who would be classed as a "typist" in the private sector was upgraded to a "secretary" in government, for example, the official job-to-job comparison could diagnose a federal pay shortfall while the academic person-to-person comparison could find a federal pay premium. Similarly, some perceived a syndrome of "grade creep" in which federal workers were pushed up into higher grades of the civil-service pay schedule than their actual tasks warranted, which could also account for the discrepancies between the two approaches.[6]

The regression equations pointing to a pattern of federal overpayment, meanwhile, were sometimes derided as academic mumbo jumbo or (more frequently) simply ignored. There were some isolated attempts to reconcile the conflicting conclusions of the two approaches. The Government Accountability Office, a respected analytical unit that reports to Congress, tried in a voluminous 1994 report to determine why scholars and federal paymasters came up with such different answers.[7] One potential driver of the discrepancy was technical: the surveys used to set private-sector benchmarks for federal pay examined only larger companies, which tend to pay more than smaller companies. If federal standards are anchored on big-company pay scales, federal workers as a group would do better than otherwise-comparable private workers who work at a mix of big and small operations. Another factor the GAO highlighted was very far from technical. Women and minorities tend to earn less than white men do in the private sector. The academics comparing pay levels tacitly incorporate gender and ethnic disparities into their models as just one of those factors that determine private-sector compensation. Federal pay policies deliberately and explicitly forswear any distinctions along race or gender lines, and the GAO attributed much of the discrepancy between the sectors to the government's practice of bringing women and minorities up to white-male compensation levels.

Another attempt to account for the difference between the two approaches came from the academic side. An economist named Brent Moulton surveyed his colleagues' prior studies in 1990, generally admiring their methods but concerned that their focus was too coarse. Some of them, for example, had controlled for workers occupations (along with education, age, and so on) and still found a sizable federal premium. But Moulton argued that it wasn't enough to take into account the broad occupational categories—"professional and technical," for example, or "handlers and laborers"—since the federal workforce was not just tilted toward the higher-skilled categories, but *within* each category had a disproportionate fraction of high-end jobs.[8] His analysis looked deeper into the detail of occupational classifications for a finer-grained comparison of federal and private workers. Moulton also introduced more refined controls for geographic differences that could distort comparisons, distinguishing not just between urban and rural locales (as had some prior studies) but across particular metropolitan areas.

Moulton's ambition to include so many detailed factors in his regression equations meant that he was piling a lot of computation onto a small collection of data, but he managed to come up with some statistically sturdy findings. He couldn't fully reconcile the conflict between the academic and official approaches—he still found a small federal premium—but he narrowed the average difference to about 3 percent. Even more valuably, his approach made it clear that the real issue was not an across-the-board disparity between the sectors, but gaps between federal and private pay that differed in both size and direction across categories of workers. Federal employees in big cities had no advantage over private-sector workers, for example, but he found a hefty federal premium in small cities and rural areas.[9] Whites were paid the same in both sectors, but minorities did substantially better in government. Federal and private pay scales were essentially the same for administrative and professional workers, but even after accounting for workers' characteristics, Moulton found premium federal pay for clerical and blue-collar employees.

Running regressions is one way to separate unjustified pay disparities from those rooted in perfectly reasonable differences. Another way to test whether compensation gaps are real or illusory is to see whether people organize their lives in response to those gaps, since millions of workers are less likely than a single researcher to be mistaken about where the good deals can be found. The labor economist Alan Krueger noticed that the difference between average pay in the federal government and the private sector varied over time. In the 1950s the average pay level in the federal government was just a little above the private average. The federal edge climbed sharply in the 1960s and 1970s, and then eased a bit in the 1980s (when Krueger's data ended). The variation over time in the difference between federal and private pay, Krueger realized, could be exploited to untangle comparability puzzles.

One possibility was that the ups and downs in relative pay simply reflected changes over time in the mix of jobs across sectors, with federal averages rising and falling as Washington hired more or fewer rocket scientists, financial analysts, and other high-end workers. If the federal government's workforce was changing, but how well it paid people in each position was not changing, then the relative appeal of federal work, on average, would be the same over time. However, if part of this difference was a real federal premium—sometimes federal paymasters were much more generous than private employers, and sometimes not—then workers' interest in federal jobs would perk up when the difference was large. Krueger gathered data on the number of people submitting applications for federal work, and carefully matched it to the time trend of the gap in federal and private pay. He found that as average federal pay increased, the number of applicants for federal jobs went up roughly in parallel. On the reasonable assumption that people are more likely to line up for federal jobs when such jobs in fact beat the alternatives, this pattern suggested that real pay premiums (not just different mixes of workers) account for some of the gap between federal and private averages.[10]

The desultory debate between academics and practitioners over federal–private comparability had mostly died down by the early 1990s. This was not because the alternative approaches had been reconciled— jobs-based and worker-based comparisons still yielded wildly different answers—but because the academics noticed that, despite their rather uncharacteristic consensus, nobody beyond the narrow brotherhood of labor economists seemed to be paying any attention. The scholars mostly moved on to other issues. Federal pay policy stayed more or less the same, and private-sector compensation patterns became increasingly skewed (the bottom falling, the top rising) from year to year.

Comparisons beyond the Federal Workforce

A few years after his analysis of applicants lining up for federal jobs, Krueger teamed with Lawrence Katz to produce a benchmark study of pay differentials inside and outside government.[11] (It is worth mentioning that both Katz and Krueger are two of the most distinguished labor economists at work today and also a bit left-of-center in their politics, with no animus against government workers.) This study, unlike the others cited so far, examined state and local as well as federal workers. It was based on late-1980s data drawn from the Current Population Survey (CPS), an ongoing project of the Census Bureau that is less comprehensive but more current than the once-a-decade national census. Each March the CPS team asks detailed questions of a large sample of Americans and distributes the results (shorn of names, but with profiles of individuals that include their earnings, work and educational histories, and other characteristics) to eager researchers. This let Katz and Krueger estimate relative wage levels in the private sector, the federal government, and state and local government, controlling for gender, race, educational attainment, years of experience, full-time versus part-time status, and urban versus nonurban locale.

The results of their study suggest that by 1988 a sharp difference between more- and less-educated workers could be seen in the relative rewards of government work. Let's focus on their findings for white workers in urban areas with five years of work experience.[12] College-educated workers earned a little extra on average (5 percent for men, 2 percent for women) if they worked in the federal government. But these more educated workers, as a group, were paid less in state and local government than were those in the private sector—18 percent less for men, and 4 percent less for women. Less-educated workers, conversely, earned systematically more in government. People whose education had stopped at high school could do a little better if they worked in state and local government (4 percent more for men, 10 percent more for women) and better still if they worked for the federal government (16 percent for men, 28 percent for women).

Like any study, this one has its limits. Its data sources permit only general attention to levels of education, lumping top MDs, MBAs, and PhDs together with the alumni of any four-year college into the broad category of college graduates. There is no way for even the cleverest labor economist to account for motivation, discipline, innate intelligence, and other characteristics that assuredly matter but that the surveys simply don't address. But this benchmark study suggests that by 1988, a long time before wage inequality reached recent peaks, government was already dissenting from the market's pronouncement that more-educated workers should be paid a lot more than less-educated workers.

Another study uncovered a few more clues. Using a similar approach to Katz and Krueger, and covering a partly overlapping time period, James Poterba and Kim Rueben analyzed pay differentials between the private sector and state and local government. Their study controlled for years of school, years of experience, location (inside or outside a metropolitan area), marital status, and race, and they found that the public-sector advantage for less-educated workers increased in the 1980s and early 1990s. Earnings for more-educated workers, conversely, grew more slowly in government than in the private sector.[13]

Poterba and Rueben's results suggested that the widening public-sector advantage at the lower end of the skills distribution was driven mostly by the eroding prospects of less-educated workers in the private sector, and not by improving public-sector pay for such workers.[14] In other words, the gap happened not because government changed, but because the rest of the economy changed.

As they differentiate among categories of work and workers, Poterba and Rueben illustrate the complicated picture of comparative pay. They find that state and local government paid a premium in the early 1990s to men working as bus drivers, orderlies, cleaners, and teachers, and for women working as practical nurses, receptionists, orderlies, cleaners, and schoolteachers. But they find a public-sector pay *shortfall* for men working as physicians—and also as truck drivers. (The trucking industry, in contrast to most of the private economy, is still heavily unionized.) There was a public-sector discount for women working as registered nurses, but not licensed practical nurses, and as college teachers, but not primary and secondary teachers.[15] While men at all educational levels had earned more in the private sector than in state and local government in 1979, by 1991 less-educated men earned a modest premium in government. College-educated men, conversely, earned 8 percent less than those in private industry, while men with postgraduate degrees earned 10 percent less. For women working in government in 1991 there was rough parity or a modest premium at all education levels, and the difference between public and private pay was not sharply different from what it had been twelve years earlier. There was some evidence, though, that the public-sector pay edge was rising for less-educated women and falling for more-educated ones.[16]

So far we have seen three basic strategies for hunting out differences in the worlds of work within and outside of government: comparing jobs, comparing workers, and drawing inferences from people's job choices. A study by William J. Moore and Robert J. Newman applies all three strategies to a tightly focused question: how well do Houston's public-transit workers fare, compared to people doing the same jobs in Houston's private sector?[17] In contrast to the sweeping landscapes of the other studies (and their inherent sacrifice of detail and precision) this analysis is a miniaturist portrait. It looks at only one city, only one year (1988), and only three job titles, none of them particularly lofty—cleaners, bus drivers, and mechanics. (See Appendix Table 1.) Cleaners were near the bottom of the Houston job market, earning less than $6 an hour in the private sector. Bus drivers made a modest $7.61 in wages and benefits. Private-sector mechanics did a bit better, with earnings of a little more than $11 putting them into the lower edge of Houston's middle class. Moore and Newman found a strong, negative link between how well these categories of workers fared in the private sector and their relative treatment by Houston Metropolitan Transit. Cleaners earned much more in government; public bus drivers had nearly as generous an edge over their counterparts in business; and mechanics did only slightly better in the public sector. All three kinds of public workers were less likely to quit (or get themselves fired) than were their private-sector counterparts, but public-sector cleaners, with the most to lose if they left government, clung especially tightly to their jobs.

Caveats, Complications, and One More Study

The literature sampled here is revealing, but short of conclusive, for three related reasons. The first is methodological uncertainty. There is room for honest disagreement about how to control for factors that blur the picture of relative pay. Labor economists form a fairly tight guild, and most of them make it a point to read others' work in their areas of interest, both to keep up with good ideas and to challenge shortcuts or shoddy methods. But distilling wisdom about the world out of impure data is an inexact art. Conclusions are never identical from one study to another. One dissenting analysis (not published in a

Appendix Table 1   Data on Houston Transit Workers, 1988

	Private-sector total compensation (per hour)	Public relative to private compensation	Public relative to private "separation rate"
Cleaners	$5.94	183%	14%
Drivers	$7.61	169%	45%
Mechanics	$11.16	116%	46%

Source: William J. Moore and Robert J. Newman, "Government Wage Differentials in a Municipal Labor Market: The Case of Houston Metropolitan Transit Workers," *Industrial and Labor Relations Review* 45(1) (October 1991): 151, Tables 2 and 3.

peer-reviewed journal, but by a respectable think tank) argues that properly adjusting for the special demands of government work shows that there was only a trivial premium for state workers as of 1989, and a much larger discount for local workers.[18] The weight of scholarly judgment, however, tilts heavily in the other direction, and it would be surprising if the dissenters turned out to be right and the mainstream wrong—surprising, but not impossible.

The second reason concerns limitations on data. The big official surveys from which researchers mine the raw numbers they try to refine into truth capture only the kinds of relatively coarse information—age, education level, years of experience, industry of employment, and so on—that can be gathered in short interviews and entered on a standard survey form. Unmeasured characteristics that surely matter in comparing relative pay, whether of the workers (differences in native ability, energy, or diligence) or of the work (differences in safety, tedium, status, or difficulty that occupational categories mask), can confound even artful analysis.

The third factor is related to the second. People surely react to differential prospects inside and outside government, and choose to work where their abilities, both measured and unmeasured, are best rewarded. Recall from Chapter 2 that American colleges and universities are increasingly segmented into a hierarchy of more- and less-selective schools, so that it is becoming less reasonable to expect that one college graduate will be pretty much like any other. If college-educated men, as a class, are badly paid in state and local government, the college-educated men who are nonetheless willing to work in state and local government may be less productive than average—in ways that alternative employers notice, but surveys do not—and hence not underpaid at all. Similarly, if women without academic credentials fare especially well in the federal government, the women who get federal jobs may possess aptitudes that belie their limited formal schooling. And so on. (Moore and Newman, in the study just cited, found Houston transit workers to be more educated and experienced than their worse-paid counterparts outside government.) Indeed, in theory everyone in the workforce should sort themselves out in response to premiums and discounts until nobody can do any better by switching sectors. To the extent this actually happens, any apparent government premium or discount would be illusory, the artifact of imperfect measurement.[19] Government would have more capable janitors and receptionists than the rest of the economy, and less capable analysts and attorneys, but everyone would be earning a fair wage.

One final study is worth summarizing here, in part because it is fresher (published in 2003) than most of the pay comparability literature and in part because it deals ingeniously with this problem of invisible differences between public and private workers. George Borjas, another widely respected labor economist, set out to update and extend his colleagues' earlier efforts to investigate differences in public and private compensation.[20] He warms up with a set of standard regression analyses to track the trend, from 1960 to 2000, in overall wage gaps between the sectors (first the raw numbers, then the same series carefully adjusted for workers' education, age, race, and locale). Borjas's findings on the patterns are in line with most of the other studies discussed here, but carry the story forward by a decade or so, and thus spot a few interesting details. The unadjusted figures show both men and women earning more in government throughout the forty-year period, though the relative edge is much larger for women.[21] Once workers' education, race, and other characteristics are factored in, relative pay in government turns slightly negative for men, with the public-sector average running a bit below the private-sector average through the whole period. The pattern for women is more surprising. Women still do better in government, but their edge over women outside government dwindles over the decades to something close to parity by the late 1990s. What drives this trend, Borjas finds, is local government. In the mid-1970s a woman working in local government earned 10 percent more than a statistically comparable woman working in the private sector. In 2000, she earned 10 percent less. (The discussion of schoolteachers in Chapter 3 casts some light on what might be going on here.)

Borjas then measures the dispersion of wages—the difference between better-paid and worse-paid workers—across and within the sectors. In the 1960s and early 1970s—as government was staffing up with high-end workers to educate the baby boom and run Great Society programs, and before middle-class prosperity started to unwind in the private economy—government had a broader range of pay scales than did the private sector. But this pattern reversed itself, first tentatively and then dramatically, and by 2000 disparities in private-sector pay were far wider than in government.[22] Looking specifically at the gaps between college-educated and high-school-educated workers, Borjas found that the payoff to higher education grew sharply in the private sector but only shallowly in government. Even *within* narrowly defined categories of workers—people of the same age, education level, race, or region—wage inequality has been expanding in the private sector but has been muted in government.

So far Borjas's contributions have been valuable but limited: extending the pay-gap analysis into the 1990s, and providing some additional detail on the story told in earlier studies. But his familiarity with the mechanics of the underlying data sources let him go a step beyond. Like most analysts working this field, his main data source was the detailed supplemental questionnaire administered each year under the Commerce Department's CPS program. Some people, Borjas knew, were included in the sample for two consecutive years. And some fraction of these people who were surveyed twice happened to switch the sector in which they worked—from business to government, or from government to business—between the first and the second survey. Not a big fraction—most people don't change jobs from one year to the next, let alone sectors—but the overall samples are large enough that Borjas was able to identify 34,454 sector-switchers who had been surveyed both as public workers and as private workers.[23]

Prior studies mostly relied on sophisticated but fallible statistical techniques to attempt fair comparisons between different workers inside and outside government. But Borjas was able to look at the exact same people on either side of the public–private divide. This cuts through the fog that inevitably confounds efforts to compare people using coarse and incomplete survey measurements. Instead of trying to imagine what Steve the corporate lawyer and Nancy the school nurse would earn if they worked in the other sector, you can just follow Steve and Nancy as they move and find out. Borjas had found a way to make the economist's mantra—"all other things being equal"—hold fairly close to true.

Borjas divided his 34,454 sector-switchers, over a twenty-two-year period, into "quitters"—people who left government—and "entrants"—people who came into government from private jobs the prior year. He used each worker's private-sector wage (either the year before starting or the year after leaving a government job) as the benchmark of his or her bottom-line earning power. Then he worked his labor-economist toolkit to get as precise as possible a fix on who quit, and who entered, as the gulf between the sectors widened. Until the late 1970s, remember, government and business had roughly similar ranges in the rewards of work. Then wage dispersion widened dramatically in the private sector, while it stayed fairly narrow in the public sector. As this trend played itself out, Borjas discovered, workers with a lot of earning power became more and more likely to leave government, and less and less likely to join it. One sentence from his cautious, technical article tells the story: "In short, the substantial widening of wage inequality in the private sector and the relatively more stable wage distribution in the public sector created magnetic effects that altered the sorting of workers across sectors, with high-skill workers becoming more likely to end up in the private sector."[24]

This is not a particularly startling discovery, in light of the rest of the evidence assembled here. But Borjas reached the conclusion in a more direct way and with fresher data than the other studies cited, making it hard to brush off the sobering results as statistical hocus-pocus.

What to Make of the Studies

The economic historians Claudia Goldin and Robert Margo have documented the "great compression" of the American wage structure in the 1940s and 1950s, a long rein of centripetal forces in the labor market that narrowed disparities between workers and shaped the middle-class culture of the early postwar decades.[25] Earnings gaps shrank both across groups (between blacks and whites, men and women, more-educated and less-educated workers), and within groups (a tighter pay distribution among white women taking their first jobs right out of high school, for example, or among college-educated males with ten years of work experience). The public sector shared in this midcentury tightening of the earnings distribution. In the 1970s, this process began to reverse itself in the private economy. For a complex set of reasons—including rising trade and immigration, changing technology, shifts in labor laws and institutions, and a weakening of cultural scruples against disparate rewards—the earning power of less-skilled workers (and particularly males) crumbled in the private sector, while the prospects of better-educated workers soared. This "great *de*compression" has mostly missed government.

Notes

1: Two Worlds of Work

1. Rick Bragg, *I Am a Soldier, Too: The Jessica Lynch Story* (New York: Knopf, 2003). Private Lynch's goal to teach kindergarten, and the lure of military education benefits, are discussed on pages 9 and 29 in *I Am a Soldier, Too;* the limited options she, her siblings, and friends faced are discussed on pages 30–32.

2. Terms of Robertson Foundation gift agreement quoted in Michael Powell, "At Princeton, Feeling Failed; Family Seeks Return of $525 Million, Saying University Has 'Abused' Gift," *Washington Post,* October 8, 2003, p. A3.

3. William Robertson is quoted in the *Washington Post* article cited above. A longer statement, in Robertson's own words, appears in "After Alma Mater Gets Your Money, It Just Might Misplace Your Mission," *San Francisco Chronicle,* October 4, 2003, p. B17. Robertson claimed that fewer than 5 percent of graduates ended up in the kinds of public service that motivated his parents' gift. Princeton disagreed, stating that its data showed that about a third of the Wilson School's 1,923 alumni took some sort of government job after graduation (quoted in John Hechinger and Daniel Golden, "Fight at Princeton Escalates over Use of a Family's Gift," *Wall Street Journal,* February 7, 2006, p. 1).

4. The appellate court eventually vacated the "front pay" award—because it found it sloppily calculated—but did not challenge the principle of compensation for the loss of a government job. *Peyton* v. *DiMario,* 287 F.3d 1121 (D.C. Cir, 2002).

5. Budget figure (for both 2003 and 2004) from Bernard Wysocki Jr., "National Institutes of Health Is Under Fire," *Wall Street Journal,* June 22,

2004, p. A4; NIH share of federal research funding from Rand Corporation study cited in Wysocki.

6. Rick Weiss, "Salary, Conflict-of-Interest Policies at NIH Are Questioned," *Washington Post,* March 25, 2004, p. A21.

7. Compensation comparison from Association of American Medical Colleges and NIH data cited in Weiss and received through the Freedom of Information Act.

8. Wallace's Balinese research in particular, and the peculiarities of island ecology in general, are discussed in David Quammen, *The Song of the Dodo: Island Biogeography in an Age of Extinction* (New York: Touchstone, 1996). See esp. pp. 49–52.

9. The figure for federal white-collar executive branch employment in June 2002 (147,080) is from the Office of Personnel Management's FedScope data system. The Bureau of Labor Statistics reports 22.9 million government workers overall in 2002; the Office of Management and Budget's tally was 22.8 million.

10. The figure for imprisoned Americans is from the U.S. Department of Justice, Bureau of Justice Statistics, accessed May 2006 at http://www.ojp .usdoj.gov/bjs/prisons.htm. The figure for federal civil servants is from the Bureau of Labor Statistics source identified in note 14 below. Both figures are for 2005.

11. For some discussion of this shifting federal–state balance see John D. Donahue, *Disunited States* (New York: Basic Books, 1997).

12. Information on civilian employment can be found at the Census Bureau's Governments Division web site, http://www.census.gov/govs; information on military force strength can be obtained from the Defense Department at http://web1.whs.osd.mil/mmid/military/ms9.pdf. The numbers cited here were assembled from data obtained in August 2003 and were drawn from the 2002 version of the five-year Census of Governments.

13. Table 1.1 presents the total of full-time and part-time jobs for the civilian sector, since in many cases data aren't available on the more logical "full-time equivalent" (FTE) basis. This overstates somewhat the size of the payroll in areas where part-time work is common (such as postal and, to a lesser extent, education) relative to those where it is rare (such as law and security.) The military categories include only those members of the reserves and the National Guard who were on active duty in one of the four services. Counting backup forces would obviously increase the defense category considerably, but misleadingly, since those *not* on active duty spend the vast majority of their time working for somebody other than the military.

14. Most of the numbers used here come from the Bureau of Labor Statistics' National Employment, Hours, and Earnings survey program, downloaded via the BLS's exemplary data extraction service in May 2006. Figures for the uniformed military come from the Office of Management and Budget, *Budget of the United States Government, Fiscal Year 2007*, Historical Table 17.5.

15. Enrollment and other statistics from U.S. Department of Education, National Center for Education Statistics, *Digest of Education Statistics 2001*, Table 65, "Public and Private Elementary and Secondary Teachers, Enrollment, and Pupil/Teacher Ratios: Fall 1955 to Fall 2001."

16. Ibid., Table 172, "Total Fall Enrollment in Degree-Granting Institutions, by attendance status, sex of student, and control of institution: 1947 to 1999."

2: Relic of the Middle-Class Economy

1. For an erudite statement of the case that it's pretty much okay, see Finis Welch, "In Defense of Inequality," *The American Economic Review* 89(2) (May 1999): 1–17.

2. Gini coefficient trend data are from the Census Bureau's Current Population Survey Table F-4, "Gini Ratio for Families by Race and Hispanic Origin of Householder, 1947 to 2004," accessed September 2006 at http://www.census.gov/hhes/www/income/histinc/f04.html. Technically the Gini coefficient measures only the *amount* of inequality, and could rise even if the poor became much poorer and the rich became much richer with no change in the middle class. Other measures, though, make it clear that the middle three-fifths of the income distribution lost ground to the top.

3. Like almost all the income numbers used here, this is from the Census Bureau's Current Population Survey. Family income for 2001 is from Table FINC-06, "Percent Distribution of Families, by Selected Characteristics within Income Quintile and Top 5 Percent," accessed September 2003 at http://ferret.bls.census.gov/macro/032002/faminc/new06_000.htm.

4. Data for Figure 2.1 are drawn from Current Population Survey Historical Income Tables (Families), Table F-33, "Families by Total Money Income 1967–2004," accessed May 2006 at http://www.census.gov/hhes/income/histinc/f23.html. Mean family income is not available for 1967, so 1968 was substituted as the base year. A separate data series, based on tax returns, reinforces the picture of the prosperous pulling away from the middle. In 1977 only one in every 1,667 tax returns reported adjusted gross income exceeding $200,000 (in 2000 dollars). By 2000 more than one in fifty reached this level. Brian Balkovic, "High-Income Tax Returns

for 2000," *Statistics of Income Bulletin,* Spring 2003, Internal Revenue Service (Figure A, page 11).

5. Peter Gottschalk and Timothy M. Smeeding, "Cross National Comparisons of Earnings and Income Inequality," *Journal of Economic Literature* 35(2) (June 1997): 643–644, esp. Figure 1.

6. Carola Frydman and Raven E. Saks, "Historical Trends in Executive Compensation 1936–2003," Harvard University Economics Department Working Paper, November 15, 2005, Table 6, p. 45. See also Kevin J. Murphy and Jan Zabojnik, "CEO Pay and Appointments: A Market-Based Explanation for Recent Trends," *American Economic Review* 94(2) (May 2004): 192–196.

7. Thomas Piketty and Emmanuel Saez, "The Evolution of Top Incomes: A Historical and International Perspective," NBER Working Paper 11955, January 2006, pp. 4–5.

8. During the 1980s work hours for men age twenty-five to sixty-five actually increased by only one-tenth as much—3.2 percent versus 31 percent—among the best-paid as they did among the worst-paid, despite the fact that tax rates dropped for the former and rose for the latter. See Joel Slemrod and Jon Bakija, *Taxing Ourselves* (Cambridge and London: MIT Press, 1997), Table 4.2, p. 107.

9. March 2002 Current Population Demographic Supplement, Table PINC-09, "Source of Income in 2001—Number with Income and Mean Income of Specified Type in 2001 of People 15 Years Old and Over by Age, Race and Hispanic Origin, and Sex," accessed July 2003 at http://ferret.bls.census.gov/macro/032002/perinc/new09_001.htm.

10. Thomas Piketty and Emmanuel Saez, "The Evolution of Top Incomes: A Historical and International Perspective," NBER Working Paper 11955, January 2006, Figure 2.

11. Peter Gottschalk, "Inequality, Income Growth, and Mobility: The Basic Facts," *Journal of Economic Perspectives* 11(2) (Spring 1997): 21–40. See also Lawrence F. Katz and David H. Autor, "Changes in the Wage Structure and Earnings Inequality," in *Handbook of Labor Economics,* ed. Orley Ashenfelter and David Card, vol. 3A (Amsterdam: Elsevier, 1999) pp. 1463–1555.

12. Gottschalk, "Inequality, Income Growth, and Mobility," Table 1, p. 37.

13. Gottschalk, "Inequality, Income Growth, and Mobility," p. 37, esp. notes 18 and 19.

14. Peter Gottschalk and Enrico Spolaore "On the Evaluation of Economic Mobility," *Review of Economic Studies* 69(238) (2002): 191–208.

15. Markus Jantti et al., "American Exceptionalism in a New Light: A Comparison of Intergenerational Earnings Mobility in the Nordic Countries,

the United Kingdom, and the United States," Institute for the Study of Labor, Bonn, Discussion Paper No. 1938, January 2006.

16. Moshe Buchinsky and Jennifer Hunt find that mobility across the wage spectrum slowed during the 1980s. "Wage Mobility," NBER Working Paper 5455, February 1996. Chul-In Lee and Gary Solon find little or no change in recent decades in economic mobility from one generation to the next. "Trends in Intergenerational Income Mobility," NBER Working Paper 12007, February 2006. For a longer-term perspective, see Joseph P. Ferrie, "The End of American Exceptionalism? Mobility in the U.S. Since 1850," NBER Working Paper 11324, May 2005.

17. The statistical workers who assemble the Current Population Survey maintain no fewer than fifteen alternative definitions of income, and have measured changes in inequality for each measure. For the standard definition—simple money income, not including capital gains—inequality grew by 11.6 percent between 1979 and 2003. For the most comprehensive measure, which takes account of most taxes and transfer programs, inequality increased by 10.8 percent during the same period. These comparisons are based on figures in U.S. Census Bureau, Historical Income Tables, Table RDI-5, "Index of Income Concentration by Definition of Income, 1979 to 2003," accessed June 2006 at http://www.census .gov/hhes/income/histinc/rdi5.html.

18. Calculated from *Economic Report of the President* 2006, U.S. Government Priority Office (Washington, DC: 2007) Tables B-1 and B-101.

19. The 1970 figure is from "Foreign-Born and Total Population," Immigration and Naturalization Service, http://www.ins.usdoj.gov/stats/308; the 2002 figure is from U.S. Department of Commerce, Bureau of the Census, press release, "Foreign-Born Population Passes 32 Million, Census Bureau Estimates," released March 10, 2003.

20. Since new immigrants tend to cluster at the extremes of the income distribution, growth in immigration also chips away at the middle-class economy even if the earnings of native workers aren't affected.

21. For some historical context on this issue, see Jeffrey G. Williamson, "Globalization, Labor Markets, and Policy Backlash in the Past," *Journal of Economic Perspectives* 12(4) (Autumn 1998): 51–72.

22. See Alan S. Blinder, "Offshoring: The Next Industrial Revolution?" *Foreign Affairs*, 85(2) (March/April 2006): 113–128.

23. In the mid-1970s the labor economist Jan Tinbergen wrote that the earnings distribution was largely determined by a "race between technological development and access to education" (Jan Tinbergen, "Substitution of Graduate by Other Labor," *Kyklos* 27 [1974]), quoted in Katz and Autor, "Changes in the Wage Structure and Earnings Inequality," p. 1465.

24. While the decline of manufacturing as a share of the economy and, to an even greater extent, the labor market started in the 1940s—and hence can't explain the acceleration of wage inequality nearer the end of the century—it is generally seen as contributing to the declining earning power of less-educated men. Urban Institute, "Widening Wage Inequality," accessed June 2003 from LexisNexis Database (Current Issues Universe, R008–22) at http://www.lexisnexis.com/ciuniv.

25. For an authoritative study of the hollowing out of the middle of the skills distribution, see David H. Autor, Lawrence F. Katz, and Melissa S. Kearney, "The Polarization of the U.S. Labor Market," NBER Working Paper 11986, January 2006.

26. Thomas Lemieux finds that virtually all of the increase in wage inequality can be explained by the pattern of college and postgraduate education and rocketing returns to high-end training. Thomas Lemieux, "Post-Secondary Education and Increasing Wage Inequality," Working Paper 12077, National Bureau of Economics Research, March 2006.

27. For one good sample of the rich literature on this issue, see Steven G. Allen, "Technology and the Wage Structure," *Journal of Labor Economics* 19(3) (April 2001): 440–483.

28. Current Population Survey PINC-3, "Educational Attainment—People 25 Years Old and Over by Total Money Earnings in 2003"; and Historical Income Table P-19, "Years of School Completed—People 25 Years Old and Over by Mean Income and Sex: 1967 to 1990." The definition of educational attainment for post-1990 data differs from the earlier series. Since the 2003 figure excludes people with five or more years of postsecondary education who failed to earn any graduate degree, it may overstate somewhat the rise in the earnings premium for postgraduate education. I use a mid-1970s figure here for consistency with other comparisons over time, but it is worth noting that the education premium was actually lower—and thus the comparison with the present starker— a few years earlier or later. For commentary on the contribution of technological change to earnings inequality, see for example George E. Johnson, "Changes in Earnings Inequality: The Role of Demand Shifts," *Journal of Economic Perspectives* 11(2) (Spring 1997): 41–55, esp. p. 51; Peter Gottschalk, "Inequality, Income Growth, and Mobility: The Basic Facts," *Journal of Economic Perspectives* 11(2) (Spring 1997): 21–40, esp. Figure 5, p. 31; and Thomas Kane, "Beyond Tax Relief: Long-Term Challenges in Financing Higher Education," *National Tax Journal* 50(2) (1997): 336.

29. U.S. Department of Education, National Center for Education Statistics, *Digest of Education Statistics 2001*, Table 171, "Historical Summary of Fac-

ulty, Students, Degrees, and Finances in Degree-granting Institutions: 1869–70 to 1999–2000." The education premium did actually decline somewhat in the late 1970s as newly graduated baby boomers hit the labor market, but more recently the bonus skilled workers command has continued to increase even in the face of rising education levels. Gottshalk, "Inequality, Income Growth, and Mobility," Figure 5, p. 31, traces the late-1970s dip in the education premium and its almost steady climb since the early 1980s.

30. In 1939 only 6 percent of workers were college graduates and 68 percent lacked a high-school diploma. By 1996 28 percent had at least a bachelor's degree and less than 10 percent lacked a high-school education. Daron Acemoglu, "Technical Change, Inequality, and the Labor Market," *Journal of Economic Literature* 40(1) (March 2002): 7–72, esp. p.14 and Figure 1, p. 15.

31. Caroline M. Hoxby and Bridget Terry estimate that the growing diversity of the college-educated explains about one-quarter of the earnings differences among degree-holders, returns to underlying ability differences explain a third, and quality segmentation among colleges and universities explains five-twelfths. "Explaining Rising Wage and Income Inequality among the College Educated," NBER Working Paper 6873, 1999.

32. From Current Population Survey, Annual Social and Economic Supplement, March 2004, Income Table 6, "Percent Distribution of Families, by Selected Characteristics within Income Quintile and Top 5 Percent in 2003," accessed September 2004 at http://ferret.bls.census.gov/macro/032004/faminc/new06_000.htm.

33. Nicole M. Fortin and Thomas Lemieux, "Institutional Changes and Rising Wage Inequality: Is There a Linkage?" *Journal of Economic Perspectives* 11(2) (Spring 1997): 94.

34. The 2002 figures are from data provided by Donna Hirsch of the Bureau of Labor Statistics in July 2003. The 2006 figures are from "Union Members in 2006," Bureau of Labor Statistics press release, January 25, 2007.

35. For a fine assessment of this theme, see James Peoples, "Deregulation and the Labor Market," *Journal of Economic Perspectives* 12(3) (Summer 1998): 117–130.

36. For a thorough exploration of this issue, see David Card, "The Effect of Unions on the Structure of Wages: A Longitudinal Analysis," *Econometrica* 64(4) (July 1996): 957–979. Fortin and Lemieux ("Institutional Changes and Rising Wage Inequality," pp. 89–90, esp. Table 2) see lower organization rates as responsible for 21 percent of the increase in male wage dispersion between 1979 and 1988. The effect for women is different, since (as will be taken up later in this book) many of the unionized

women are relatively high-skilled public sector workers who would be well paid in any event. Richard Freeman also finds that declining unionization accounts for about a fifth of the growing wage gap. See Freeman, "Labor Market Institutions and Earnings Inequality," *New England Economic Review* (May–June 1996): 164; and *When Earnings Diverge: Causes, Consequences, and Cures for the New Inequality in the U.S.* (Washington, D.C.: National Policy Association, 1997), p. 40. More recent work confirms the equalizing effect of unions for male earnings economy-wide but amplifies that the story doesn't apply to women. David Card, Thomas Lemieux, and D. Craig Riddell, "Unionization and Wage Inequality: A Comparative Study of the U.S., UK, and Canada," NBER Working Paper 9473, January 2003.

37. See Peter Gottschalk and Timothy M. Smeeding, "Cross National Comparisons of Earnings and Income Inequality," *Journal of Economic Literature* 35(2) (June 1997): 633–687; and Thomas J. Volgy, John E. Scharz, and Lawrence E. Imwalle, "In Search of Economic Well-Being: Worker Power and the Effects of Productivity, Inflation, Unemployment, and Global Trade on Wages in Ten Wealthy Countries," *American Journal of Political Science* 40(4) (November 1996): 1233–1252.

38. Katz and Autor, "Changes in the Wage Structure and Earnings Inequality," pp. 1477–1478.

39. The predilection of some industries, and some companies, to offer compensation beyond what straightforward economics would predict is discussed in Lawrence F. Katz and Lawrence H. Summers, "Industry Rents: Evidence and Implications," *Brookings Papers on Economic Activity* (1989): 209–275.

40. Two researchers (Dan Devroye and Richard Freeman) studied the earnings distribution of workers in America, Sweden, Germany, and the Netherlands to see how much of the variance could be attributed to differences in skills. Instead of educational attainment—a notoriously noisy measure of skills, especially for international comparisons—they used a standardized measure of numeracy and literacy developed by the Organization for Economic Cooperation and Development. They found that measured differences in skills explained only 7 percent of differences in earnings. In fact, they discovered, there is more earnings inequality for American workers with the *same* measured skills than for workers in the other three countries across the entire skills spectrum. Dan Devroye and Richard Freeman, "Does Inequality in Skills Explain Inequality of Earnings Across Advanced Nations?" NBER Working Paper 8140, February 2001.

41. Thomas Piketty and Emanuel Suaz explore the evidence suggesting shifts in cultural norms in the course of affirming the broad trend using

tax evidence—a different data source than most of those referenced in this chapter. Piketty and Suaz, "Income Inequality in the United States 1913–1998," NBER Working Paper 8467, September 2001, pp. 21–30.

42. Edward L. Glaeser attributes American inequality in large part to ethnic heterogeneity, which undermines the sense of commonwealth that could otherwise motivate egalitarian politics. He also notes the importance of deliberately inertial political institutions, and of cultural attitudes toward work, luck, and the future that let Americans tolerate an internationally exceptional level of inequality. Edward Glaeser, "Inequality," NBER Working Paper 11511, July 2005, esp. pp. 13–18, 20–23.

43. For a discussion of this theme, see Robert H. Frank and Philip J. Cook, *The Winner-Take-All Society* (New York: Free Press, 1995).

44. The Rehabilitation Act of 1973, for example, required federal workplaces to make affirmative efforts to hire and accommodate people with disabilities, embodying higher (and much earlier) standards than those set for the private economy in the Americans with Disabilities Act passed seventeen years later.

45. Data from the various Bureau of Labor Statistics survey programs are accessible through the Bureau's "Public Data Query" tool at http://data.bls.gov. Unless otherwise indicated, the data cited here are from that source; cover the most recent period available; and were accessed in June 2004.

46. Pay figures in this paragraph are averages for all occupations, and are calculated from Occupational Employment Statistics as of May 2005, accessed June 2006 at http://data.bls.gov/oes/industry.

47. It does turn out, however, that even sophisticated comparisons suggest a big-company pay premium that can't be explained away by clear-cut differences in the work or the workers. See Katz and Summers, "Industry Rents: Evidence and Implications."

48. Government compensation officials, especially in the federal government, orient their thinking to the characteristics of particular jobs. Scholars studying comparative pay patterns, conversely, focus on the characteristics of particular workers. As a later section observes, this disparity in approaches has created a fundamental and enduring difference of opinion not just about the magnitude of the federal–private pay gap, but about whether the gap is positive or negative.

49. Background on the Occupational Employment Statistics Program, and links to its data, can be found at http://www.bls.gov/oes/oes_emp.htm#overview.

50. Figures cited here are from the data file "May 2005 National 3-digit NAICS Industry-Specific Estimates" accessed June 2006 at http://www.bls.gov/oes/oes_dl.htm#2005_m.

51. For some purposes, of course, private pay levels for jobs that are mostly associated with government are interesting indeed—just not for the current broad-gauge comparison.

52. The 2005 comparisons are based on data accessed June 2006 at http://www.bls.gov/oes/oes_dl.htm#2005_m. One job category that technically met the conditions for inclusion—"stock clerks and order fillers"—has been left out because it was borderline in terms of scale, and because the public and private pay difference was so enormous (public pay roughly double private pay) that it seems dubious that the positions were really comparable.

53. Descriptive characteristics of SOC43–6011, Executive Secretaries and Administrative Assistants, from OES online data system, accessed June 2004 at http://www.bls.gov/oes/2003/may/oes436011.htm.

54. State and local government workers at the ninth decile earned 3.58 times as much as those at the first decile in 1998. For the private sector, the ratio was 4.03. The difference between business and government in this measure of near-the-top and near-the bottom wage dispersion in 1998—about 13 percent—is roughly the same as the growth in the ninth-to-first earnings ratio for all male workers from 1983 to 1998. The 1998 comparisons are from the BLS National Compensation Survey, and cover only earnings from work. The 1983–1998 comparison is based on data from the March CPS Supplement and includes all money income, so it is only roughly comparable. (Current Population Survey, Historical Income Inequality Table IE-2, "Measures of Individual Earnings Inequality for Full-Time, Year-Round Workers by Sex: 1967 to 1999," accessed June 2001 at http://www.census.gov/hhes/income/histinc/ie2.html.)

3: Safe Harbor

1. From Bureau of Labor Statistics, Occupational Employment Statistics program, May 2005 Occupational Employment and Wage Estimates, National Cross-Industry Estimates spreadsheet, accessed June 2006 at http://www.bls.gov/oes/oes_dl.htm#2005_m. In this version, the economy-wide figures include government as well as the private sector. Teachers and teachers aides are excluded.

2. From Bureau of Labor Statistics, Occupational Employment Statistics program, May 2005 Occupational Employment and Wage Estimates, National NAICS 3-digit Industry Specific Estimates spreadsheet, accessed June 2006 at http://www.bls.gov/oes/oes_dl.htm#2005_m.

3. March 2005 Economic and Social Supplement, Family Income Table FINC-06, "Percent Distribution of Families, by Selected Characteristics

within Income Quintile and Top 5 Percent in 2004." This data source refers to a point half a year or so earlier than the Occupational Employment Statistics data, but for present purposes the imprecision is minimal.

4. CPS Historical Income Table F-12, "Earners—Families (All Races) by Median and Mean Income: 1947 to 2001," accessed May 2007 at http://www.census.gov/hhes/income/histinc/f12.html.

5. As it happens, I grew up in my town's cop neighborhood, with one police family next door, another across the street, and a third (a close friend's family) two doors down.

6. Current Population Survey, Personal Income Table PINC-03, "Educational Attainment—People 25 Years Old and Over, by Total Money Earnings in 2004, Work Experience in 2002, Age, Race, Hispanic Origin, and Sex," accessed June 2006 at http://ferret.bls.census.gov/macro/032005/perinc/new03_154.htm.

7. U.S. Department of Justice, Bureau of Justice Statistics, "State and Local Law Enforcement Statistics Summary," accessed July 2004 at http://www.ojp.usdoj.gov/bjs/sandlle.htm#education.

8. The figures for detectives are from 2003 Occupational Employment Statistics data.

9. Rural-Metro, a pioneer in private fire protection, is discussed in Pamela Varley, *Igniting the Passions: Private vs. Public Fire Service in Suburban Phoenix,* Kennedy School of Government Case Program C-16-92-1166 (Cambridge, Mass.: Harvard University, 1992).

10. Bureau of Labor Statistics press release, "Union Members in 2003," January 21, 2004.

11. Thomas Farragher, "On Street, Police Unions Tactics Questioned," *Boston Globe,* July 22, 2004, p. 1.

12. Russell L. Smith and William Lyons, "The Impact of Fire Fighter Unionization on Wages and Working Hours in American Cities," *Public Administration Review* 40(6) (1980): 568–574.

13. Casey Ichniowski, Richard B. Freeman, and Harrison Lauer, "Collective Bargaining Laws, Threat Effects, and the Determination of Police Compensation," *Journal of Labor Economics* 7(2) (April 1989): 191–209.

14. David T. Methe and James L. Perry, "The Impacts of Collective Bargaining on Local Government Services: A Review of Research," *Public Administration Review* 40(4) (July–August 1980): 359–371.

15. Timothy D. Chandler and Rafael Gely, "Protective Service Unions, Political Activities, and Bargaining Outcomes," *Journal of Public Administration Research and Theory* 5(3) (July 1995): 295–318.

16. Stephen J. Trejo, "Public Sector Unions and Municipal Employment," *Industrial and Labor Relations Review* 45(1) (October 1991): 166–180.

17. Robert G. Valletta, "Union Effects on Municipal Employment and Wages: A Longitudinal Approach," *Journal of Labor Economics* 11(3) (July 1993): 545–574.

18. For example, see William J. Moore and John Raisian, "Union-Nonunion Wage Differentials in the Public Administration, Educational, and Private Sectors: 1970–1983," *The Review of Economics and Statistics* 69(4) (November 1987): 608–616.

19. USPS Annual Report, 2003, Operating Statistics Tables pp. 45–51.

20. These wage and benefit budget figures are from the Office of Management and Budget, *Budget of the United States Government, Fiscal Year 2004,* Analytical Perspectives Volume, Table 11.4, "Personnel Compensation and Benefits."

21. The postal service's role as the vanguard of federal unionism is discussed in Richard J. Murphy, "The Difference of a Decade: The Federal Government," *Public Administration Review* 32(2) (March–April 1972): 108–113.

22. The relevant statute is 39 U.S.C. § 101(c).

23. *Embracing the Future: Making the Tough Choices to Preserve Universal Mail Service,* Report of the President's Commission on the U.S. Postal Service, July 2003, p. 119. For a discussion of this dispute see U.S. Government Accountability Office, "Bold Action Needed to Continue Progress on Postal Transformation," Statement of Comptroller General David Walker before the Senate Committee on Government Affairs, November 3, 2003, pp. 37–40.

24. Those eager to sample the technical debate over comparability can refer to Michael L. Wachter, Barry T. Hirsch, and James W. Gillula, "Postal Service Wage Comparability: What Is the Appropriate Comparison?" Industrial Relations Research Association Paper 1997A-56, for one point of view and the (rather informal) statement of James Medoff, http://www.ustreas.gov/offices/domestic-finance/usps/documents/shtml (accessed November 2007) for the other.

25. "U.S. Postal Service: Data on Career Employee Diversity," September 15, 2003, GAO-03-745R, p. 11.

26. Current Population Survey, March 2002 supplement, PINC-03, "Educational Attainment—People 25 Years Old and Over, by Total Money Earnings in 2001, Work Experience in 2001, Age, Race, Hispanic Origin, and Sex." The data were collected in 2002 but refer to 2001, and so are not strictly comparable to the 2002 postal service salary number, though the gap is slight.

27. Figure 3.1 is based on wage and salary accrual data for federal government enterprises—as noted in the text, almost exclusively the postal service—from the National Income and Product Accounts maintained by the Com-

merce Department's Bureau of Economic Analysis, Tables 6.6B and 6.6.C, various years, and on Current Population Survey Historical Tables, Table P-17 (for 1990 and earlier) and P-24 (for years after 1990).

28. 2003 President's Commission report, p. 109.

29. PINC-03, "Educational Attainment—People 25 Years Old and Over, by Total Money Earnings in 2001, Work Experience in 2001, Age, Race, Hispanic Origin, and Sex."

30. An interesting theoretical discussion of the draft versus reliance on volunteers can be found in Thomas W. Ross, "Raising an Army: A Positive Theory of Military Recruitment," *Journal of Law and Economics* 37(1) (April 1994): 109–131.

31. Comparisons are for people age twenty-five and older. For 1974 and 1984 the source is Current Population Statistics Historical Income, Table P-17, "Years of School Completed—People 25 Years Old and Over by Median Income and Sex: 1958 to 1990"; for 2001 it is Table P-16, "Educational Attainment—People 25 Years Old and Over by Median Income and Sex: 1991 to 2001." Note that the difference between "educational attainment" and "years of school completed" means the figures aren't directly comparable, though the trend is far too stark to be driven by changes in the measurement details. It was not merely a matter of differences in education levels, but applied across the board. In 1974 a moderately well-paid, full-time male worker (at the ninetieth percentile of the earnings distribution) made about 3.8 times as much as his moderately badly paid counterpart (at the tenth percentile). By 1986 the ratio was 5-to-1, and by the turn of the century closing in on 6-to-1. For women, the ratio went from just over 3 to 4.6. CPS Historical Statistics, Table IE-2, "Measures of Individual Earnings Inequality for Full-Time, Year-Round Workers by Sex: 1967 to 2001."

32. Military pay numbers for Figure 3.2 are straight pay plus the basic housing allowance for E-3 enlisted personnel with two or three years of active service from the Defense Finance and Accounting Service, accessed June 2003 at http://www.dfas.mil/money/milpay/priorpay. The civilian comparison is a weighted average of male and female mean earnings for high-school educated workers age eighteen to twenty-four who work full time year round.

33. Detailed unpublished results from this survey were generously provided by my colleague Robert Blendon, who directed it.

34. Army records cited by Karen Schaler, "All That You Can Be," *The New Yorker,* July 26, 2004, p. 29. It is worth noting that a commanding officer's approval is required for cosmetic surgery, and that breast-enlargement patients need to pay for their own implants.

35. Beth Asch et al., *Military Recruiting and Retention after the Fiscal Year 2000 Military Pay Legislation,* RAND Corporation report prepared for the Secretary of Defense, RAND, 2002.

36. Beth J. Asch, James R. Hosek, and John T. Warner, National Defense Research Institute Report, "Enlisted Personnel," RAND Corporation, 2001, p. v.

37. 2002 RAND study, pp. 56–57.

38. U.S. Government Accountability Office, Report to the Ranking Minority Member, Senate Committee on Veterans Affairs, "Veterans' Education Benefits: Comparison of Federal Assistance Awarded to Veteran and Non-Veteran Students," GAO-02-368, February 2002.

39. 2001 RAND study, p. 26.

40. Joshua D. Angrist, "Estimating the Labor Market Impact of Voluntary Military Service Using Social Security Data on Military Applicants," *Econometrica* 66(2) (March 1998): 249–288. A summary of Angrist's results is on Table V, p. 281.

41. 2001 RAND study, p. 31.

42. The poll of military families cited earlier found that 72 percent had been in the army for more than five years, but only 39 percent planned to re-enlist.

43. Figure 3.3 is based on data from U.S. Department of Education, National Center for Education Statistics, *Digest of Education Statistics 2002,* Table 77, "Estimated Average Annual Salary of Teachers in Public Elementary and Secondary Schools: 1959–60 to 2001–02." The NCES appears to use National Income and Product Account data from the Commerce Department as its reference point, which is reasonable, and averages wage and salary data for two consecutive years to come up with a comparison for the academic-year numbers for teachers, which is commendable but, considering other sources of noise in the data, perhaps unduly fastidious.

44. As of the 1999–2000 school year, the most recent for which full data are available, 42 percent of public elementary and secondary teachers had a master's degree, about 5 percent had an education specialist's degree, and nearly 1 percent had a doctorate. U.S. Department of Education, National Center for Education Statistics, *Digest of Education Statistics 2002,* Table 68, "Teachers in Public and Private Elementary and Secondary Schools, by Selected Characteristics: 1999–2000."

45. National Education Association, "Status of the American Public School Teacher 2000–2001," Washington, DC, 2003, p. 5.

46. Statistics in this section are from the NEA's "Status of the American Public School Teacher 2000–2001" report, except where noted otherwise. The NEA may not be a wholly impartial source, perhaps, but this report

is based on a fairly large and well-conducted survey that yields data both fresher and more detailed than the numbers provided by the Department of Education, which I use as a cross-check wherever possible. Income and other comparative data for groups other than teachers are drawn from the appropriate tables of the Census Bureau's Current Population Survey reports.

47. Data reported by the College Board and published in the U.S. Department of Education, National Center for Education Statistics, *Digest of Education Statistics 2000* (Table 129, for years prior to 1995) and *Digest of Education Statistics 2002* (Table 135, for 1995 onward).

48. Sean P. Corcoran, William N. Evans, and Robert M. Schwab, "Changing Labor-Market Opportunities for Women and the Quality of Teachers, 1957–2000," *American Economic Review* 94(4) (May 2004): 234.

49. NEA, "Status of the American Public School Teacher," Table 76.

50. Robert D. Putnam, *Bowling Alone: The Collapse and Revival of American Community* (New York: Simon & Schuster, 2000). Putnam's discussion of civic associations is concentrated in Chapter 3 and summarized in Figure 8, p. 54.

51. NEA, "Status of the American Public School Teacher," Table 77.

52. And probably, too, to a certain kind of man. As the male fraction of public-school teachers has fallen, there are hints that the men who opt for teaching careers are differentially family-focused and unobsessed with earning power. Male teachers are actually more likely than their female counterparts to be married, to have school-age children at home, and to dedicate their free time to youth groups. NEA, "Status of the American Public School Teacher," pp. 93 and 100.

53. Charlie LeDuff, "Seizing the Moment, and Defying Expectations," *New York Times,* October 9, 2003, p. A33.

54. Ida Strauss, "The Emerging Relationship," in *Collective Bargaining in the Public Service,* eds. D. K. Krueger and Charles Smith (New York: Random House, 1969), p. 11.

55. "Developments in Public Administration," *Public Administration Review* 18(1) (Winter 1958): 67–87.

56. Richard J. Murphy, "The Difference of a Decade: The Federal Government," *Public Administration Review* 32(2) (March–April 1972): 108–113. This is also the source for the discussion of Kennedy's 1962 executive order and its sequels.

57. Early institutional and legal developments in public-sector unionism, especially in New York City, are discussed in James L. Perry and Charles H. Levine, "An Interorganizational Analysis of Power, Conflict, and Settlements in Public Sector Collective Bargaining," *The American Political Science Review* 70(4) (December 1976): 1185–1201.

58. John Kincaid, "Constitutional Federalism: Labor's Role in Displacing Places to Benefit Persons," *PS: Political Science and Politics* 26(2) (June 1993): 173.

59. Sources for this paragraph are Murphy, "The Difference of a Decade"; Carl W. Stenberg, "Labor Management Relations in State and Local Government: Progress and Prospects," *Public Administration Review* 32(2) (March–April 1972): 102–107; and David B. Lipskey and John Drotning, "The Influence of Collective Bargaining on Teachers' Salaries in New York State," *Industrial and Labor Relations Review* 27(1) (October 1973): 18–35.

60. "FEC Releases Final PAC Report for 1979–80 Election Cycle," Federal Election Commission press release, February 21, 1982.

61. Marick F. Masters, "Federal-Employee Unions and Political Action," *Industrial and Labor Relations Review* 38(4) (July 1985): 612–628; quotation from page 628.

62. Data in this paragraph are from the Bureau of Labor Statistics press release, "Union Members in 2006," Table 3, "Union Affiliation of Employed Wage and Salary Workers by Occupation and Industry," released January 2007, and for years prior to 1990, from unpublished historical data provided by the Bureau of Labor Statistics.

63. "PAC Activity Increases in 1995–96 Election Cycle," Federal Election Commission press release, April 21, 1997.

64. Political contribution data for 1989–2004 are from OpenSecrets.org, accessed June 2006.

4: Backwater

1. In a perceptive 1993 book, Derek Bok lamented the gap between top rewards in public service and other fields of endeavor—a gap that has widened considerably since Bok wrote *The Cost of Talent: How Executives and Professionals Are Paid and How It Affects America* (New York: Free Press, 1993).

2. Franklin's aversion to paying public officials—seconded, though probably not sincerely, by Alexander Hamilton—is discussed in Ron Chernow, *Alexander Hamilton* (New York: Penguin Press, 2004) p. 230. John Adams's disapproval (in principal) to dependence on public employment for one's livelihood is conveyed in a letter to his son, excerpted in David McCullough, *John Adams* (New York: Simon & Schuster, 2001), p. 415.

3. Zachary Goldfarb, "Hill Salary Site Proves Too Big a Hit," *Washington Post*, September 27, 2006, p. A25.

4. Partnership for Public Service, "Back to School: Rethinking Federal Recruiting on College Campuses," *The Public Manager* (May 2006): 12.

5. Paul E. Dwyer, "Salaries of Members of Congress: A List of Payable Rates and Effective Dates, 1789–2006," Congressional Research Service Report 97–1011, Library of Congress, revised June 2006.

6. A Gallup survey on a proposed 1987 raise, even though the increase was strongly endorsed by President Reagan, found more than three out of four Americans objecting. In 1989 a CBS News/New York Times poll discovered 84 percent opposed to a congressional raise. The America Talks Issues organization asked 1,500 voters in 1994 about the notion of "increas[ing] the salaries and benefits of members of Congress to encourage the best people to go into government." Only 5 percent scored this an 8 or higher (on a scale of zero to 10) as an improvement in American government. When the countercase was posed—"reduce the salaries and benefits of members of Congress to let them know that we really want spending cuts and that cuts should start at the top with themselves"—few disagreed. The largest group of respondents (43 percent) rated this proposal a perfect "10," and an additional 25 percent gave it an 8 or 9. A 1999 Gallup poll for CNN and *USA Today* found 74 percent disapproval for a rather timid boost in congressional salaries that had just been enacted.

7. Even legislators too lightly endowed with acumen or scruple to thrive as doctors, lawyers, or entrepreneurs could no doubt prosper as used-car salespeople.

8. Dwyer, "Salaries of Members of Congress," footnote 2.

9. The average for families in the middle fifth is a better benchmark than the overall average, which is skewed by the extremes, particularly the upper extreme. Congressional pay data for Figure 4.1 are from Dwyer, "Salaries of Members of Congress"; family income data are from Current Population Survey Historical Income Table F-3, "Mean Income Received by Each Fifth and Top 5 Percent of Families (All Races): 1966 to 2001." These are also the data sources for Figure 4.2.

10. It is nothing new for a Wall Street executive or a captain of industry to make a financial sacrifice for a prestigious stint in the Cabinet. But the scale of the sacrifice today can be startling. When Henry M. Paulson Jr. was tapped to be Treasury secretary in mid-2006, he swallowed a 99.5 percent pay cut from his prior job running Goldman Sachs. Eric Dash, "After $38 Million Last Year, the Pay Is Not the Issue," *New York Times,* May 31, 2006, p. C5. Paulson's prior compensation of $30 million was not entirely typical, to be sure.

11. Those interested in perusing federal pay scales, from the lowliest GS-1 (about $18,000 in mid-2004) to the top of the Executive Schedule (nearly $175,700), can consult the Office of Personnel Management's pay tables, available at http://www.opm.gov/oca/04tables/html/es.asp.

12. It is worth noting that the job at the top paid twice as much for George W. Bush as for his predecessor, Bill Clinton. John F. Kennedy reportedly said of the presidency that "the pay is good and I can walk to work." The salary of $100,000—which the wealthy Kennedy actually turned down— *was* a fairly impressive sum in 1961. It doubled to $200,000 in the Nixon administration, but stayed at that level until 2001. Bill Clinton almost certainly would have made more money between 1993 and 2001, his years in the White House, had he stuck with private practice when he graduated from law school.

13. Like the other public opinion data cited here, the Rasmussen poll is from the Lexis-Nexis public opinion archives.

14. Current Population Survey, Money Income in 2005, Table PINC-11, "Income Distribution to $250,000 or More by Sex: 2005," accessed September 2006 at http://pubdb3.census.gov/macro/032006/perinc/new11_000. htm. Note that "money income" includes investment as well as earned income.

15. Most figures in this paragraph are from Julianne Basinger and Sarah H. Henderson, "Hidden Costs of High Public Pay," *The Chronicle of Higher Education*, November 14, 2003, p. 3. The growth in the number of public university presidents earning more than $500,000 is from Sam Dillon, "Ivory Tower Executive Suite Gets CEO-Level Salaries," *New York Times*, November 15, 2004, p. A18.

16. Caroline M. Hoxby and Andrew Leigh, "Pulled Away or Pushed Out? Explaining the Decline of Teacher Aptitude in the United States," *American Economic Review* 94(4) (May 2004): 238–239.

17. Gardiner Harris, "F.D.A.'s Drug Safety System Will Get Outside Review," *New York Times*, November 6, 2004, p. A9.

18. Quotes and specific references in this paragraph are from Kevin Johnson and Toni Locy, "Low Pay Squeezes FBI Agents—and Perhaps U.S. Security," *USA Today*, April 5, 2004, p. 1A.

19. The unedifying story of Dr. Laura Callahan is told by William P. Dizzard III, "Callahan Resigns from Homeland Security Department," *Government Computing News*, March 26, 2004.

20. Eric Lipton, "High Contractor Pay Lures Counter-Terrorism Officials," *New York Times*, June 18, 2006, p. 1.

21. Judith M. Labiner, "Looking for the Future Leaders of Government? Don't Count on Presidential Management Interns," Brookings Institution Center for Public Service Working Paper, August 22, 2003, p. 9.

22. Ibid., pp. 11–12 and 17.

23. Paul Light, "In Search of Public Service," The Brookings Institution, June 2003, pp. 4–9.

24. The Harvard, Council for Excellence in Government, and Weekly Reader survey data are from Lexis-Nexis Academic Universe public opinion archives.

25. The report of the first Volcker commission is "Leadership for America: Rebuilding the Public Service" (National Commission on the Public Service, 1989); the second is "Urgent Business for America: Revitalizing the Federal Government for the 21st Century" (National Commission on the Public Service, 2003).

26. A good overview of reform efforts can be found in Jonathan D. Breul and Nicole Willenz Gardner, *Human Capital 2004* (New York: Rowman & Littlefield, 2004).

5: A Twisted Transformation

1. Ronald Coase's "The Nature of the Firm" was originally published in *Economica* 4 (November 1937): 386–405.

2. Indeed, contractual sophistication showed up much earlier. For a summary of a well-developed insurance contract drafted a century and a half before Columbus sailed, see Humbert O. Nelli, "The Earliest Insurance Contract. A New Discovery," *Journal of Risk and Insurance* 39(2) (1972): 215–220.

3. Some additional commentary on how recent developments, especially but not exclusively in information technology, make some classic assumptions of market efficiency less fanciful than they used to be can be found in John D. Donahue and Richard J. Zeckhauser, "Government's Role When Markets Rule," in *Governance Amid Bigger, Better Markets,* eds. John D. Donahue and Joseph S. Nye Jr. (Washington, D.C.: Brookings Institution Press, 2001). A useful examination of what I term the splitting theme in the private sector is Carliss Y. Baldwin and Kim B. Clark, *Design Rules: The Power of Modularity* (Cambridge, Mass.: MIT Press, 2000).

4. For a useful discussion of this theme, see Naomi R. Lamoreaux, Daniel M. G. Raff, and Peter Temin, "Beyond Markets and Hierarchies: Toward a New Synthesis of American Business History," *The American Historical Review,* 108(2) (April 2003): 404–433.

5. Relevant books include E. S. Savas, *Privatization: The Key to Better Government* (Chatham, N.J.: Chatham House, 1988) and *Privatization and Public-Private Partnerships* (Washington, D.C.: Congressional Quarterly Press, 1999); John D. Donahue, *The Privatization Decision: Public Ends, Private Means* (New York: Basic Books, 1989); and Elliott Sclar and Richard Leone, *You Don't Always Get What You Pay For* (Ithaca, N.Y.: Cornell University Press, 2001). A good source on the Bush administration's com-

petitive sourcing campaign is David Walker et al., *Improving the Sourcing Decisions of the Federal Government,* Final Report of the Commercial Activities Panel, distributed by the U.S. Government Accountability Office, April 2002.

6. It is possible, in some circumstances, to structure arrangements that motivate outside suppliers to translate ill-defined mandates into just what the government would have wanted had it been able to specify its requirements in advance. See Murray Horn, *The Political Economy of Public Administration* (Cambridge: Cambridge University Press, 1995).

7. "Performance management" has become an ascendant theme in public-sector reform. The basic notion is to hone the definitions of public employees' tasks so that expectations are crystal clear, then to measure their performance carefully and frequently and hold them accountable for results. I admire many of the proponents of performance management, both scholars and practitioners, and ardently share their goal of boosting efficiency and accountability. But the characteristics that make a task suitable for performance management also tend to make it suitable for privatization. There may be relatively few functions that are well specified and easy to evaluate where privatization would not generate a bigger payoff than developing performance measures to improve internal delivery.

8. The story of IBM's exit from making desktop PCs is just one example of a far broader trend, and is described in Jed Graham, "Manufacturer Sanmina Proves to Be an Asset for Cost-Cutting IBM as $5 Billion PC Pact Inked," *Investors' Business Daily,* January 9, 2002, p. 14. A few years later IBM got out of the PC business altogether.

9. Some background on this trend can be found in Lisa Gelman and David Dell, *HR Outsourcing Trends* (New York: Conference Board, 2002), and in Corporate Leadership Council, *Strategic HR Outsourcing: A Quantitative Assessment of Outsourcing Prevalence and Effectiveness* (Washington, D.C.: Corporate Executive Board, 2003).

10. Barry Newman, "Making Great Art Is What Terry Kester Does for Jeff Koons," *Wall Street Journal,* May 29, 2002, p. 1.

11. Paul Light commissioned a heroically ambitious but less than fully convincing effort to estimate the headcount of nongovernmental personnel delivering federally funded services. See *The True Size of Government* (Washington, D.C.: Brookings Institution Press, 1999).

12. The most frequently cited empirical reference on local privatization is the series of surveys undertaken in 1982, 1998, 1992, and 1997 by the International City and County Management Association. Each year more than three thousand local governments and about fifteen hundred

county governments were queried about their service delivery practices, with a response rate ranging between 36 and 46 percent for cities and roughly half that for counties. At the state level, a similarly respectable but limited survey effort has been undertaken by the Council of State Governments. See Keon S. Chi and Cindy Jasper, *Private Practices: A Review of Privatization in State Government* (Lexington, Ky.: Council of State Governments, 1998).

13. These examples are from the U.S. Department of Commerce, Bureau of the Census, *Statistical Abstract of the United States 2001* (Washington, D.C.: U.S. Government Printing Office, 2002), various tables, and from the "American FactFinder" feature of the Census Bureau's web site (http://factfinder.census.gov/), which provides demographic, economic, and other data with great precision and at a rather alarming level of detail.

14. Steven Minicucci and John D. Donahue, "A Simple Estimation Method for Aggregate Government Outsourcing," *Journal of Policy Analysis and Management* 23(3) (Summer 2004): 489–507.

15. The report, "Competitive Sourcing, Fiscal Year 2003" (Office of Management and Budget, May 2004), is heavy on process and projections and remarkably shy about job numbers. The 2,729 figure was arrived at by taking the agency-by-agency numbers of jobs that were studied for potential privatization in Table 2, page 6, and multiplying those by the percentage of such studied jobs, in each agency, that actually went to contractors in Appendix C. Some of the studies were still ongoing when the report was issued, so the final tally of job switches could be somewhat higher.

16. I am indebted to Richard Zeckhauser for this strategy of approaching a contentious issue on a comparative basis—that people who disagree about the *absolute* wisdom of some approach can search for consensus on where it works best (or least badly) and where its benefits are small (or its costs most ruinous).

17. The notion of "inherently governmental" tasks, which has long served as the touchstone for federal decision rules on outsourcing, is (aside from the extreme cases) too ambiguous to be very helpful.

18. Michael E. Motley, "A Look at Other Countries' Postal Reform Efforts," U.S. Government Accountability Office, GAO/T-GGD-96-60, January 25, 1996.

19. Background on this quiet splitting of postal functions can be found in Mary Elcano, R. Andrew German, and John T. Pickett, "Hiding in Plain Sight: The Quiet Liberalization of the United States Postal System," in *Current Directions in Postal Reform,* eds. Michael Crew and Paul Kleindorfer (Norwell, Mass.: Kluwer Academic, 2000), and in U.S. Government Accountability Office, "A Primer on Postal Worksharing," GAO-03-927, July 2003.

20. *Embracing the Future: Making the Tough Choices to Preserve Universal Service,* Report of the Presidential Commission on the U.S. Postal Service, July 31, 2003.

21. William Burrus, president of the American Postal Workers Union, as quoted in Christopher Lee, "Panel Recommends Leaner Postal Service," *Washington Post,* July 24, 2003, p. A19.

22. These figures are from the Census Bureau's electronic data files maintained by the Governments Division, State and Local Employment and Payroll series, for 2002.

23. U.S. Department of Education, National Center for Education Statistics, *Digest of Education Statistics 2002,* Table 80, "Staff Employed in Public Elementary and Secondary School Systems, by Functional Area, 1949–50 to 2000."

24. The figures on the breakdown of internal versus external service delivery in this paragraph were calculated from the U.S. Department of Education, National Center for Education Statistics, *Digest of Education Statistics 2002,* Table 164, "Total Expenditures for Public Elementary and Secondary Education, by Function and Subfunction."

25. These comparisons are from the Bureau of Labor Statistics Occupational Employment Survey database, and are for 2003.

26. Kirsten Lundberg, "Private Food Service in Houston's Public Schools?" Kennedy School of Government Case C-15-01-1622, 2001.

27. Government Accountability Office, "School Lunch Program: Role and Impacts of Private Companies," Report RCED-217, August 1996.

28. Representative John L. Mica (R-Fla.) emphasized that federal rules in place on September 11 did not require screeners to confiscate box cutters. Relevant segments of his November 1, 2001 testimony were reprinted in "A Nation Challenged: Excerpts from Debate on Airport Security Bills," *New York Times,* November 2, 2001, p. B6.

29. The political debate over lumping or splitting passenger screening can be traced in Elisabeth Bumiller, "Bush to Increase Federal Role in Security at Airports," *New York Times,* September 28, 2001, p. A1; Lizette Alvarez, "Bush's Approach on Plane Security Chosen by House," *New York Times,* November 2, 2001, p. A1; Matthew Wald, "At Airports, New Watchdog Is Taking Over," *New York Times,* January 27, 2002, p. E16; and Nicholas Lemann, "The McCain Code," *The New Yorker,* February 4, 2002, pp.43–51. Gerald Dillingham provides a clear contemporary primer on the options in "Weaknesses in Airport Security and Options for Assigning Screening Responsibilities," U.S. Government Accountability Office GAO-01-1165T, September 21, 2001.

30. Jon Hilkevitch, "Airport screener turnover plunges," *Chicago Tribune,* February 18, 2003, p. 2.

31. "Republican Zealotry," *New York Times,* October 28, 2001, p. D12.

32. Two Nobel economists faced off on this question of whether high-quality airport screening could be delegated successfully. James Heckman argued that a public form of organization for screeners was "not needed and probably counterproductive" since an upgraded contractual framework was eminently feasible. Joseph Stiglitz countered that the instinct to cut costs would inevitably erode service quality if the function remained private. Louis Uchitelle, "Now, Uncle Sam Wants You," *New York Times,* November 25, 2001, p. D3. It may be that the whole debate was of secondary importance if, as seems likely, it is no longer possible using only hand weapons, to hijack a plane full of knowingly doomed passengers.

33. The three market leaders were the Argenbright Security unit of Britain's Securicor; the Globe Aviation unit of Sweden's Securitas; and Huntleigh Security, a subsidiary of ICTS of the Netherlands.

34. Federal Procurement Data Center, "Federal Procurement Report, Fiscal Year 2002," April 16, 2003, p. 2. The center has more recent data posted for other categories, but as of 2006 was behind schedule in posting its usual tallies of top contractors.

35. These general categories and spending numbers are from the "Federal Procurement Report," pp. 7–9; the Lockheed-Martin numbers are from pp. 15–18; and the totals for the three large consulting firms are from pp. 14–15.

36. Scott Shane and Ron Nixon, "In Washington, Contractors Take On Biggest Role Ever," *New York Times,* February 3, 2007, p. A1.

37. Ibid.

38. Ibid. See also Bernard Wysocki Jr., "Is U.S. Government 'Outsourcing Its Brain'?" *Wall Street Journal,* March 30, 2007, p. A1.

39. This trend is discussed in Bryna Sanger, *The Welfare Marketplace: Privatization and Welfare Reform* (Washington, D.C.: Brookings Institution Press, 2003).

40. The CEO of American Management Systems, which concentrates on state and local rather than federal contracting, announced a major strategic shift to focus on the burgeoning demand for outsourced IT services in the public sector. Anitha Reddy, "Fairfax's AMS Sets Sights on Outsourcing," *Washington Post,* December 4, 2003, p. E5.

41. Corporate IT outsourcing raises its own set of concerns. Much of the debate centers on shifting work overseas to take advantage of a divide in the working world related to, but different from, the one at issue here.

Security anxieties arise as well, as related in John Schwartz, "Experts See Vulnerability as Outsiders Code Software," *New York Times*, January 5, 2003, p. B1.

42. Harvard's Kennedy School of Government, where I teach, contracts out much of the routine work of installing hardware, maintaining servers, and extricating clueless faculty from the messes we get ourselves into. But a formidably competent IT director and her crack staff form the core of the operation.

43. This trend is discussed in a (generally enthusiastic) study by Yu-Che Chen and James L. Perry, "IT Outsourcing: A Primer for Public Managers" (Washington, D.C.: IBM Endowment for the Business of Government, 2003), pp. 10–11.

44. A team led by Nobel laureate Joseph Stiglitz produced a crisp application of classic economic principles to underscore that there are many domains that government should stay out of as IT reshapes the options. But the report specifies that employing technology to "improve the efficiency with which public services are provided" is an entirely appropriate public task. Joseph Stiglitz, Jonathan Orzag, and Peter Orzag, "The Role of Government in a Digital Age," report commissioned by the Computer and Communications Industry Association, October 2000.

45. U.S. Government Accountability Office, "Human Capital: Selected Agencies' Use of Alternative Service Delivery Options for Human Capital Activities," GAO-04-679, June 2004.

46. GAO-04-679, p. 13. For another perspective, see Janice Koch, "HR Outsourcing in Government Organizations: Emerging Trends, Early Lessons," Conference Board, 2004.

47. The Occupational Employment Survey reports suppress much of the information on avionics technicians in the industry that includes the United Space Alliance—probably to preserve confidentiality, because USA constitutes all or most of the avionics technicians employed in that industry. Avionics technicians earn about $43,000 in government, about $47,000 in transportation equipment manufacturing, about $52,000 in air transportation, and about $39,000 in air transport support. The average salary for aerospace engineers is nearly the same in business and government, though in government it is lower on the high end and higher on the low end.

48. NASA eventually shifted its aspirations from oversight to what it called "insight"—a less intensive form of monitoring that left much to the contractor's discretion. Some shuttle managers became intensely concerned that the growing knowledge gap between NASA and USA imperiled flight safety and called for reuniting decision-making authority with flight op-

erations, either by unwinding the delegation or by making shuttle operations more conventionally private.

49. My familiarity with the shuttle operations contract dates from work I did
in 2001–2002 with the RAND Corporation, but all facts cited are from
publicly available documents, including the report of that task force,
"Alternate Trajectories" (RAND, 2002). Relevant press reports include
R. Jeffrey Smith, "Experts Critical of Shuttle Program's Budget Cuts,"
Washington Post, February 3, 2003, p. A1, and Greg Schneider, "Cost-
Conscious NASA Relies on Contract Firms," *Washington Post,* February 3,
2003, p. A17.

50. Neil King Jr. and Russell Gold, "Army to Rebid Halliburton Contract,"
Wall Street Journal, September 7, 2004, p. A3.

51. The vice president for government affairs of Blackwater USA is quoted in
David Barstow, "Security Companies: Shadow Soldiers in Iraq," *New York
Times,* April 19, 2004, p. A1.

52. Some of these issues are addressed by Peter W. Singer in *Corporate Warriors* (Washington, D.C.: Brookings Institution Press, 2002).

53. General Downing and Thomas W. O'Connell are quoted in Eric Schmitt
and Thom Shanker, "Big Pay Luring Military's Elite to Private Jobs," *New
York Times,* March 30, 2004, p. A1.

54. Lockheed's largest customer, accounting for roughly $25 billion, was the
U.S. public sector, primarily but not exclusively the federal government.
An additional $5 billion was for sales to foreign governments. Much of
this, of course, was for the aircraft and other hardware that nobody
would expect governments to make for themselves. But a large and growing share was for IT services, consulting, and other functions that could
be done internally. Lockheed Martin 2003 Annual Report, Notes to Consolidated Financial Statements, p. 68.

55. The roots of this shift were discerned more than thirty years ago when a
labor expert attributed the new focus on public workplaces in part to "an
awareness among many unions that their strength in private industry is
on the wane, and that the public service represents a virtually untapped
field for productive organizational efforts." Carl W. Stenberg, "Labor
Management Relations in State and Local Government: Progress and
Prospects," *Public Administration Review* 32(2) (1972): 103.

56. One could also counter that it is a very good thing that the transformation has stalled, to the extent that it centers on outsourcing. A shallow
variant of this is that no policies that damage workers' interests should
ever be adopted—an issue I take up, though of necessity in a cursory way,
in the next chapter. A subtler variant questions whether cost savings
from delegation should count as real efficiency gains. If the only effect of

delegating commodity tasks is lower pay and leaner benefits for workers, then cost savings cannot be considered an improvement in efficiency but a simple reshuffling of wealth: taxpayers are better off at workers' expense. This argument is correct, but there are often other consequences from delegation—advantages due to specialization, managerial focus, and optimal scale—that produce efficiency gains at nobody's expense.

6: Finding the Future

1. Paul C. Light, *Government's Greatest Achievements: From Civil Rights to Homeland Defense* (Washington, D.C.: Brookings Institution Press, 2002).

2. Private performance would worsen by less than government's performance would improve, both because the marginal payoff to talent is likely higher in the sector where talent has been scarcer, and because easing less-skilled workers' motives to shelter in government would make the public sector more flexible with no corresponding damage to the private sector.

3. These figures are calculated from Current Population Survey Table PINC-10, "Wage and Salary Workers—People 15 Years Old and Over, by Total Wage and Salary Income in 2005, Work Experience in 2005, Race, Hispanic Origin, and Sex," and are for people who work full time for fifty weeks or more. Data accessed September 2006 at http://pubdb3.census.gov/macro/032006/perinc/new10_001.htm.

4. The demographics of differential growth in high-skilled and low-skilled populations, and the economic implications, are discussed in David T. Ellwood, "The Sputtering Labor Force of the 21st Century: Can Social Policy Help?" National Bureau of Economic Research Working Paper 8321, June 2001.

5. President's Commission on the U.S. Postal Service, 2003, p. 132.

6. The state and local figure, for fiscal year 2002, is from the Census Bureau's Governments Division, "State and Local Government Finances by Level of Government and by State," at http://www.census.gov/govs/estimate02. The federal figure for the same year is from the Consolidated Federal Funds Report at http://www.harvester.census.gov/cffr/asp/Reports.asp.

7. Labor economist George Borjas, in the most recent systematic estimate of public–private pay differentials, finds that women working for the federal government earn significant premiums; but all other groups—women in state and local government, and men at every level—earn less than statistically comparable private-sector workers, as of 2000. Borjas doesn't consider benefits or employment levels, but his estimates undercut the notion that large personnel savings are even theoretically available. George J. Borjas, "Wage Structures and the Sorting of Workers into the Public Sector," in *For*

the People: Can We Fix Public Service?, eds. John D. Donahue and Joseph S. Nye (Washington, D.C.: Brookings Institution Press, 2003), p. 35, Figure 3.3.

8. Total government expenditure of $3.1 trillion is from Office of Management and Budget, *Budget of the United States, Fiscal Year 2005*, Historical Table 15.4. Outlays for federal items in this paragraph are from the Fiscal 2005 budget, Historical Table 3.2. State and local items are from the Census Bureau's "State and Local Government Finances by Level of Government and by State." Two respected tax analysts estimate that the 2001–2003 tax changes will cost $275 billion in 2010, even if they are not made permanent and if no changes are made to the Alternative Minimum Tax. William G. Gale and Peter Z. Orszag, "Bush Administration Tax Policy: Revenue and Budget Effects," *Tax Notes*, October 4, 2004, Table 1, p. 106.

9. The 2005 deficit of $318 billion is from FY 2007 Budget of the United States Government, Table 1.3, "Summary of Receipts, Outlays, and Surpluses or Deficits, 1940–2011"; nondefense employee compensation of $128 billion is from Bureau of Economic Analysis, National Income and Product Account Table 3.10.5, "Government Consumption Expenditures and General Government Gross Output," accessed electronically in June 2006, http://www.bea.gov/national/nipaweb/TableView.asp? SelectedTable=101&FirstYear=2005&LastYear=2007&Freq=Qtr&3 Place=y.

10. My ethicist colleague Arthur Applbaum has suggested that America's low-risk, low-reward public sector could be viewed as a device for shoring up the moral legitimacy of our high-risk, high-reward private economy, since if workers can choose which game they want to play the rules can't be attacked as unfair. This is an ingenious interpretation, though if that is indeed our collective rationale for America's separate economies, the ethical strategy is both utterly unconscious and rather clumsily applied.

11. The main source for the history of the SES is "Report on the Senior Executive Service," prepared for the Office of Personnel Management by the National Academy of Public Administration, December 2002.

12. Until 2003 there were six separate levels of the SES, but legislation that year, in a concession to the reality that most were clustered at or near the top, substituted a single "band" for base pay topping out near the ceiling for political appointees, or about $155,000. Kay Coles James, director of OPM, "Memorandum for Heads of Departments and Agencies," Office of Personnel Management, December 16, 2003.

13. Hay Management Consultants, "Comparative Analysis of SES Base Salary, Total Annual Cash Compensation, Benefits, and Total Remuneration," October 31, 1996, summarized in NAPA report, p. 59.

14. NAPA report, p. 81.

15. In the first year of my 1990s stint in Washington, I naively decided not to award a performance bonus to an SES staff member, on the grounds that he had performed rather badly. I was quickly informed—not just by this worker, but by his abler SES colleagues and personnel officials—that such distinctions transgressed the unwritten rules of departmental management. NAPA report, 2002, p. 23.

16. Kay Coles James, director of OPM, "Memorandum for Heads of Departments and Executive Agencies," Office of Personnel Management, February 12, 2004.

17. Federal Civilian Workforce Statistics, Office of Personnel Management, February 2006, p. 76.

18. The specific performance rating figure, for 2000, is below two-tenths of 1 percent rated less than "fully satisfactory," and is from the NAPA report cited earlier, p. 23. The separation figure is from Office of Personnel Management data at http://www.fedscope.opm.gov.

19. The quote in the first sentence of this paragraph is from the NAPA report, p. 23. The other studies mentioned are summarized and excerpted in the NAPA report: "The U.S. Office of Personnel Management in Retrospect," Merit Systems Protection Board, 2001; and "The Senior Executive Service: Views of Former Federal Executives," Merit Systems Protection Board, 1989. The last quote in the paragraph is from page 42 of the report, extracted from James Colvard, "Senior Executive Service Had High Hopes."

20. Harvard University, surely not the most squeamish nonprofit in this regard, is a case in point. Jack Meyer managed Harvard's endowment for fifteen years, delivering spectacular results but rankling faculty, staff, and alumni with the lofty compensation he and his staff collected. Early in 2005 Meyer and his top deputies decamped to the for-profit sector where eight-figure paychecks raise fewer eyebrows.

21. The empirical study by George Borjas cited in the appendix finds that only 2.5 percent of private-sector workers move into public jobs in any given year. Borjas, "Wage Structures and the Sorting of Workers into the Public Sector," Table 3.1, p. 45.

22. The share of Cabinet and sub-Cabinet appointees' prior careers spent in government was about 26 percent in the Eisenhower administration and about 55 percent in George W. Bush's first term. John D. Donahue, "In-and-Outers: Up or Down?" in Donahue and Nye, *For the People*, Table 4A-1, p. 67.

23. The Pennsylvania Associators figure in David Hackett Fisher, *Washington's Crossing* (Oxford: Oxford University Press, 2004). Their origins and organization are described on pp. 26–28.

Appendix: The Evidence on Comparative Compensation

1. Some analysts suggest the right wage is generally *above* the walk-away point, but for present purposes we can bypass the "efficiency wage" literature.

2. President John F. Kennedy quoted in Sharon P. Smith, "Pay Differentials between Federal Government and Private Sector Workers," *Industrial and Labor Relations Review* 29(2) (January 1976): 184.

3. The private-industry average was $5,380 in 1963 and $9,867 in 1974; the corresponding figures for federal civilian pay were $6,993 and $14,083. These numbers are wages and salaries for full-time equivalent employees from the Commerce Department's National Income and Product Accounts, Table 6.6, various years.

4. Smith, "Pay Differentials between Federal Government and Private Sector Workers," Table 3, p. 195. The reference is to her regressions explaining wage rates. The analysis of overall earnings is comparable.

5. For example, Steven F. Venti, "Wages in the Federal and Private Sectors," in *Public Sector Payrolls*, ed. David Wise (Chicago: University of Chicago Press, 1987), found a 4 percent federal premium for men and a 22 percent premium for women. Joseph Gyourko and Joseph Tracy, "An Analysis of Public and Private-Sector Wages Allowing for Endogenous Choices of Both Government and Union Status," *Journal of Labor Economics* 6(2) (April 1988): 229–253, found an overall federal premium of about 18 percent. Other interesting empirical analyses include Matthew Black, Robert Moffitt, and John. T. Warner, "The Dynamics of Job Separation: The Case of Federal Employees," *Journal of Applied Econometrics* 5(3) (July–August 1990): 245–262; and Jeffrey Perloff and Michael L. Wachter, "Wage Comparability in the U.S. Postal Service," *Industrial and Labor Relations Review* 38(1) (October 1984): 26–35.

6. Brent R. Moulton, "A Reexamination of the Federal-Private Wage Differential in the United States," *Journal of Labor Economics* 8(2) (1990): 276 and 278.

7. U.S. General Accounting Office, "Federal/Private Sector Pay Comparisons," Report OCE-95-1, December 1994.

8. Moulton, "A Reexamination of the Federal-Private Wage Differential in the United States," Table 2, p. 277.

9. Ibid., Table 4, p. 290.

10. Alan B. Krueger, "The Determinants of Queues for Federal Jobs," *Industrial and Labor Relations Review* 41(4) (July 1988): 567–581. Figure 1, p. 571, tracks the trends in relative wages and applicant queues.

11. Lawrence Katz and Alan B. Krueger, "Changes in the Structure of Wages

in the Public and Private Sectors," *Research in Labor Economics* 12 (1991): 137–172.

12. Calculated from Katz and Krueger, Table 1, p. 145. The focus on relatively new workers is meant to better reflect recent labor market trends.

13. James M. Poterba and Kim S. Rueben, "The Distribution of Public Sector Wage Premia: New Evidence Using Quantile Regression Methods," NBER Working Paper W4734, May 1994.

14. Ibid., pp. 23–24.

15. Ibid., Table 7, p. 33.

16. Ibid., Table 6, p. 32.

17. William J. Moore and Robert J. Newman, "Government Wage Differentials in a Municipal Labor Market: The Case of Houston Metropolitan Transit Workers," *Industrial and Labor Relations Review* 45(1) (October 1991): 145–153.

18. Dale Belman and John Heywood, "The Truth about Public Employees: Underpaid or Overpaid?" Economic Policy Institute Briefing Paper, 1993.

19. The adjustment could take place in many ways, of course. Government employers could select from applicant queues through a range of legitimate or questionable criteria; public jobs could become unpleasant enough that workers were just compensated by the higher pay; and so on. Dale Belman and John S. Heywood explore the possibility that relatively high-paying states employ an overqualified workforce in "State and Local Government Wage Differentials: An Intrastate Analysis," *Journal of Labor Research* 16(2) (Spring 1995): 196–198.

20. George J. Borjas, "Wage Structures and the Sorting of Workers into the Public Sector," in *For the People,* eds. John D. Donahue and Joseph S. Nye. For the record, George is a colleague and he undertook this project in part at my urging.

21. Borjas, "Wage Structures and the Sorting of Workers into the Public Sector," Figure 3-2, p. 33, and Figure 3-3, p. 35.

22. Ibid., Figures 3-4 to 3-9, pp. 37–44.

23. The methodology and results of Borjas's work with the 1979–2001 "Outgoing Rotation Group" sample are described in ibid., pp. 44–51.

24. Ibid., p. 52.

25. Claudia Goldin and Robert A. Margo, "The Great Compression: The Wage Structure in the United States at Mid-Century," *Quarterly Journal of Economics* 107(1) (February 1992): 1–34.

Index